712.60942 BuS

Green Desire

Green Desire

Imagining Early Modern
English Gardens

Rebecca Bushnell

CORNELL UNIVERSITY PRESS
Ithaca & London

First published 2003 by Cornell University Press

Printed in the United States of America

Library of Congress Cataloging-in-Publication Data
Bushnell, Rebecca W., 1952–
   Green desire : imagining early modern English gardens / Rebecca Bushnell.
      p. cm.
Includes index.
   ISBN 0-8014-4143-9 (cloth : alk. paper)
   1. Horticultural literature—England—History—16th century.   2. Horticultural
literature—England—History—17th century.   3. Gardening—England—History—
16th century.   4. Gardening—England—History—17th century.   5. English litera-
ture—Early modern, 1500–1700—History and criticism.   6. Gardens in literature.
I. Title.
   SB318.34.G7B87   2003
   635′.0942′09031—dc21

                                                                    2003004297

Cloth printing   10 9 8 7 6 5 4 3 2 1

Contents

Illustrations

Acknowledgments

This book took longer to write than I hoped, and it has grown like an unruly vine. The first piece was an essay written for the volume *The Historical Imagination: History, Rhetoric, and Fiction, 1500–1800*, edited by Donald R. Kelley and David Harris Sacks (published in 1977 by Cambridge University Press for the Woodrow Wilson International Center for Scholars and used by permission). It profited greatly from the editing of Don Kelley and David Sacks, and parts of that essay are included in revised form in chapter 6. Chapter 2 began as an essay, "The Gardener and the Book," published in *Didactic Literature in England 1500–1800*, ably edited by Natasha Glaisyer and Sara Pennell (Aldershot: Ashgate, 2003), and it is reprinted in revised form by permission of the editors and publishers. Lectures were the seeds of the other chapters, and I can only offer blanket thanks to all those audiences who have enlightened me over the years. At the end of the process, two anonymous readers for Cornell University Press wisely prodded me to make the book's argument stronger, and Bernhard Kendler once again stepped forward graciously and swiftly to help bring it to fruition. Kay Scheuer edited the text with care and sympathy.

I owe special thanks to my colleagues at Penn, particularly Phyllis Rackin, who has shaped my thinking about nature and gender in the early modern period and who is always an incisive reader. Peter Stallybrass (a better gardener than I) took the time to read the whole manuscript at the end and offered me enthusiastic support and guidance.

Other scholars from Penn and elsewhere, including Roger Abrahams, Crystal Bartolovich, Kevin Brownlee, Marina Brownlee, Rita Copeland, Margreta De Grazia, Heather Dubrow, Mary Fissell, Beverly Haviland, John Dixon Hunt, Elizabeth Hyde, Cary Mazer, Andrew McRae, Lisa New, Maureen Quilligan, Barbara Riebling, Laurie Shannon, Bill Sherman, Julie Solomon, Wendy Wall, and David Wallace contributed key ideas and friendship. The themes for this book were explored in several graduate seminars, and I am indebted to many of the brilliant graduate students I have collaborated with at Penn.

This book has also benefited from the patient assistance of a generation of research assistants, who will be happy to know that it is finally done: Suzanne Daly, Catherine Michaud, Jose Serrano, Sarah Brockett, Ruth Toner, and Tom Lay. The staff of the University of Pennsylvania Library were always helpful, especially Michael Ryan, Dan Traister, Hilda Pring, and John Pollack, as were the staffs of Dumbarton Oaks, the Lindley Library of the Royal Horticultural Society, and the Folger Shakespeare Library. Betty W. Johnson, a fierce gardener, lent me books from her own library as well as offered me sensible advice.

I could not have completed this book without the leave time given to me by Sam Preston, dean of the School of Arts and Sciences: he had faith I would finish the book, and I could not disappoint him. Thanks are also due to Jennifer Knapp and Allison Rose and to my fellow deans—David Balamuth, Walter Licht, Ramin Sededi, Rick Beeman, and Joe Farrell—who tended efficiently to my administrative work for three months. My family tolerated my obsessive work habits and gave me solace.

Introduction

People often assume that anyone who writes about gardening must also be a great gardener, but this is not necessarily true. I myself have tended a small plot with some satisfaction but little success. In fact, we recently moved to a new house partly to escape the tangled chaos of an old garden, finding refuge in a tidy landscape that someone else mows and prunes.

What I most remember about gardening at my old house is the exhausting work. I really did like growing things, but I just could not bear the strain. Many battles were fought and lost there against a guerrilla band of arrogant wisteria vines, flotillas of weeds that swept away all in their path, and a ragged patch of sedum that buzzed with angry bees all August. Every inch of that garden resisted my advances.

So how have I come to write about gardening in early modern England, aside from either a desire for revenge or a wish to inhabit a fantasy world of knot gardens and topiary? It all started when I wrote my last book, *A Culture of Teaching,* which dealt with the theory and practice of early English humanist education. Constantly stumbling over comparisons of teaching to gardening in humanist pedagogical treatises, I dug into contemporary English gardening manuals to see what these similes might have meant in their time. There I found that both teachers and gardeners asserted nature's authority while also insisting that people can master anything in nature—whether a child's disposition or a flower's hue. Nature was everywhere in early modern writing and always alien.

Because of the intense surge of ecological activism and theory in the past forty years, writing about nature is burgeoning these days, whether in cultural or literary fields, or in descriptions of growing your own piece of Eden. The last two decades of the twentieth century saw the emergence of "ecocriticism," which knits together environmental studies and literary criticism in a new "earth-centered" approach to literary studies.[1] Although earlier classics such as Raymond Williams's *The Country and the City*, which dismantled the rhetoric of British rural fictions, shaped many of its terms, this new critical movement has focused primarily on nineteenth- and twentieth-century American culture and has close ties to the politics of ecological activism. This movement in literary studies forms only one strand of contemporary nature writing, which encompasses the political, cultural, and philosophical and asks us to rethink the relationship between human beings and nature and the very concept of the natural.

Even a little reading of this body of work immediately reveals how difficult it is to write about nature and culture. Any discussion of this topic must submit to the paradox that, even if you think that culture constructs nature, "there can be nothing that is not 'nature'—it has no opposite."[2] Nature is what *is* or is "real" in the world. The most toxic chemical substance and the most exquisite flower alike are composed of the elements that constitute "nature." To look at it another way, it is also hard to think of something that is purely "natural." A long time ago C. S. Lewis put the problem succinctly: if you try to posit an opposition between nature as something "not interfered with" and culture as the product of interference, you won't get far, since "in the real world everything is continuously 'interfered with' by everything else; total mutual interference . . . is of the essence of nature."[3] Yet, human beings persist in opposing nature and "not nature," needing a nature outside of ourselves, even while we map it according to social structures, perceptions, and needs.

For, indeed, even today one of the most powerful—and most controversial—concepts of the new nature writing is that "'nature' is a hu-

---

[1] Cheryl Glofelty and Harold Fromm, *The Ecocriticism Reader: Landmarks in Literary Ecology* (Athens: University of Georgia Press, 1996), p. xviii.

[2] Neil Evernden, *The Social Creation of Nature* (Baltimore: Johns Hopkins University Press, 1992), p. 20.

[3] C. S. Lewis, *Studies in Words*, 2d ed. (Cambridge: Cambridge University Press, 1967), p. 45.

man idea": in William Cronon's words, "far from inhabiting a realm that stands completely apart from humanity, the objects and creatures and landscapes we label as 'natural' are in fact deeply entangled with the words and images and ideas we use to describe them."[4] This concept is controversial because to deny nature this kind of independence from the human might seem to diminish its power and its very reality. That is not true: knowing how we "think nature" will not stem the power of a flood or quench a fire. But this knowledge will help us understand how, when we invoke the authority or privilege of nature, we may in fact not always be doing nature any good.[5]

Insofar as it is socially constructed, the category of nature is also historically contingent, for every era creates its own nature. In retrospect we can see that Western ideas of nature underwent the reclassifications recounted by Michel Foucault in *Les Mots et les Choses*, or *The Order of Things*, as well as the reevaluation narrated by Keith Thomas in his *Man and the Natural World: A History of the Modern Sensibility*. Over the course of three centuries, Thomas tells us, the relationship between English people and other species, animal and vegetable, altered fundamentally, for "only a few hundred years [before today] the idea that human cultivation was something to be resisted rather than encouraged would have been unintelligible."[6] Yet in our time resisting human encroachment on nature has become a cultural imperative or at least a matter of serious political debate.

All such discourses, whether for or against nature, seek to obscure their own historicity and contingency. The point of something being natural is that it is always "a priori," or in the Aristotelian sense, "the natural . . . is the Given."[7] Aristotle defined "*phusis*" or nature as "whatever each thing is like (*hoion hekaston esti*) when its process of coming to be is complete."[8] This kind of thinking avoids the question of how you know a "coming-to-be" is complete in an organic world where things are always mutating. Who says a thing has come to be what it is? Is a

[4] William Cronon, "Introduction: In Search of Nature," in *Uncommon Ground: Rethinking the Human Place in Nature*, ed. Cronon (New York: W. W. Norton, 1996), p. 20.

[5] Ibid., pp. 23–56, for the argument that awareness of the "constructedness" of nature is not anti-environmentalist: all the essays in Cronon's volume seek to critique the notions of nature as a "naïve reality" (p. 34) and "moral imperative" (p. 36).

[6] Keith Thomas, *Man and the Natural World: A History of the Modern Sensibility* (New York: Pantheon, 1983), p. 14.

[7] Lewis, *Studies*, p. 45.

[8] Ibid., p. 34.

plant what it *is* as a bud, a flower, or a fruit? According to Aristotle only two things lie outside *phusis*—mathematics and God—but I am sure he implicitly believed that the philosopher, too, occupies this territory, a position that gives him the right to say what is.

If we recognize nature's status as the "given," we can understand why the advocates of culture might strive to grant it the status of the natural. In his essay on the social and semiotic dimensions of myth-making, Roland Barthes argued insightfully that the French bourgeoisie wished, through their rites of celebration and consumption, to transform "the reality of the world into an image of the world, History into Nature." That is, he saw that "the bourgeois class has precisely built its power on technical, scientific progress, on an unlimited transformation of nature: bourgeois ideology yields in return an unchangeable nature." Any such argument claiming to be based in nature posits that its premises and practices precede culture and are thus "universal" and "eternal."[9] In so arguing, we tend to transform the "necessary" into the natural, where "necessity becomes, therefore, the standard of nature."[10]

It is not surprising, then, that these days the easiest way to sell something is to claim that it is "all-natural," as if that were a token of inherent goodness and desirability. As Jennifer Price has observed about the way the store The Nature Company markets products, "in modern America we 'graft on' to nature manifold positive values: authenticity, simplicity, reality, uniqueness, purity, health, beauty, the primitive, the autochthonous, adventure, the exotic, innocence, solitude, freedom, leisure, peace."[11] But who is to say that nature is always good? C. S. Lewis sensibly noted the contradiction in our thinking that a man's actions may be unnatural and thus bad, but a man who rises above nature is good. Depending on how you look at it, "the natural element in a man [i]s something morally better or worse than what he might make of it."[12] If, as the geographer Yi-fu Tuan has written in his book *Escapism*, culture is escapism in the best sense, nature has become for us the essence of what we cannot escape, and therefore it evokes both the

[9] Roland Barthes, *Mythologies* (Paris: Editions du Seuil, 1957); trans. Annette Lavers (London: Jonathan Cape, 1972), pp. 141–42.

[10] Evernden, *Social Creation*, p. 60.

[11] Jennifer Price, "Looking for Nature at the Mall: A Field Guide to the Nature Company," in Cronon, *Uncommon Ground*, pp. 186–202; p. 190.

[12] Lewis, *Studies*, p. 52.

terror and the pleasures of the real.[13] Any argument we might make on behalf of nature, in the end, thus tells us as much about our fears and hopes for culture as it does about what lurks in the woods and blooms in the fields.

Intervening in the midst of all this heady confusion and debate over the meaning of nature in our time, *Green Desire* examines a local argument about nature and culture that took place in English gardening manuals of the sixteenth and seventeenth centuries. A great deal was at stake then, socially and theologically, in the matter of human mastery over nature, and English philosophers, poets, and artists argued constantly about it. Since then copious scholarship has been devoted to telling how the English Scientific Revolution transformed our view of nature. This story has gained the status of myth, populated by its heroes Francis Bacon, William Harvey, Robert Boyle, and Isaac Newton, yet this tale has also attracted the inevitable criticism to which all myths must someday submit. Many scholars have now questioned the idea of the Scientific Revolution itself, and how revolutionary it was, though perhaps few have gone as far to claim, as Steven Shapin did, that "there was no such thing as the Scientific Revolution."[14] Whether or not you want to call it a "revolution," the seventeenth century did witness fundamental changes in how the English understood their connection to nature, however unevenly such changes may have occurred across social ranks.

This book's modest contribution to that story is its discovery of the passionate debate about nature that took place not just in the universities, gentleman's societies, and literary salons, but also in nursery and market gardens and modest households, and in particular, in the

---

[13] Yi-fu Tan, *Escapism* (Baltimore: Johns Hopkins University Press, 1998).

[14] Steven Shapin, *The Scientific Revolution* (Chicago: University of Chicago Press, 1996), p. 1. One of the most useful things about Shapin's little book is the extensive bibliographical essay at the end, to which I refer the reader seeking an overview of the vast field of scholarship on this subject. In my own work, I have found particularly helpful Shapin's own *A Social History of Truth: Civility and Science in Seventeenth-Century England* (Chicago: University of Chicago Press, 1994); Charles Webster, *The Great Instauration: Science, Medicine, and Reform, 1626–1660* (New York: Holmes and Meier, 1976); Barbara Shapiro, *Probability and Certainty in Seventeenth-Century England: A Study of the Relationship between Natural Science, Religion, History, Law, and Literature* (Princeton: Princeton University Press, 1983) and *A Culture of Fact: England 1559–1720* (Ithaca: Cornell University Press, 2000); Thomas, *Man and the Natural World;* and William Eamon, *Science and the Secret of Nature: Books of Secrets in Medieval and Early Modern Culture* (Princeton: Princeton University Press, 1994).

pages of common gardening manuals printed in England from the middle of the sixteenth century onward. For the most part, this genre of nature writing has been thoroughly ignored by historians of both science and garden culture. Historians of science have their sights set on bigger game, and most serious garden historians dismiss these how-to books as tedious and naïve.[15] They have attracted the interest of antiquarians and writers of popular gardening histories, who have found them charming but have not subjected them to sustained analysis.[16] Penelope Hobhouse's *Gardening through the Ages: An Illustrated History of Plants and Their Influence on Garden Styles—from Ancient Egypt to the Present Day* is typical in its approach, which encloses in its broad historical swath pieces of the old books, focusing on details that would make them familiar and appealing to the modern gardener.[17] Like Hobhouse, modern gardeners mostly care for these writings of the past because they would like to make the spirit of old gardens live in the present: witness the titles of Rosemary Verey's *Classic Garden Design: How to Adapt and Recreate Garden Features of the Past* and Graham Stuart Thomas's *Recreating the Period Garden*.[18] The double appeal of quaint history and contemporary relevance is expressed neatly by the jacket copy of Oxford University Press's reissue of Thomas Hill's sixteenth-century garden manual *The Gardeners Labyrinth:* "Those who like Hill relish the feel of good rich soil, 'the delectable sights and smels of the flowers,' the sweetness of a home-grown melon, will not only find his tips invaluable, but will also catch a glimpse of what life was like in late sixteenth- and early seventeenth-century England."[19]

[15] See for example, Michael Charlesworth, ed., *The English Garden: Literary Sources and Documents* (Mountfield, East Sussex: Helm Information, 1993).

[16] While not particularly scholarly, Martin Hoyles's books on gardening books are an invaluable source of information: see his *Gardeners Delight: Gardening Books from 1560 to 1960* (London: Pluto Press, 1994), and *Bread and Roses: Gardening Books from 1560 to 1960* (London: Pluto Press, 1995).

[17] Penelope Hobhouse, *Gardening through the Ages: An Illustrated History of Plants and Their Influence on Garden Styles—from Ancient Egypt to the Present Day* (New York: Simon and Schuster, 1992). For similar popular histories of gardening (as opposed to garden design), see Neil Fairbairn, *A Brief History of Gardening* (Emmaus, Pa.: Rodale, 2001), and Anthony Huxley, *An Illustrated History of Gardening* (New York: Lyons Press, 1978; rpt., 1998), which differs in its focus on the developments of the craft (lawn care, propagation, irrigation, etc.).

[18] Rosemary Verey, *Classic Garden Design: How to Adapt and Recreate Garden Features of the Past* (London: Congdon and Weed, 1986), and Graham Stuart Thomas, *Recreating the Period Garden* (London: David R. Godine, 1985).

[19] Thomas Hill, *The Gardeners Labyrinth*, edited and with an introduction by Richard Mabey (Oxford: Oxford University Press, 1987).

Curiosity and affection first led me to spend time with these eccentric old books: affection for the writers' love of their craft, and curiosity about their arguments and debates about nature. But it was also compelling to witness these fairly ordinary men writing about making art and transforming themselves as well as their surroundings. I thus credit these early English garden books with articulating a kind of everyday "garden theory." One may not find in them the kind of high garden theory that John Dixon Hunt has been seeking for landscape architecture, "theory as contemplation, the deep understanding of praxis from within."[20] But my project does respond to one part of Hunt's call to think about the intellectual traditions of landscape architecture: that is, I want to "discover within the activities of garden art and landscape architecture themselves the grounds of an adequate theory." I take these garden manuals on their own terms, investigating the "detailed and strategic dialogue between theory and practice" that took place at every level of writing about the garden in the early modern period.[21]

Green Desire thus mostly concerns books, writing, and rhetoric and not garden design or garden history, although those topics, of course, come into it. But my approach is also new because it focuses on the rhetoric of the "how-to" books and not on more elevated texts, literary, scientific, or philosophical. Throughout the argument, both the poets—Milton, Marvell, and Shakespeare—and the scientists—Bacon, Hartlib, and Evelyn—do enter into the story. The mixture of genres is deliberate but unusual insofar as the literary and scientific texts appear here to explain the garden manuals. Literary readers are now all familiar with the New Historicist use of everyday or very banal texts to explicate high literary genres, when this historical criticism strives to root literary texts in their contemporary cultural and historical moments. So perhaps it will seem perverse to some readers that canonical literature is brought in here to interpret the garden manuals, and not the other way around.

I have chosen this ordering for two reasons. First, arguments, images, and ideas shared by the manuals and the literary and scientific texts should bolster my appeal to have the manuals taken seriously, be-

---

[20] John Dixon Hunt, *Greater Perfections: The Practice of Garden Theory* (Philadelphia: University of Pennsylvania Press, 2000), p. xi; see also his essay on seventeenth-century garden theory in the same book.
[21] Ibid., p. 8.

cause they engaged important social and intellectual issues. Second, I want to argue that the scientific and literary discourses of nature seeped into the more practical writing about gardening, for example, when the literary image of the "flower woman" began to appear in how-to books about flower gardening, or the language of scientific "disinterest" spread through the late seventeenth-century manuals for gentlemen gardeners. Like early modern conduct or marriage manuals, the early English garden books are shot through with social and political language defined by a changing world. This book cannot possibly tell the whole story of the transformation of early modern English social and political life, but it will mark those significant points of contact between the field of practical gardening and other realms.

In recent years, some scholars have looked closely at the genre of husbandry books and agrarian literature, in particular because of their links to the literary genre of the georgic, or poems on the pleasures of the rural life. John Dixon Hunt has been perhaps the most thoughtful and prolific contributor to scholarship on the relationship between literature and landscape architecture in post-Restoration England.[22] In his book *The Georgic Revolution* Anthony Low devoted serious attention to sixteenth- and seventeenth-century husbandry books pursuing the georgic moralization of labor (though he had little patience for men like the entrepreneurial manual writer Gervase Markham).[23] In 1992 Michael Leslie and Timothy Raylor edited the fascinating collection of essays *Culture and Cultivation in Early Modern England: Writing and the Land,* which explores the intricate connections between literary and agrarian discourses.[24] Andrew McRae's *God Speed the Plough: The Representation of Agrarian England, 1500–1660* is the most comprehensive and compelling study of the social and intellectual dimensions of agrarian writing in this period.[25] I am indebted to all these scholars for

[22] For other works by Hunt, see *The Genius of the Place: The English Landscape Garden, 1620–1820,* ed. John Dixon Hunt and Peter Willis (Cambridge: MIT Press, 1988), and *Garden and Grove: The Italian Renaissance Garden in the English Imagination, 1600–1750* (Philadelphia: University of Pennsylvania Press, 1986).

[23] Anthony Low, *The Georgic Revolution* (Princeton: Princeton University Press, 1985).

[24] Michael Leslie and Timothy Raylor, eds., *Culture and Cultivation in Early Modern England: Writing and the Land* (Leicester: Leicester University Press, 1992).

[25] Andrew McRae, *God Speed the Plough: The Representation of Agrarian England, 1500–1660* (New York: Cambridge University Press, 1996).

ambition. In the end, the garden writers of the end of the seventeenth century succeeded all too well in suppressing the memory of those early English gardeners and their dreams of mastery.

I myself would hope that many different sorts of readers would find pleasure from this book. Some might read it because they are students of early modern English culture, to explore an unfamiliar genre that engages problems of art, nature, gender, social status, and work. But I am also hoping for readers interested in gardening itself, who might come to care about these manuals and their authors. They are odd, to be sure, and I would not recommend that modern gardeners follow much of their advice, but we can indeed see something of ourselves in these men and women and their green desires. These books helped to shape many of our contemporary ideas of the art, from the fashion value of flowers to the strange dignity and pleasure of garden labor—and this is their story.

❦ 1 ❦

Composing Gardens

Most gardeners cannot get enough of books, along with rare bulbs, shiny tools, and carloads of compost. Bookshops hardly know how to handle them all. The Borders bookstore in Philadelphia has set up sections on general gardening, Asian gardening, fruits and vegetables, landscaping, flowers and flower arrangement, annuals and bulbs, perennials, flowers divided alphabetically, and plants including cacti, ferns, herbs, marijuana, and mushrooms. The shelves extend then to books on wildflowers, lawn care, trees and shrubs, and finally farming and livestock, completing a taxonomy that stretches from bonsai to chickens. One wonders how to account for this appetite for garden books. Surely the appeal of gardening is that it is so unlike reading: sweating rather than thinking, breathing fresh air rather than the dust of the study.

Of course, gardeners read to get advice about what to plant, where to plant it, and how to keep it alive. But even then every gardener knows that the wisdom found in books is not the same as that earned by growing things. Garden knowledge gained from experience is always local. What works even for your neighbor may not work for you, and even then, as trees grow or fall, or buildings rise, you may have to change your ways. But the rules in books never change, and they speak without knowing the gardener's strength, place, time, and wealth.

Writers of garden books do recognize this problem. They often caution the reader to think of his or her own ground, place, and station in life. As John Brookes advises in *The Garden Book*, "get back to reality, forget the stately layouts that you might have seen and think about the type of garden you really need. . . . This will provide much food for thought, for the permutations of possible requirements among even a family of four, considering their diverse ages, and various likes and dislikes, are endless."[1] *Taylor's Master Guide to Gardening* tracks the changing needs we have in our lives from youth to retirement, when "the body lodges a protest" and "reluctantly, we cut back, maybe even move to a smaller property."[2] The writers of the first English gardening books also hoped that people would plant a *suitable* garden: as John Parkinson put it in his *Paradisi in Sole,* "although many men must be content with any plat of ground . . . because a more large or convenient cannot bee had to their habitation: Yet I perswade my selfe, that Gentlemen of the better sort and quality, will provide such a parcell of ground to bee laid out for their Garden . . . as may be fit and answerable to the degree they hold."[3] Sensible gardening demands decorum, both natural and social.[4]

But even though the books tell us to be careful and to stay down to earth, most people read them because they are books of dreams about what might be as much as about what is. As Jamaica Kincaid has written, no real garden can outdo that dream: "I shall never have the garden I have in my mind, but that for me is the joy of it: certain things can never be realized and so all the more reason to attempt them."[5] Modern books and catalogues excite these cravings with lush illustrations of someone else's garden, which allow readers to fantasize that they might be their own.[6] Lacking such pictorial resources, early mod-

---

[1] John Brookes, *The Garden Book* (New York: Crown, 1984), p. 8.

[2] *Taylor's Master Guide to Gardening* (Boston: Houghton Mifflin, 1994), p. 3.

[3] John Parkinson, *Paradisi in Sole: Paradisus Terristris or A garden of all sorts of pleasant flowers* (London, 1629; rpt., New York: Dover, 1991), p. 3.

[4] On class assumptions at stake in modern ideas about gardening, see Mara Miller, *The Garden as an Art* (Albany: State University of New York Press, 1993), pp. 35–36: "A sense of stability and of the predictability of one's tenure—often perquisites of middle and upper-class status . . . are prerequisites for gardening and imply both a certain kind of privilege in relation to the passage of time and the habit of thinking on a certain temporal scale, which may become part of the definition of social class. . . . Gardens also imply leisure—the leisure to enjoy them but more importantly the leisure to have become educated, in whatever senses may be relevant to the particular gardenist's culture." On decorum, see Derek Attridge, "Puttenham's Perplexity: Nature, Art, and the Supplement in Renaissance Poetic Theory," in *Literary Theory/Renaissance Texts,* ed. Patricia Parker and David Quint (Baltimore: Johns Hopkins University Press, 1986), p. 269.

[5] Jamaica Kincaid, *My Garden (Book):* (New York: Farrar, Straus and Giroux, 1999), p. 220.

[6] But see ibid., p. 62, on the special appeal of catalogues without pictures.

ern garden books rely instead on words to stir the imagination. In 1629 John Parkinson believed his books should indeed excite passion as well as instill decorum, when he told his readers who "desired to have faire flowers" "what to choose, or what to desire."[7] The garden book, that is, not only teaches *how* to have what you want, but it will also tell you *what* to desire.

What did it mean in 1629 when Parkinson thought of telling his reader "what to desire"? The emotions conveyed by the word "desire" sprawled as widely in Parkinson's time as they do in our own. In its most neutral meaning, "desire" could be coolly construed as a need or want expressed politely: the word is found in the Parliament records referring to sober petitions and in dry orders for consumer goods. Yet from its first recorded uses in Middle English (from the French *désir*), "desire" also carried the tinge of longing, beyond want, whether sexual or otherwise. Once one left the world of polite discourse, "desire" connoted something improper. Certainly, in the religious language of Protestant early modern England, this kind of desire lived with the devil and was best feared and mastered.

Desire was also associated with ambition: a drive as dangerous in that time as sexual longing. It is no coincidence that the word stamps Shakespeare's great plays of political striving, and in particular, *Macbeth, Richard III, Coriolanus,* and *Hamlet.* When Macbeth begs that light not see his "black and deep desires," he confesses his need not for some *thing* or some one else, but for himself to be more or to be other than what he is now. In early modern England, an aristocrat burning to excel might be admired, but ambition, whether in a prince or a shoemaker, was symptomatic of worrying changes taking place across social ranks. Despite the government's and church's earnest promulgating of an orthodoxy of social order and hierarchy, English society was on the move in the cities and the countryside. Old forms of agriculture were being disrupted by the practice of enclosing common fields, large households were breaking up, people were moving to cities to make new lives, new professions were being established, and the influx of money and goods from trade was creating a new breed of wealthy entrepreneurs.[8] As Keith Wrightson has observed, as tradi-

---

[7] Parkinson, *Paradisi*, epistle to the reader.

[8] There is a substantial literature on the question of social and economic change in England in this period; see, among others, Lawrence Stone, "Social Mobility in England, 1500–1700," *Past and Present* 33 (1966): 16–55; A. Fletcher and J. Stevenson, eds., *Order and Disorder in Early Modern England* (Cambridge: Cambridge University Press,

tional distinctions of status were thus breaking down, "social mobility was recognized as a structural feature of society, an element of dynamism which, in the context of a society acutely conscious of social stratification, served to confirm and highlight rather than abrogate social distinctions."[9] Desiring, in that context, meant not being content with your given lot and yearning for a new identity, better than that with which you were born. But, then, even more so than before, people were concerned to *define* the object of social desire and thus to mark and protect social differences.

Unlike "need," desire implies a certain excess: you can desire what you really do not need. As such, desire is also infinitely malleable. Parkinson knew only too well what has become a theme of modern cultural studies: people need to be told what to want, since that hunger does not necessarily well up spontaneously from within them. Today, while people of course still lust for sex and power, perhaps the most complex engine of desire is global consumer culture. It is almost impossible to escape the barrage of images and words designed to make us want things we do not need or never even imagined coveting. At the beginning of the seventeenth century when Parkinson wrote, consumer culture had already begun to take hold in England's urban centers—and certainly in the gardener's world.[10] The growing appetite for consumer items, whether fine lace or rare garden bulbs, or a stately house and a stunning garden, intersected with the desire that fueled social ambition, since it was implied that possessing such things signaled social advancement. All the more so, people felt that desire for things—and green desire—had to be managed and guided, in a world still anxious about social mobility and the value of decorum, whereby your possessions and behavior should clearly reveal your station in life.[11]

This book tells the story of how the writers of early English garden books tried to create this world of decorum and desire in the world of the garden. Rather than taking these gardening manuals at face value,

---

1985); and Frank Whigham, *Ambition and Privilege: The Social Tropes of Elizabethan Courtesy Theory* (Berkeley: University of California Press, 1984).

[9] Keith Wrightson, *English Society, 1580–1680* (New Brunswick: Rutgers University Press, 1982; rpt., 1984), p. 22.

[10] See Joan Thirsk, *Economic Policy and Projects: The Development of a Consumer Society in Early Modern England* (Oxford: Clarendon, 1978).

[11] On the functions of clothes and fashion as unstable markers of social identity, see Ann Rosalind Jones and Peter Stallybrass, *Renaissance Clothing and the Materials of Memory* (Cambridge: Cambridge University Press, 2000).

I ask how, when, why, and for whom these men wrote their prescriptions and dreams for cultivating fruits and flowers. The easy answer would be that they did it to sell books and make money, but since authors then did not profit much from their books, there must have been other reasons. The printers and writers wanted to both create and influence readers. We can look at prefaces and title pages to find out how these authors aimed to build a readership, while they also sought to generate and control the gardener's ambitions. Some professed their intention to serve their country or the interests of the "plain English husbandman," or the country gentleman or housewife; other wanted to cater to the tastes of gentry. All wanted to make something new of gardening itself, to elevate that work to the status of both profession and recreation, and thus to remake themselves. The complex desires they had for their gardens and their books, that is, cannot be disentangled from their dreams of their own lives. Even in their most banal prose, they fashioned the image of the gardener as sensualist, man of wit, lover of God, and creator of wealth.

In order to frame the story of garden writing, this chapter surveys the flourishing practices of English gardening from the sixteenth to the early eighteenth century, and in particular, the remarkable diversity of early modern gardeners, all wanting something different from their work: a paltry wage, a comfortable household, a profitable business, a magnificent estate, or scientific knowledge. In particular, it considers the ways in which gardening offered a path to self-improvement for all ranks of men, even those who would have been wary of ambition. It considers who among them might have been reading the books produced, when writers and printers became critical players in shaping the identity of a gardener as someone who reads and works to better himself and his world. The chapter ends by reviewing how some of these men themselves surveyed the history of their art. Their fabricated histories reveal how they variously imagined their own origins, when they wrote themselves into the story of gardening's progress over the centuries.

The Complete Gardener

Turning back to the sixteenth century, how do we know who was working in English gardens, what they were doing, and what their status was? What did they aspire to be? The stories of the botanists and plant collectors have been told many times, and the gardens of the great have been celebrated in gardening histories, but the traces of the lives of weeding women, market gardeners, seedsmen, and nursery-men remain buried in civic records or household account books. Agri-cultural and social historians have begun to mine the archives to tell their stories. As John Harvey directed in his edition of John Galpine's nursery catalogue: "As a corrective to an undue reliance upon literary history of gardening as an art form, we have to turn away from the books which tell us what planters thought they were trying to achieve, to contemporary records of what was actually possible"; that is, we must dig out the scraps of bills for seeds and plants and scribbled de-signs that are all that remain of real gardens.[12] Even then, many of these documents come from great estates, and thus they may present only a partial picture.

Green Desire does not claim to tell the real story of these gardeners, which is a task for future generations of garden historians. However, to display the gap between what garden writers "thought they were trying to achieve" and "what was actually possible," this book needs to lay out for those readers unfamiliar with garden history what we know now about the practice of gardening in England up through the early eighteenth century. Mara Miller reminds us that even today not all gardeners are equal, since "we apply to gardens the same hierar-chical distinction between artist, who defines a vision, and craftsman, who carries out the vision of another: gardenists (designers and theo-rists, although they sometimes do some of the labor), are superior to gardeners, who dig the holes."[13] By the eighteenth century, the class system of English gardeners was highly complex: there were nursery-men and seedsmen, market gardeners, botanists, "plain" gardeners, and "florists," among others, each vying for business. Some of these types of gardener were in fact relatively new: the *Oxford English Dic-tionary* lists as the first occurrence of the term "florist" Sir Henry Wot-ton's comment in 1623 that his work "hath given me acquaintance with some excellent Florists (as they are stiled)," meaning someone who grows flowers purely for decorative purposes.[14] Garden manuals played an important part in shaping the identity and status of a per-

[12] John Harvey, introduction to *The Georgian Garden: An Eighteenth-Century Nursery-man's Catalogue* (Stanbridge: Dovecote Press, 1983), p. 7.

[13] Miller, *Garden as an Art*, p. 80.

[14] Ruth Duthie, *Florists' Flowers and Societies* (Haverfordwest, Dyfed: C. I. Thomas and Sons, 1988), p. 5.

son called a gardener, whether florist, botanist, man of leisure, or householder, and in generating the language used to describe this work, including profession, calling, art, and science, as well as labor.[15]

Sustaining the gardens of the gentry and the botanists who compiled herbals were the hands and minds of weeding women and laboring men. In recent years, several scholars have unearthed the lives of "servants-in-husbandry," young men and women who were employed and boarded as agricultural laborers. Ann Kussmaul estimates that "between one-third and one-half of hired labor in early modern agriculture was supplied by servants in husbandry."[16] Most worked in the fields, plowing, sowing, and reaping, but some also helped to prepare and maintain kitchen and pleasure gardens, great and small. The records for estate gardens rarely list the wages of such men and women, since many were casual workers, but we do glimpse them occasionally. The garden accounts for Hampton Court in 1696 list a large staff divided among the head gardeners, a permanent group of laborers, and workers paid by the day for digging and weeding (men at two shillings to one shilling and sixpence a day, the women at eight pence a day).[17] Such diggers and weeders may not have been dignified with the name of "gardener," but without them, none of these gardens would have been possible (see figure 1 for a sympathetic depiction of male and female garden labor, with a group of feckless aristocrats partying in the background). Who can say what they thought of the gardens they cultivated?

Sometimes garden books directly addressed the "country housewife" and the "English husbandman," whose work helped to sustain the household economy. The social category of husbandman was formally distinct from the status of yeoman, traditionally a more prosperous and better-educated farmer. But husbandman defined an occupation of farming, as well as a social rank. So Gervase Markham, a gentleman, could call himself a husbandman[18] when he meant one

---

[15] On the development of the professions, see Rosemary O'Day, *The Professions in Early Modern England, 1450–1800: Servants of the Commonweal* (Harlow: Longman, 2000).

[16] Ann Kussmaul, *Servants in Husbandry in Early Modern England* (Cambridge: Cambridge University Press, 1981), pp. 4–5.

[17] Miles Hadfield, *A History of British Gardening* (London: John Murray, 1979), p. 153.

[18] See David Cressy, *Literacy and the Social Order: Reading and Writing in Tudor and Stuart England* (Cambridge: Cambridge University Press, 1980), p. 126: "Contemporary commentators sometimes had difficulty in separating the husbandmen from the

FIGURE 1. Pieter van der Heyden, *Spring*. Reproduced by permission of the Metropolitan Museum of Art, Harris Brisbane Dick Fund, 1926 (26.72.57).

who "with discretion and good order tilleth the ground in his due seasons, making it fruitfull to bring forth Corn and plants, meete for the sustenance of man."[19] Markham's *English Housewife* and *English Husbandman* both include advice on the culture of flowers, herbs, and fruit, while neither housewife nor husbandman would have been labeled by the term "gardener" alone.[20]

---

yeomen in their classifications of the social order. The problem continues for modern historians, not least because the activity of husbandry was the source of yeoman profits. . . . In practice the distinction between yeomen and husbandmen was one of esteem." But see also Wrightson, *English Society*, p. 33, on a distinction between husbandman and yeoman according to stability of income and net worth.

[19] Gervase Markham, *The English Husbandman* (London, 1613; rpt., New York: Garland, 1982), sig. a3r.

[20] Thus Thomas Hill (using the pseudonym of Dydymus Mountain) observed in *The Gardeners Labyrinth* (London, 1594; rpt., New York: Garland, 1982), that "the husband-

For many, however, the gardener was a permanent household servant, better than mere day laborers. The characteristics of William Lawson's gardener make him sound like the ideal household help: "Such a Gardner as will conscionably, quietly and patiently travell in your Orchard, God shall crowne the labors of his hands with joyfulnesse, and make the cloudes droppe fatnesse upon your Trees, hee will provoke your love, and earne his Wages, and fees belonging to his place."[21] As Lawson's prose suggests, a good gardener was a valuable domestic asset, and such men were increasingly well rewarded. Household records from the seventeenth century indicate that before the Civil War, gardeners were usually paid far less than male cooks and more along the lines of butlers (way below ten pounds a year). After the Restoration the head gardener could command a higher salary, surpassing those of butlers: in 1660–1700, the annual wages of butlers ranged from three to ten pounds sterling, whereas those of head gardeners ranged from four to twenty pounds.[22] If one were privileged to be a royal gardener, of course, one could make considerably more and pave the way to social advancement.

It was this sort of English gardener, and especially the gardeners who served peers and kings and queens, who often gained some fame and fortune, especially in the latter half of the seventeenth century and the early eighteenth century. When Moses Cook published a book on fruit-tree cultivation in 1679, the title page advertised him as "Gardener to that great Encourager of Planting, the Right Honorable, the Earl of Essex."[23] John Evelyn attributed the gardens at Essex's estate to Cook, noting that they were "very rare, and cannot be otherwise, having so skillful an Artist to governe them as Mr. Cook, who is as to the Mechanic part not ignorant in Mathematics, and pretends to Astrology."[24] The John Tradescants, elder and younger, worked as gardeners for several noble patrons. The elder Tradescant gardened for

man or Gardener, shal enjoy a most commodious and delectable Garden, which both knoweth, can, and will orderly dress the same" (p. 3).

[21] William Lawson, *A New Orchard and Garden* (London, 1618; rpt., New York: Garland, 1982), p. 3.

[22] J. T. Cliffe, *The World of the Country House in Seventeenth-Century England* (New Haven: Yale University Press, 1999), p. 101.

[23] Moses Cook, *The Manner of Raising, Ordering, and Improving Forest and Fruit Trees* (London, 1679), title page.

[24] John Evelyn, *Diary*, ed. E. S. De Beer, 6 vols. (Oxford: Clarendon Press, 1955), 4:200.

FIGURE 2. Charles II receiving a pineapple; after Hendrik Danckerts. Reproduced by permission of the Victoria and Albert Picture Library.

the Cecils, the Wottons, and later the Duke of Buckingham, before he was appointed keeper of the royal gardens at Oatlands. The younger Tradescant started as his father's assistant and succeeded him at Oatlands in 1638 (at a magnificent salary of 100 pounds a year).[25] John Rose, who was "keeper of St. James' garden" for Charles II, has been immortalized by his association with the painting of a gardener presenting a pineapple to the king (see figure 2).[26] Whether or not this painting in fact depicts Rose or the first pineapple (the association has been contested), it evokes the gravity and intimacy of the relationship

[25] Prudence Leith-Ross, *The John Tradescants: Gardeners to the Rose and Lily Queen* (London: Peter Owen, 1984), p. 106.

[26] See Hadfield, *History of British Gardening*, p. 126. Hadfield points out several reasons why we should doubt this identification.

between the gardener and his royal master. The gardener may bow before his majesty, but he occupies the same garden space, and he can offer his king something as rare as jewels.[27]

Other kinds of gardeners made a living by working for themselves: the market gardeners, seed sellers, and nurserymen (which included those estate gardeners who later branched out into selling). Housewives and husbandmen had long brought their surplus produce to market in town and cities, and men had been growing orchard fruit to sell since the beginning of the sixteenth century. According to Ronald Webber, it was Henry VIII who first encouraged commercial fruit production at the orchard of his "fruiterer," Richard Harris.[28] Not until the mid-sixteenth century, however, did men and women around towns and cities begin to make serious money by tending their own or rented gardens and selling the produce. Dutch and French immigrants catalyzed market gardening in England when they introduced new root crops and their commercial production, as well as the growing of flowers and seeds for income. The practice flourished in London, and then throughout the south of England near the towns that relied on their produce.[29] By the end of the seventeenth century, market gardening was a major enterprise, serving a consumer appetite for more varied fruits and vegetables: Malcolm Thick estimates that English market gardeners worked 10,000 acres in 1660, but more than 110,000 acres by 1721.[30]

Such market gardens produced vegetables and bush fruit and not ornamental flowers; instead, commercial growing of flowers and fine fruits thrived in the nursery gardens that supplied both the market gardeners and small and large estates. Some of these nurserymen had been market gardeners at first, while others had gained their experience as estate gardeners. Many became successful businessmen and significantly advanced English horticulture.[31] As early as the sixteenth

---

[27] See John Ozell's translation of Boileau's "Epistle to my Gardener," where the Gardener is called "Thou ruler of my garden" (in John Dixon Hunt, ed., *The Oxford Book of Garden Verse* [Oxford: Oxford University Press, 1993], p. 82).

[28] Ronald Webber, *The Early Horticulturalists* (Newton Abbot: David and Charles, 1968), p. 31. See also H. Frederic Janson, *Pomona's Harvest: An Illustrated Chronicle of Antiquarian Fruit Literature* (Portland, Ore.: Timber Press, 1996).

[29] Malcolm Thick, "Market Gardening in England and Wales," in *Agrarian History of England and Wales*, ed. J. Thirsk (Cambridge: Cambridge University Press, 1985), p. 503.

[30] Ibid., p. 507.

[31] For a comprehensive account of the beginnings of the nursery business in England, see John Harvey, *The Early Nurserymen* (London: Philamore, 1974). See also

century, several nursery gardens were already established in London and Westminster, including that of Henry Russell, where one could buy fruit trees and flowers, and John Banbury's nursery in Tothill Street. Ralph Tuggy, often cited by both John Parkinson and John Gerard for his "rarities," opened a flower nursery in Westminster in 1620.[32] After the Restoration Thomas Hamner purchased fruits and flowers from several London nurserymen: for example, he paid one nurseryman for twenty-three different kinds of gillyflowers at eighteen pence the root, and another for plants and seeds of anemones (nineteen different kinds of roots, at prices ranging from sixpence for an ounce of "Rebecca starrs" seeds to one root of "Bella Ciba" at one shilling, sixpence).[33] Several nurserymen were confident enough of their skill that they also wrote about their practice. John Rea, who composed an influential gardening book on flower culture, was a nurseryman in Kinlet in Shropshire. In the late seventeenth century Thomas Fairchild, later author of *The City Gardener*, established his nursery in Southwark, where he became well known for his efforts in plant hybridization as well as for his "curious garden."[34] The most famous of the nursery gardens was the Brompton Park nursery, established in 1681 by four men who had been gardeners to the great: Roger Looker, John Field, Moses Cook, and George London. In 1687, with Looker and Field dead and Cook retired, Henry Wise joined with London to build a massive and profitable operation that stayed in business until 1851. Wise and London themselves produced a popular translation of a French garden book, published as *The Retir'd Gardener* in 1706.

A commercial market for seeds flourished along with the nursery business. There had always been an informal market for exchange of seeds, and garden books advised the reader to save seeds. But gardeners were also buying new kinds of seed. Most of the evidence about the traffic in seeds mentions vegetable crops, yet, as Thick reports, "flower seeds, of which little evidence of commercial production has

Thick, "Market Gardening," p. 525: "Many of the early nurserymen were former gardeners in noble or gentle households, and such establishments continued to supply recruits to the trade who, having learnt their skills in private gardens, saw the commercial opportunities in setting up their own businesses."

[32] See Michael Leapman, *The Ingenious Mr. Fairchild: The Forgotten Father of the Flower Garden* (London: Headline, 2000), pp. 53–54. Also see Harvey, *The Early Nurserymen*, passim.

[33] See *The Garden Book of Sir Thomas Hanmer*, intro. Eleanour Sinclair Rohde (London: Gerald Howe, 1933), pp. 166–75.

[34] See Leapman, *Ingenious Mr. Fairchild*, passim.

been found, were nevertheless demanded by the creators of pleasure gardens and sold by men whose lists of wares contained ever more varieties."[35] In 1673, while the seedsman John Reynolds's inventory was overwhelmingly invested in vegetables and herbs, he also had in stock thirty pounds of poppy and three pounds of stock gillyflower seeds plus "divers small quantities of fine seeds and flower seeds."[36]

With this trade in seed as well as plants came anxiety about quality control and bad business practices. When supplying the needs of horticulture became good business, some men and women saw the advantage in cheating the market. Hugh Platt complained about buying corrupt artichoke seed,[37] and Richard Gardiner reviled as traitors to their country those whose seed was "olde and dead" or "false and counterfeit."[38] Thus the business of gardening attracted the suspicions about market practices endemic to a developing consumer economy. Gardening had ceased to be merely the practice of monks laboring inside their walls or householders working for their own subsistence: it had become a way to get somewhere in the world, whether through labor, craft, business acumen, or fraud.

In London this growth of market and nursery gardening, with all the accompanying hazards, led in 1605 to the formation of the Worshipful Company of Gardeners, a guild chartered in an effort to control the proliferation of entrepreneurial gardeners. While a gardeners' guild had existed since the reign of Edward III, this charter represented the first attempt to oversee what was called "the trade, crafte, or misterie of Gardening, planting, grafting, setting, sowing, cutting, arboring, rocking, mounting, covering, fencing and removing of plantes, herbes, seedes, fruites, trees, stocks, setts, and of contryving the conveyances to the same belonging." Its purpose was also to exclude "certain ignorant and unskillful persons who had taken upon themselves to practice the said trade, not having been apprenticed thereto, [and] had sold dead and corrupt plants, seeds, stocks, and trees." The second royal charter in 1616 "prohibited any person inhabiting the City or within six miles thereof ('other than such our subjects as shall garden for their own household use and private spending') from using or exercising

---

[35] Malcolm Thick, "Garden Seeds in England before the Late Eighteenth Century: I. Seed Growing," *Agricultural History Review* 38 (1990): 67.

[36] Ibid., p. 116.

[37] Hugh Platt, second part of *The Garden of Eden* (London, 1675), p. 130.

[38] See Thick, "Garden Seeds," p. 106.

the 'art or mystery of gardening' . . . without the license of the Company." Some applicants for membership in the Company were excluded because they were only "husbandmen" who had not served apprenticeships.[39]

However, despite all these efforts, the Company was not very successful in exerting its control over the garden business. Men continued to pour into the city to hire themselves out as gardeners,[40] and, in any case, the City of London was never receptive to the Company's claims, only granting the members freedom of the city in 1659.[41] The Company proposed to "incorporate ten garden designers, 150 noblemen's gardeners, 400 gentlemen's gardeners, 100 nurserymen, 150 florists, twenty botanists, and 200 market gardeners; and to establish a system of technical correspondence, employment agencies and supervision of all gardeners and apprentices" throughout England and Wales, but the scheme never worked.[42] The Company's story thus signals both men's desire to control gardening as a complex "mystery" and the difficulty of doing so when gardening had become as much as a business as a craft and when it offered such a promising route to self-improvement.

The "occupation" of gardener was not limited to those men and women who made their living by garden work. Among the gardeners of early modern England we must also count gentlemen, scholars, clergymen, and aristocrats who thought of themselves as scientists or scholars of horticulture, while they gardened too. Notable among these were the herbalists John Gerard and John Parkinson, William Turner, Thomas Johnson, Nicolas Culpeper, and William Coles. These were multitalented men, some of low and some gentle birth, with cir-

---

[39] Arnold F. Steele, *The Worshipful Company of Gardeners of London: A History of Its Revival, 1890–1960* (London: Worshipful Company of Gardeners of London, 1964), pp. 31–37.

[40] "At this time, the Company's problems were further compounded by the fact that hundreds of country labourers were moving into the London area to work on the grounds of Hampton Court and Kensington Palace, and on the gardens of the Duke of Beaufort and the Earls of Chesterfield, Sunderland, Rutland, Bedford, Devonshire and Craven. At one time as many as five hundred were employed, with only ten 'able masters' and forty other professed gardeners, many of whom afterwards posed as gardeners. Thus the Company not only faced continuing difficulties with controlling the markets, but it appeared to have little influence over the employment of recognised gardeners in the seats of power" (ibid., p. 41).

[41] Leapman, *Ingenious Mr. Fairchild*, p. 84.

[42] Steele, *Worshipful Company*, p. 41.

cles of acquaintance ranging from nurserymen to kings. Most started as apothecaries or barber-surgeons, but they came to take on many occupations including those of author and gardener. The first notable English herbalist, William Turner, was the son of a tanner, but he studied medicine at Cambridge, where he became a cleric and passionate religious reformer. During that time he published his *Newe Herball*, based on his observation of British plants.[43] John Gerard was a barber-surgeon, admitted to the freedom of the Barber-Surgeon's Company in 1569; however, he also served as a gardener to William Cecil in the Strand and at Theobolds, while overseeing his own garden in Holborn, where he cultivated more than a thousand herbs and plants. A legal document relating to a land transaction in 1605 lists him as "herbarist to James I."[44] Thomas Johnson, a freeman of the Apothecaries' guild, emended and enlarged Gerard's *Herbal* significantly in 1633, since even in its own time the book was criticized as a messy unattributed translation of Rembert Dodoens's herbal *Pemptades*. John Parkinson, who earned fame both for his gardening book *Paradisi in Sole* (1629) and his massive herbal *Theatrum Botanicum* (1640), was also well connected, although we know less of his life. Like Gerard, he was born outside London, but by 1616 he was a practicing London apothecary with a garden at Long Acre. His *Paradisi in Sole* is prefaced by letters of testimonial from fellows in his craft, a doctor, and a knight, noting that he served as apothecary to James I and as the "botanicus regius primarius" to Charles I.

The portraits of Gerard and Parkinson decorating their books exude their pride in their status (see figures 3 and 4). Both bear their coats of arms and are encircled by their Latin titles. Gerard's portrait announces that he is a "civis" or citizen as well as a surgeon of London, and his elaborate dress speaks of his being a man of substance. Parkinson's portrait notes he is an apothecary, and his dress is also elegant in the style of his time. Yet both men are marked as gardeners, too: Gerard holds a potato plant, and Parkinson what appears to be a rose campion, signaling their plantsmanship. While these men clearly served other men, whether as apothecaries or gardeners, as herbalists they

---

[43] John Gilmour, *British Botanists* (London: Collins, 1946), p. 10.
[44] Eleanour Sinclair Rohde, *The Old English Herbals* (London: Longmans, Green, 1922; rpt., New York: Dover, 1971), p. 103. See also Frank J. Anderson, *An Illustrated History of the Herbals* (New York: Columbia University Press, 1977).

FIGURE 3. Portrait of John Gerard, from his *Herball* (1597). Reproduced by permission of the Folger Shakespeare Library.

FIGURE 4. Portrait of John Parkinson, from *Paradisi in Sole* (1629). Reproduced by permission of the Annenberg Rare Book and Manuscript Library, University of Pennsylvania.

thought of their works as contributing to the health and wealth of England and of themselves as men of honor and learning.

The seventeenth century witnessed the emergence of academic botanists who succeeded the herbalists, spanning the world of scholarship and gardening practice. The first Chair of Botany in Britain was established at Oxford in 1669, with Robert Morison as the occupant. Morison himself had come from a gentle background; he learned his botany while in exile in France during the Interregnum, when he studied with the French king's botanist and supervised the Duke of Orleans's garden at Blois. But a botanical garden had bloomed at Oxford since 1621;[45] it was first designed and planted by Jacob Bobart, a man of obscure origins (he was also a local innkeeper). Bobart's son, who succeeded his father in that garden, was appointed the Oxford Professor of Botany after Morison, showing that more than one road led to such a grand title. John Ray, their contemporary, was educated at Cambridge and taught there until 1662, when he left after refusing to assent to the Act of Uniformity. While not holding an academic post Ray produced a massive amount of botanical research, in particular, his *Historia Plantarum Generalis* (1686–1704), describing "all known plants" and covering "plant anatomy, physiology and morphology."[46] Men such as Morison and Ray, as well as Leonard Plunkenet and Nehemiah Grew, who published his *Anatomy of Plants* in 1682, did live in a world apart from many of the writers discussed in this book, where they busied themselves with anatomizing and classifying dried specimens. But while they may have lived at a distance from the gardens where the work was done, by the end of the seventeenth century their groundbreaking scholarship on plant propagation did begin to transform the world of practical gardening.

English botany and gardening also thrived in the intellectual circles dedicated to furthering the spirit of Baconian science. There gentlemen began to preach the benefits of gardening as a means to improve the English land and the English people—not excluding the gentleman himself. With works such as his *Sylva Sylvarum* and his vision of scientific research sketched out in his utopian *New Atlantis*, Francis Bacon had marked a new direction for horticultural experiments, both for

---

[45] There was no botanical garden at Cambridge until 1759; the Royal Garden at Edinburgh was founded in 1667; the Apothecaries' Garden in Chelsea in 1673 (Gilmour, *British Botanists*, p. 14).

[46] Ibid., p. 18.

gain and for the advancement of knowledge. During the Interregnum, while one group gathered at Oxford under the leadership of John Wilkins and Robert Boyle to explore the new "experimental" philosophy, Samuel Hartlib and his circle promoted innovation in the agricultural sciences.[47] Hartlib's circle, which included Ralph Austen, Cressy Dimock, and John Beale, was eager to improve husbandry by designing new fertilizers, promoting drainage, and cultivating new cereal crops. They also led the way in defining the study of agriculture as an "experimental" science to be disseminated for the public good. Although these innovators' visibility dimmed after the Restoration because of Hartlib's associations with the Puritan cause, they transformed the way English gentlemen thought about agriculture, when (in Michael Leslie's words), "country gentlemen took to experimenting with new crops, new livestock techniques, new fertilizers, drainage and irrigation, ploughing, and sowing."[48] Not only market gardeners and nurserymen, then, could see their way to better living through plants; it was a direction for the gentry as well.

Following the work of the Oxford experimentalists, the Royal Society of London for the Promotion of Natural Knowledge, chartered by Charles II in 1662, encouraged the study of gardening as a noble pursuit. In his enthusiastic defense of the Society's work published in 1667, Thomas Sprat described the kind of experiments related to "vegetables" that the Society had witnessed to date:

the growth of Vegetables in several kinds of Water; . . . of hindring the growth of Seed Corn in the Earth, by extracting the Air: and furthering their growth, by admitting it: of steeping Seeds of several kinds: of inverting the Positions of Roots, and Plants set in the ground, to find whether there are values in the Pores of the Wood, that only open one way: of the decrease of the weight of Plants growing in the air: of *Lignum*

[47] For the fullest account of the activities of the Hartlib group, see Charles Webster, *The Great Instauration: Science, Medicine, and Reform, 1626–1660* (New York: Holmes and Meier, 1976). On the contribution of the Hartlib circle to the theory and practice of gardening, see John Dixon Hunt, "Historical Excursus: Late Seventeenth-Century Garden Theory," in his *Greater Perfections: The Practice of Garden Theory* (Philadelphia: University of Pennsylvania Press, 2000), pp. 180–206; see also Michael Leslie, "'Bringing Ingenuity into Fashion': The 'Elysium Britannicum' and the Reformation of Husbandry," in *John Evelyn's 'Elysium Britannicum' and European Gardening*, ed. Therese O'Malley and Joachim Wolschke-Bulmahn (Washington, D.C.: Dumbarton Oaks, 1998), pp. 131–52.

[48] Leslie, "'Bringing Ingenuity into Fashion,'" p. 141.

Fossile: of the growing of some branches of Rosemary, by only Sprinkling the leaves with water; of Camphire wood: of Wood brought from the Canaries; of a stinking Wood brought out of the East-Indies: of the re-union of the Bark of Trees after it had been separated from the Body.[49]

Gentleman amateur experimentalists, collectors of exotica, and scholars joined together in the pursuit of such curious experiments: it was Sir Kenelm Digby—collector, alchemist, and courtier—and no Oxford botanist who gave the first recorded lecture on a botanical subject in 1661.[50] Academic botanists were indeed members of the Royal Society: on December 17, 1674, John Ray read two papers on plant reproduction and the structure of seeds (discussed in chapter 5),[51] and the Society published Nehemiah Grew's work on the anatomy of plants (while employing him as "curator" of plants in 1671).[52] But John Tradescant the younger, who was neither an academic nor a courtier, was also elected a member, as was (much later) the controversial Richard Bradley, author of *New Improvements In Planting and Gardening both Philosophical and Practical* and the first horticultural journalist.

The gentlemen of the Royal Society, however, may have had some reservations about the virtues of "improvement"—especially of one's self. As Barbara Benedict has observed, while the members of the Royal Society professed their interest in public service, they disliked "professionalism"; it was left up to the press to convert their observations into practice. That press was all too willing to translate the work of the Society into popular culture, insofar as "any invention that addressed the problems of nature or the physical world was popular."[53] In the history of garden practice and garden writing, the most important member of the Royal Society was one of its founders, John Evelyn, author of *Sylva or a Discourse on Forest Trees, Acetaria* (a book on salad greens), the first *Kalendarium Hortense,* and the massive and never completed *Elysium Britannicum.* Evelyn exemplifies the gentleman gar-

---

[49] Thomas Sprat, *The History of the Royal Society of London, For the Improving of Natural Knowledge* (London, 1667), ed. Jackson I. Cope and Harold Whitmore Jones (St. Louis: Washington University Press, 1958), pp. 222–23.

[50] See Blanche Henrey, *British Botanical and Horticultural Literature before 1800,* 3 vols. (London: Oxford University Press, 1975), 1:101.

[51] See Leapman, *Ingenious Mr. Fairchild,* pp. 26–29.

[52] Henrey, *British Botanical and Horticultural Literature,* 1:135–38.

[53] Barbara M. Benedict, *Curiosity: A Cultural History of Early Modern Inquiry* (Chicago: University of Chicago Press, 2001), p. 41.

dener and virtuoso or "curious" man for whom gardening was an intellectual passion.[54] Like many of the virtuosi of his time, he collected and observed plants and rarities of nature, but he also applied his knowledge in his own garden at Sayes Court, in designs for the gardens of his friends, and in his public writings. As his books attest, he was passionately interested in translating this work into practice but less concerned about writing for the common man: as he declared in his draft of the *Elysium Britannicum,* he addressed himself not to "Cabbage-planters; but to the best refined of our nation who delight in Gardens and aspire to the perfections of the Arte."[55]

Evelyn was perhaps the greatest of the "gentleman" gardeners, some of whom were just concerned to cultivate their own country estates for what they called "honest recreation." While the Hartlib circle had urged country gentlemen to apply themselves to the new science of agriculture for the profit of themselves and England, many gentlemen professed to love gardening less for profit and more for spiritual pleasure and refreshment. We are familiar with a few of them because they chose to publish their gardening wisdom, for example John Worlidge, about whom we know little except his title as "gent.," and Ralph Austen, who was a member of Hartlib's and Boyle's groups. Several were clergymen, educated men with some leisure time, who saw gardening as a godly avocation. In these ranks William Turner and John Ray were joined by the Reverends Henry Compton, Adam Buddle, and Robert Uvedale. Robert Sharrock, who wrote an influential book on plant propagation, was a fellow at New College, Oxford, but also Archdeacon of Winchester, and was "accounted learned in divinity, in the civil and common law, and very knowing in vegetables and all pertaining thereunto."[56] Samuel Gilbert, the author of the *Florist's Vade-Mecum* and the son-in-law of John Rea, the nurseryman, was rector of Quatt in Shropshire and chaplain to Jane, Baroness Gerard of Gerard's

[54] On Evelyn, see Hunt, "Historical Excursus," in *Greater Perfections;* on Evelyn also see O'Malley and Wolschke-Bulmahn, eds., *John Evelyn's 'Elysium Britannicum' and European Gardening.*

[55] *Elysium Britannicum, or The Royal Gardens,* ed. John E. Ingram (Philadelphia: University of Pennsylvania Press, 2001), p. 42. See Michael Hunter, "John Evelyn in the 1650's: A Virtuoso in Quest of a Role," pp. 103–4, in *John Evelyn's 'Elysium Britannicum' and European Gardening.* See also Michael Leslie, "'Bringing Ingenuity into Fashion,'" on Evelyn's relationship with the Hartlib circle.

[56] Henrey, *British Botanical and Horticultural Literature,* 1:140, on Sharrock; Henrey is quoting Anthony á Wood.

Bromley—and, apparently, the man who planned her garden as well. John Laurence, chaplain to the Bishop of Salisbury and later rector of Yelvertoft in Northamptonshire, explicitly defended the clergyman's role as garden expert, when he professed in *The Clergyman's Recreation* that he wrote out of his twenty years of experience to "recommend the art of managing a garden to those of my own order, the Clergy, not to make them envy'd by Magnificence, but to make them happy." Laurence confessed that "most of the time I can spare from the necessary Care and Business of a large Parish, and from my other Studies, is spent in my Garden and making Observations toward the farther Improvement thereof" (his second book was appropriately entitled *The Gentleman's Recreation*).[57] It was always the mark of the English gentleman, in the end, not to appear to care for profit, and this indifference would remain the distinction between these men and the gardeners who labored for wages, traded in plants, or bartered their knowledge.

These gentleman gardeners were the closest in style and attitude to the aristocratic men and women whose gardens have come to mark the milestones of garden history. Few of this select group, famous though their gardens were, have left us much writing about their garden practice or dreams, and so we can only speculate (just as with the weeding women and laboring men) about their thoughts. Without these men and women—Sir Francis Carew, William Cecil, Henry Danby, Earl of Danvers, the Duchess of Beaufort, the Duke and Duchess of Bedford, Sir Henry Capel, Baron of Tewkesbury, Arthur Capel, Earl of Essex, and of course monarchs from Henry VIII to Queen Anne—English gardening would have been impoverished, literally and figuratively.[58] Their vision, curiosity, and love of splendor stimulated innovation in design and the acquisition of new plants from around the world, and their fortunes made these changes possible. In his manuscript of the *Elysium Britannicum*, John Evelyn noted that a garden requires three things—a "good purse," a "Judicious Eye," and a "skillful hand." Thus it needs three sorts of gardeners: "the person at whose charge and for whose divertissement the garden is made" (the word "divertissement" replaced the word "use" first scribbled there); "the Surveyor . . . from

---

[57] John Laurence, *The Clergyman's Recreation*, in *Gardening Improv'd* (London, 1718; rpt., New York: Garland, 1982), preface.

[58] For an excellent account of these gardens, see Roy Strong, *The Renaissance Garden in England* (London: Thames and Hudson, 1979; rpt., 1998).

whose dictates and directions the garden is contrived"; and the "immediate Labourers."[59] It was the purses and the desires of peers and gentry that supplied the nurserymen and seedsmen and employed the gardeners, both those who dictated and those who labored.

Some of the gentry do seem to have done more than just commission and inhabit these gardens. Moses Cook wrote of his master Arthur Capel, Earl of Essex, at his garden at Cassiobury in 1676, "You have not been onley a spectator but an Actor in most of what is treated of in the ensuing Lines; for, to your Eternal prayse be it spoken, there is many a fine Tree which you have Nursed up from Seeds sown by your own hands, and many thousands more which you have commanded me to raise."[60] It is said of Mary Capel, Duchess of Beaufort (Arthur's sister), who compiled a twenty-volume herbarium, that she herself was renowned for such a "Nursing Care, scarce any plant ('tho from most distant climate) can withstand."[61] As chapter 3 suggests, "nursing" plants was not necessarily seen as undignified. But when we speak of such men and women as gardeners, we must always remember the diverse group of scholars, artists, merchants, travelers, and workers who had to come together to advance the cause of English gardening and realize their dreams.

Not only were the actors in the story of English gardening thus diverse: their own identities were constantly in flux. One could be a common gardener but grow to be man of wealth and a writer through the nursery business; another might be like Gervase Markham, a gentleman, but proud to say that he lived as a husbandman. An apothecary might arrive, through his gardening and writing, to consort with kings. The culture of fruit and flowers, in short, was a form of "cultivation," whereby men and women could produce beauty and profit from the land, yet also advance or transform themselves. The irony of all this striving, however, is that everyone knew in the end that a lack of ambition was the mark of a "true" English gentleman: the kind of man for whom gardening was art, avocation, and recreation, but not a way of business.

---

[59] *Elysium Britannicum*, p. 35.
[60] Cook, *Manner of Raising*, dedication.
[61] Douglas Chambers, "'Storys of Plants': The Assembling of Mary Capel Somerset's Botanical Collection at Badminton," *Journal of the History of Collections* 9 (1997): 50.

Knowing Your Reader

As horticulture prospered and spread throughout English society, so did the business of producing garden books. Surveying Blanche Henrey's bibliography of botanical works of the period, Martin Hoyles concludes that "nineteen known gardening books [were] published in the sixteenth century, eleven concerned with herbs and eight on horticulture. In the first half of the seventeenth century, roughly the same number were published, but the second half of the century saw the figure increase fivefold."[62] As we shall see in chapter 2, the writers and printers of these books pitched them to appeal to all sorts of readers, from the monarch to the plain English husbandman and housewife. Our challenge is to disentangle the texts' claims about their readers from the reality of who could and could not read and buy books. Given the ephemeral nature of many of these books, which were small and cheap, we can only speculate as to who really owned and read them, and what they sought there. But we can see how their authors and printers wished to create a new audience of garden readers—an audience that had never existed before.

Some historians have argued that, in the early period of English printing, more books being published meant that more people were reading and had enough money to buy books. Readers drove the market for print, while the increasing availability of cheap books encouraged reading. Louis Wright was convinced that, by the time of the English Civil War, not only could more people read and write, but "there had come an unconscious development in the public taste, an increase in the appetite for printed works, a fixed habit of book-buying among citizens whose fathers, if they read at all, had been content with an almanac and the Bible."[63]

Since Wright, scholars have debated the level of literacy in England in the sixteenth and seventeenth centuries.[64] H. S. Bennett concluded

[62] Martin Hoyles, *Gardeners Delight: Gardening Books from 1560 to 1960* (London: Pluto Press, 1994), p. 9.

[63] Louis B. Wright, *Middle-Class Culture in Elizabethan England* (Chapel Hill: University of North Carolina Press, 1935), p. 81.

[64] H. S. Bennett estimates that some six thousand volumes were printed before 1557, "and the existence of such a volume of work is in itself prima facie evidence of a considerable reading public. Further, as we shall see, these volumes served a wide variety of interests, and were made available in a number of forms, so that there were many cheap little pamphlets of a few pages as well as large and expensive folios. Every kind

that increased literacy had to be connected to the growing production of books, and that the burgeoning of the printing trade should signify a new hunger for reading.[65] However, in his influential work on literacy, David Cressy criticized this kind of argument, noting that, though the output of books did increase, this could be accounted for by the increasing consumption of just a few consistent buyers.[66] Cressy made a case for a much lower level of literacy in English society than Wright and Bennett assumed, especially among those who lived in the country and who could be classified at the rank of husbandman.[67] (Cressy's evidence of the comparative illiteracy of "husbandmen" as opposed to "yeomen" is a little misleading since the line distinguishing yeomen and husbandmen was very thin.) Yet, responding to Cressy, in turn, Margaret Spufford and Tessa Watt argued separately for a much wider readership than his evidence would indicate. If ability to sign one's name indicated literacy (which is a very conservative standard), Spufford saw as encouraging the evidence that "between 1580 and

---

of taste and every sort of public were catered for" (*English Books and Readers: 1475 to 1557* [Cambridge: Cambridge University Press, 1952], p. 20). Of the period after 1557 he writes: "To speak of the reading public is to speak of a body about which we are very imperfectly informed. The output of books during the reign of Elizabeth makes it clear that reading was no longer the prerogative of a few, but at the same time we cannot estimate with any accuracy what percentage of the population could read. The detailed evidence is slender and contradictory, some writers leading us to think that a great proportion of people could read, while others suggest it was a minority" (*English Books and Readers: 1558–1603* [Cambridge: Cambridge University Press, 1965], p. 2). Cf. Sandra Clark, *The Elizabethan Pamphleteers: Popular Moralistic Pamphlets 1580–1640* (London: Athlone Press, 1983), p. 19: "Some feel that members of a highly literate society such as our own tend to minimize Elizabethan illiteracy, because they wrongly regard it as a stigma; others emphasize the 'astonishing expansion of education between 1560 and 1640' and see England in the early seventeenth century as 'at all levels the most literate society the world had ever known.' Undoubtedly, the general level of literacy was higher in London than elsewhere in the country."

[65] Bennett, *English Books and Readers: 1475–1557*, p. 29.

[66] Cressy, *Literacy and the Social Order*, p. 47.

[67] See Cressy (who doesn't follow through on the implication of his notation of the slippage between the categories of yeoman and husbandman): "The difference is clearly shown in their aggregate level of illiteracy. Yeomen had much more engagement with the world of print and script than husbandmen and this is reflected in their considerably superior ability to sign. The percentage of illiteracy in the four rural areas for which we have evidence was 35%, 27%, 73% and 33% for yeomen, compared to 79%, 79%, 91% and 73% among deponents labelled husbandmen. Yeomen had more leisure and more wealth than husbandmen, and were more likely to be able to enjoy the escapist delights of literacy as well as its practical benefits. Husbandmen, on the other hand, might have been more constantly preoccupied with subsistence. . . . While the yeoman was regarded as energetic and thrifty, the husbandman could be dismissed as clownish and rude" (p. 127).

1700, 11 per cent of women, 15 per cent of laborers, and 21 per cent of husbandmen could sign their names, against 56 per cent of tradesmen and craftsmen, and 65 per cent of yeomen."[68] In any case, as Spufford argued elsewhere, more people could read than could write.[69] Both Spufford and Watt detailed the lower social orders' consumption of chapbooks or cheap print, which included manuals of advice such as almanacs and garden books.[70] This book cannot settle this matter of literacy decisively; such evidence suggests, however, that many different sorts of people interested in rural matters might be reading and buying books. It was a matter for printers and writers to define these readers as garden book readers, whether they were rich or poor, gentlemen or husbandmen.

Sometimes printers and writers of herbals wanted to attract a professional audience of physicians and apothecaries, and they made that clear in their prefaces. William Turner hoped that his English herbal would help surgeons and apothecaries ignorant of Greek and Latin.[71] William Coles's *Adam in Eden* advertises itself as "A Work of such a Refined and Useful Method, that the Arts of Physick and Chirugerie are so clearly laid open, that Apothecaries, Chirugions, and all other ingenious Practioners, may from our own Fields and Gardens, best agreeing with our English Bodies, on emergent and sudden occasions, compleatly furnish themselves with cheap, easie, and wholsome Cures, for any part of the Body that is ill-affected." In his conclusion to his epistle, Coles deliberately defined his book's readership as professionals and the gentry, clearly believing that success lay in the direction of more educated readers.[72]

Other writers and printers of herbals, however, were thinking of

[68] Margaret Spufford, *Small Books and Pleasant Histories: Popular Fiction and Its Readership in Seventeenth-Century England* (Athens: University of Georgia Press, 1982), p. 21.

[69] Margaret Spufford, "First Steps in Literacy: The Reading and Writing Experiences of the Humblest Seventeenth-Century Spiritual Autobiographers," *Social History* 4 (1979): 407–35. See also Tessa Watt, *Cheap Print and Popular Piety: 1550–1640* (Cambridge: Cambridge University Press, 1991), pp. 7–8.

[70] See Watt, *Cheap Print*. See also B. S. Capp, *English Almanacs, 1500–1800: Astrology and the Popular Press* (Ithaca: Cornell University Press, 1979).

[71] *Garden Book of Sir Thomas Hamner*, p. 85.

[72] "To conclude, I dedicate these my Labours to the Commonwealth of Learning, to the Colledg of Physitians, Chirurgions & Apothecaries; to the Court, to the Nobility & Gentry; In fine to all those that honour this Art, and delight in the peace and welfare of their Country" (William Coles, *Adam in Eden: or, Natures Paradise. The History of Plants, Fruits, Herbs and Flowers* [London, 1657], letter to the reader).

broader audiences and experimenting with the size and pricing of their books. Generally speaking, one would think that small and cheap books were intended to attract a wide popular audience and large impressive folios a smaller but richer group of readers. Yet the publication history of Henry Lyte's translation of Rembert Dodoens's herbal suggests that one cannot easily align popularity and price. In 1578 Lyte offered his translation of *A Niewe Herball, or Historie of Plantes* in a large, amply illustrated folio edition of 779 pages (plus front matter). The front matter includes Lyte's coat of arms and a letter of dedication to Queen Elizabeth, which states that Lyte published this translation for her pleasure and the country's profit and to show himself a thankful subject. At the same time, his preface to the reader proclaims that he translated this book for the benefit of the "ignorant" if literate reader,[73] thus implying that he sought a readership extending from the queen to the common subject.

In 1606, however, William Ram decided to publish a digest of Lyte, called *Rams little Dodeons* [*sic*]: *A briefe Epitome of the new Herbal, or History of Plants . . . now collected and abbridged*, which advertises its brevity and low price:

> So, as where the geat [*sic*] booke at large is not to be had, but at a great price, which canot be procured by the poorer sort, my endeavor herein hath bin chiefly, to make the benefit of so good, necessary and profitable a worke to be brought within the reach and compasse as well of you my poore Countrymen & women, whose lives, healths, ease and welfare is to be regarded with the rest, at a smaller price, then the greater Volume is.

Further, in marked contrast to Lyte's dedication to the queen, Ram offered his version directly to "these my poore and loving countrymen whosoever and in whose hands soever it may come."[74] Despite Ram's intentions in writing a cheap and "popular" book, however, Lyte's book seems to have been more successful; only one edition of Ram's book was published, whereas Lyte's went into four editions by 1619. Wright concludes from this evidence that many people were willing to

---

[73] Henry Lyte, *A Niewe Herball, or Historie of Plantes* (London, 1578), letter to the reader.

[74] *Rams little Dodeons: A briefe Epitome of the new Herbal, or History of Plants* (London, 1606), preface.

spend the money for a folio: "Expensive as the large herbals were, the interest of the public was such that many a citizen who would have begrudged a few pence for any lesser book, parted with the price of one of the huge illustrated folios."[75] It is also quite possible, however, that the "poor" reading public at which Ram's book was aimed did not exist as he described it. Lyte's introduction, which displays the *rhetoric* of public service to the poor, shows a better sense of how the market worked. It may have appealed to a wealthier reader who liked Lyte's altruism but really wanted to add a more impressive book to his or her library.[76]

The printers and writers of husbandry books appear to have had similarly mixed intentions for their readers. As Natalie Davis has warned us in the case of French husbandry books, "we have no *sure* evidence that any of these books addressed to a rural public actually reached a peasant audience."[77] One also wonders about how available these books were, given the location of most booksellers in urban areas.[78] Husbandry manuals were indeed smaller than most herbals, implying their greater accessibility. Bennett estimates that in the first half of the sixteenth century husbandry books cost about a penny, as opposed to the much higher prices for the folio herbals.[79] Andrew McRae thinks that, even then, the early husbandry books would have been too

[75] Wright, *Middle-Class Culture*, p. 576. In the case of Gerard, Wright notes that in the Huntington Library's copy of Johnson's 1633 version of Gerard's *Herbal*, a note on the flyleaf tells us that it cost two pounds, eight shillings, on September 1, 1654 (p. 577). See also Bennett, *1558–1605*: "Up to about 1550 most herbals were of little consequence. . . . The herbalists of the second half of the century had a high standard to keep, and the day of the cheap, ill-informed little book was over. The few herbals that were printed were for the most part large and well-illustrated volumes, and also for the most part translations" (pp. 187–88). Terry Comito compares the "predominantly middle class audience" of the gardening manuals with "the aristocratic patrons of the herbals," but it is unlikely that the audiences can be separated so distinctly (since the herbals varied so much in format and size) (Terry Comito, *The Idea of the Garden in the Renaissance* [New Brunswick: Rutgers University Press, 1978], p. 21).

[76] At the same time, there is evidence that people thought that the market could support the publication of only a few such large folios at a time: in 1635, John Parkinson's massive herbal *Theatrum Botanicum* was entered into the Stationers' Register, but it did not appear until 1640, presumably because of the competition offered by Thomas Johnson's reissuing of Gerard's *Herbal* in 1633. See Henrey, *British Botanical and Horticultural Literature*, 1:80.

[77] Natalie Zemon Davis, *Society and Culture in Early Modern France: Eight Essays* (Stanford: Stanford University Press, 1975), p. 208.

[78] See Bennett, *1475–1557*, pp. 21–24. See also Davis, *Society and Culture*, p. 197.

[79] Bennett, *1475–1557*, p. 231.

expensive for anyone except gentlemen,[80] although this would depend on whether your pennies were disposable income or not.[81] In John Fitzherbert's *Book of Husbondrye*, both the front matter and the printing history suggest that many ranks of men might have read such books—if "reading" meant something besides scanning the book with one's own eyes. The frequent reprinting of this book indicates its popularity (it went through eighteen editions from 1532 to 1598, at which point it was issued in a revised and "purged" edition by the printer James Roberts).[82] The title page of the book advertised it as *A Newe tracte or treatyse moost profytable for all husbandemen: and very frutefull for all other persons to rede*, and thus designed for "husbands," "yomen," and "labourers." However, in the body of the text, Fitzherbert addressed the "yong gentleman that intendeth to thrive": this gentleman is instructed to read the book himself "from the beginnyng unto the ending," and then, "acordyng to the season of the yere [to] rede to his servauntes what chapyter he woll."[83] The book thus had a double audience of "readers" built into it: the "young gentleman" to be sure, but also the illiterate servant, who would have the book read to him if he could not decipher it for himself.[84]

All types of books on "country" or rural matters thus confronted inherent problems in fashioning a reader. Gervase Markham defined his public as "the plain English husbandman," while including himself, a gentleman by birth, in that group, since, as he recalled in his letter of dedication to Lord Clifton, for many years "wherein I lived most happily, I lived a Husbandman, amongst Husbandmen of most excellent knowledge."[85] Since he wrote as a husbandman, he told his reader, he

---

[80] Andrew McRae, *God Speed the Plough: The Representation of Agrarian England, 1500–1660* (New York: Cambridge University Press, 1996), p. 139. In general, this discussion relies on McRae's insightful account of the development of husbandry books.

[81] I am indebted to Peter Stallybrass for pointing out to me that a penny would be indeed affordable if it were just disposable income.

[82] See McRae, *God Speed*, p. 136. McRae reasons that while the book may have been originally pitched to the manorial lord, by the time Roberts's edition was issued, it was seen as more for all degrees of men (p. 145).

[83] [John] Fitzherbert, *Here begynneth a newe tracte or treatyse moost profytable for all husbandemen: and very frutefull for all other persons to rede: [The book] of Husbondrye* (London, 1532), fol. xlvi (verso).

[84] See note in Bennett, *1475–1557*, p. 28: "One writer, after advising every man to read his book, is forced to add 'or [those] that cannot rede to geve dylygent eere to the reder.'" See also Davis, "Printing and the People," in *Society and Culture*, pp. 189–226, where she discusses the phenomenon of reading such books out loud.

[85] Markham, *The English Husbandman*, front matter.

wrote for husbandmen and not "curious" men or dabblers in secrets of cultivation. He was "resolved that this I have written is fully sufficient for the plaine English husbandman."[86] Wendy Wall has observed that in thus addressing "the 'general and gentle' husbandmen of England to think of themselves as a shared collective group, Markham hails an audience that [did] not yet exist."[87] However, it was also an audience his book was designed to create.

When Thomas Hill published, probably in 1558, *A most brief and pleasaunte treatyse, teachynge howe to dress, sowe, and set a Garden,* usually considered the first gardening book printed in England, he experimented quite self-consciously with tapping into the readership both for herbals and for husbandry manuals and drawing a new "gardener" reader from this group. In his letter of dedication to Thomas Constable, he addressed husbandmen in conjunction with the more ill-defined public of those "such as have their study and delight in Gardenynge."[88] The preface is directed to "the gentle reader," but it professes the hope that "the knowledge [in this book] shall move the simple and unlettered to whom I write this my boke not only to bestow the more diligence in the dressyng, sowyng, and settyng of these and other herbes in their gardens, but to be carefull also how to avoyde noyous wormes, beastes and flyes, that commonlye harme gardens."[89] Hill thus sought a public embracing the gentleman and the husbandman, the lettered and the "simple and unlettered," all seeking profit and delight and gathered under the umbrella of the term "gardener."

Hill's simultaneous appeal to the well-to-do and the poor, seen using the book for profit and delight, is a characteristic feature of the early garden book. All the garden manuals discussed here experimented in some way with defining and expanding their readership, appealing most often to men but sometimes to women, to the rich and poor, and to those seeking profit as well as entertainment. In seeking

---

[86] Ibid., p. 58.

[87] Wendy Wall, "Renaissance National Husbandry: Gervase Markham and the Publication of England," *Sixteenth-Century Journal* 27 (1996): 776–77.

[88] *A most brief and pleasaunte treatyse, teachynge howe to dress, sowe, and set a Garden, and what propertyes also these few hearbes heare spoken of, have to our comodytie: with the remedyes that may be used against such beasts, wormes, flies and such lyke, that commonly noy gardens, gathered out of the principallest Authors in this art, by Thomas Hyll, Londyner,* dedicatory epistle. The title page does not list the date, but we assume that the first date of publication was circa 1558; the second edition was published in 1563.

[89] Ibid., preface.

readers, these books also shaped what it meant to be a gardener in early modern England—and a gardener who was a reader of books. Buying books, reading books, and practicing the garden arts became inextricably intertwined and even confused.

Histories of Garden Work

In the burgeoning printing industry of early modern England, when men were writing books of advice on subjects ranging from poetry to fishing, everyone wanted to prove that such activities were worthwhile enterprises. It was a common rhetorical move to begin these books with a history that discovers illustrious ancestors and establishes the craft's tradition. Horticultural writers too were concerned to trace their roots. As with all such forms of history in the early modern period, their own narratives of gardening were shaped by a desire to reconstruct the past to fit the present and the writer's self-image. As fantasies, such invented histories tell us much about the values held by those who composed them.

In reconstructing the history of gardening, several sixteenth-century writers started with the Latin writer Columella's *De agricultura*, book 10, 1–3, which explicitly aligns garden and social history. Columella began by recounting horticulture's origins in producing food:

So the subject which has still to be dealt with is horticulture, which the husbandman of old carried out in a half-hearted and negligent fashion but which is now quite a popular pursuit. Though indeed, among the ancients there was a stricter parsimony, the poor had a more generous diet, since highest and lowest alike sustained life on an abundance of milk and the flesh of wild and domestic animals as though on water and corn. Very soon, when subsequent ages, and particularly our own, set up an extravagant scale of expenditure on the pleasure of the table, and meals were regarded as occasions not for satisfying men's natural desires but for the display of wealth, the poverty of the common people, forced to abstain from the more costly foods, is reduced to an ordinary fare. The cultivation, therefore, of gardens, since their produce is now in greater demand, calls for more careful instructions from us than our forefathers have handed down.[90]

[90] Columella, Lucius Junis Moderatus, *On agriculture,* trans. E. S. Forster and Edward H. Heffner (Cambridge: Harvard University Press, 1955), book 10, 1–3, pp. 3–5.

Columella thus linked gardening's beginnings to social difference, suggesting that no one needed to garden seriously until the poor and the rich began to have very different diets, the former's plain and the latter's for pleasure alone. It is unclear from the passage, however, how gardening in fact was supposed to fit into this change: to supplement the diets of the poor or to grace the lavish tables of the rich?

When Conrad Heresbach, a German gentleman writing about husbandry for men like himself, adapted this story in his *Foure Bookes of Husbandry* (as translated by Barnabe Googe in 1577), he resolved this ambiguity by explaining that gardening came about for the benefit of virtuous rural folk and "old husbands." As Heresbach told the story:

> For when (as Columella sayth) in the olde time the people lived more temperately, and the poore at more libertie fedde of fleshe and milke, and suche thinges as the ground and foldes yeelded: but in the latter age when ryotte and daintinesse began to come in, and the wealthyer sort to esteeme no fare but costly, and farre fetched, not content with meane dyet, but coveting such thinges as were of greatest price, the poore people as not able to beare the charges, were banished from the costlier cates, and driven to content them selves with the basest foode. And hereof sprang at the first the planting of Orchardes, and making of Gardens, wherewith the poorest creature that was, might store his Kitchen, and have his victuals alwayes at hand, the Orchard and Garden serving for his Shambles, with a great deale more commendable and hurtlesse dyet. Herein were the olde husbandes very careful, and used alwayes to judge, that where they founde the Garden out of order, the wife of the house (for unto her belonged the charge thereof) was no good huswyfe.[91]

Heresbach's version adjusts Columella's story to focus on the poor who first cultivated orchards and gardens in order to create a "commendable and hurtlesse" diet, as opposed to the riot and daintiness of the rich's "cates." Orchards and gardens became part of the ideal orderly, economical, and *modest* household, corresponding to Heresbach's image of the virtuous bourgeois country gentleman whom his book was designed to support.

But when Thomas Hill in turn adapted Columella's history of gar-

---

[91] Conrad Heresbach, *Foure Bookes of Husbandry, collected by M. Conradius Heresbachius,* trans. Barnabe Googe (London: Richard Watkins, 1577), fol. 48r–v.

dening in *The Gardeners Labyrinth* he constructed the tale differently, reading instead into the story a common desire for the *pleasures* of fruits and herbs, which drove the need to garden:

Columella reporteth [in] lib 10. that the Ancient husbandmen so slen-
derly looked unto (or rather forced of) Gardens, that they in furthering
the groweth and yield of their fruits and hearbes, bestowed small travail
and diligence. And as they appeared negligent in their labours of the
Garden, so were they well pleased with a mean living, insomuch that the
common host fed and lived willingly on grass and simple hearbes. But
after the age and people were reformed, and brought by the instruction
of the Epicure, to a more delight of themselves in coveting to feede on
daintie hearbes and Sallates, with meats delectable, and taking an
earnester care for the pleasing of their mouths, they laboured then to become skillful, and to use a greater care about the ordering and apt dressing of Garden plots, by well fensing and comely furnishing of their
ground, with sundry needful and delectable trees, plants, and hearbes: in
which travels and diligence of the husbandmen, to good successe and
commoditie ensuing, procured not only the willing carriage of hearbs,
fruits, and other commodities farre off to be exercised unto Cities and
market townes, by which these through the sale obtained a daily gaine
and yearely revenew, for the aide of their houshold charges, but allured
them also to place and frame gardens, as well within Cities and Townes
as fast by, that a cost bestowed, might after possesse the procreation and
delight of minds, besides the proper gaine made by the fruits, floures,
and hearbes, gathered in them. The Garden plots at length, grewe so
common among the meaner sort, that the charge and the chiefest care of
the same, was committed unto the wife, insomuch that these accounted
not the wife of the house, to be a huswife indeede, if shee bestowed not a
paine and diligence as Cato reporteth in the weeding, trimming, and
dressing of the Garden.[92]

This passage is worth citing at such length because of the way in which this "history" of gardening extends Columella's brief sketch of social history to tell a more contemporary English story. It avoids the distinction between rich and poor set up by both Columella and Heres-

[92] Dydymus Mountain [Thomas Hill], *Gardeners Labyrinth*, pp. 2–3.

bach; rather, according to this tale the garden began as a place for the common people to eke out their sustenance by toiling just a little. Once they "were reformed" to the taste of "the Epicure," these people worked harder, laboring to become skillful not so much for mere sustenance but "for the pleasing of their mouths." Hill thus, in effect, completely reversed the story as it was told by Heresbach. Rather than separating the rich-idle-pleasure connection from the poor-laboring-profit one as Heresbach did, Hill implied without disapproval that more attention to taste and a desire for pleasure motivated all gardeners, without distinction of ranks. Instead, for Hill, the class and gender differentiation came later, after this work for pleasure produced a surplus of "commoditie" to be taken to urban markets. Only then did Hill mention the "meaner" gardener and the role of women in producing profit.

Hill and Heresbach thus outlined two ways of looking at the complex relationship of labor and leisure, class and gender, pleasure and profit in the history of the garden. In Heresbach's vision, with his concern to establish husbandry as the virtuous work of the country gentleman, sensuality or pleasure was separated from garden work; this work then became morally valuable as opposed to the excess and riot of the wanton urban rich. For Hill, who was writing for a new class of gardeners and especially those who gardened for a living, the desire to garden originated in sensual pleasure. The drive to produce pleasure may have led to a kind of excess, but not an excess of delight—rather a surplus of goods, which could be managed by the common gardener and housewife. Pleasure was part of the economy of gardening that could be converted into gain.

Inventing gardening history thus set a pattern for defining the practice according to the distance between the rich and poor, the pursuit of pleasure and profit, and the complex status of work in that balance, where labor was neither denigrated nor exclusively the province of the poor. Where the story's focus narrowed to the culture of flowers, in particular, and as the seventeenth century progressed, however, the balance tipped toward pleasure and knowledge as the motivation for gardening for the gentry, with an accompanying drift toward thinking of garden history in terms of great men. In John Evelyn's translation of Jean de la Quintinie's *The Compleat Gard'ner*, the account begins with the image of Adam as the first gardener, who was "Created in a Garden, and received Orders after his Transgression, to till the Earth and to get his Maintenance out of it by the Sweat of his Brows." From Adam, the text traces a line to the Patriarchs who "were those first Fruit and Kitchin-Gardners" yet required the "Service of some principal Domestick to help them in their Gardens, who disdained not to take the Name of that we commonly understand by the Term of Gard'ner." Thereafter, with "distinction of Degrees and Fortunes, it hapned that the pleasures of Sight and Smell, inspired some Persons with the Curiosity to gratifie them with Flowers. . . . Thus was the Culture of Flowers begun indeed by such Gard'ners as those we just now mentioned, because there were no others that could do it."[93] The differences from Hill here are quite instructive, especially where status structures the historical account. The story might begin with Adam's fall into labor[94] but it soon moves to displacing work to a "domestic" called the gardener.[95] Flower gardening began with "curious" men, who wished to gratify their senses, but they still needed gardeners to do the work. Whereas Hill's gardener worked for his own delight and profit, La Quintinie's did it to gratify curiosity—pleasing both the senses and the mind (the text goes on to chart a subdivision between "florists" and "plain gardeners," where the former are clearly superior).

By the time of the publication of the first recognized English history of gardening in Stephen Switzer's *Ichnographia Rustica, or, The Nobleman, Gentleman, and Gardener's Recreation* (1718), Columella's little group of common people and the rich had been replaced by a parade of great gardeners, starting with God, Adam, and the Patriarchs. In charting his garden genealogy, Switzer (himself a professional nurseryman) marched beyond the Patriarchs to the great kings of Egypt and Persia and the Greeks and Romans, past the "dark ages," up to his own time. Unlike the story that Hill told, Switzer's tale unrolls a long chain of aristocratic, royal, literary, and finally scientific and "gentleman" gardeners. He complained about those who would restrict history to political and military events, precisely because gardening

[93] Jean de la Quintinie, *The Compleat Gard'ner,* trans. John Evelyn (translation of *Instruction pour les jardins fruitiers et potagers*) (London, 1693; rpt., New York: Garland, 1982), preface.

[94] On this trope of tracing husbandry back to Adam, see Anthony Low, *The Georgic Revolution* (Princeton: Princeton University Press, 1985), pp. 135–42; and McRae, *God Speed,* chap. 3.

[95] See also Evelyn's own construction of the history of the garden in his *Elysium Britannicum,* where he tells a story of gardening's origin in the exile from Paradise, pp. 29–30.

history embraces many sorts of different people: for "in this [gardening] there is a general Entertainment to every busy and Intelligent Person; and an Imitation of the Practices of those great Virtuosos is in some measure or other in the Power of every Rank or Degree of Mankind. . . . So that the History as well as the Practice of Gardening may not be an unwelcome Subject; and we are assured that the Romans . . . had as great a value for the Memoirs of Men of Wit, Literature, or any other private Accomplishments as they had for the greatest Politicians and Captains."[96] While Switzer might profess that he was concerned with every "rank or degree," what he really cared about was the "busy and intelligent person." This person was not Hill's and Heresbach's common man but rather the gentleman of wit. Switzer's narrative thus records the advancement of knowledge through gardening, not sustaining the household or growing food for markets. The line from Hill and Heresbach to Switzer, then, while it redefines the social status of gardeners, also reorients horticultural work and pleasure. We move from the notion that garden work provides sensual pleasure, as well as profit, for all people, to the idea that gardening work resembles a gentleman's other aesthetic and scientific pursuits.

When we ourselves look back at the history of English gardening, as Hill or Switzer did, we surely also look to find ourselves in that history. Many recent histories of English gardening begin in earnest in the seventeenth century, with the gentlemen gardeners who either owned their own estates or designed those of noble men and women. In *The History of the Modern Taste in Gardening* (1782), Horace Walpole made it very clear that he thought that from the beginning gardening implied property ownership, since "gardening was probably one of the first arts that succeeded to that of building houses, and naturally attended property and individual possession."[97] Such is still the assumption of many garden book readers, even though their own plot might be relatively modest. The books considered here, however, unfold a less uniform and staid image of the gardener enclosed within his sheltering garden walls. These garden manuals show us men (and some women) not content with the status quo, jostling each other in the markets, experimenting, grafting and pruning, envisioning new designs—and, of

---

96 Stephen Switzer, *Ichnographia Rustica, or, The Nobleman, Gentleman, and Gardener's Recreation* (London, 1718; rpt., New York: Garland, 1982), p. 56.

97 Horace Walpole, *The History of the Modern Taste in Gardening* (1782), ed. John Dixon Hunt (New York: Ursus Press, 1995), p. 17.

course, writing and printing books. Many of the men who wrote these books wanted something new for themselves and for their readers—the readers they created as gardeners. These books not only disseminated the changing practices of gardening in the sixteenth and seventeenth centuries; they helped to shape that practice and the image of the English man and woman's garden as a place of dreams.

❧ 2 ❧

The Printed Garden

What makes someone want to buy a garden book? How does one choose? Such purchases conclude elaborate if implicit negotiations between book sellers and buyers, when publishers try to anticipate what makes a book desirable and readers come to browse and maybe buy. In deciding what to print, a seller must somehow gauge what the reading public wants: Garden dictionaries or encyclopedias? Practical advice for day-to-day cultivation? Picture books? And what sort of plants will interest them? Will roses always be in demand or is something else now in vogue? And what about regional markets: will an English gardener shop differently from an American one?

Buyers come to the bookstore usually needing something: they may want to keep deer from eating their plants or to propagate a cactus. Yet they find themselves leafing through a book that they did not expect to see. One might intend to bring home a guide to cultivating tomatoes but be seduced by a book promising perennials that flower luxuriantly from March to November. Rather than getting a practical manual, one purchases a book filled with visions of earthly delight.

What makes a garden book desirable depends on many intangibles of taste and need, unique to each reader. The previous chapter outlined how early writers saw themselves as serving many types of "gardeners," from England's queen down to the illiterate husbandman. But how were the books fashioned to attract these different gardeners? And how, in turn, did a book's design as well as content influence garden practice? A book is not a neutral container of information. As D. F. McKenzie has observed, "the material forms of books, the non-verbal elements of the typographic notations within them, the very disposition of space itself, have an expressive function in conveying meaning."[1] So the size, type, advertising, organization, and illustrations all can tell us much about how early modern English people imagined gardening as a social, recreational, professional, and scientific practice. At the same time, the existence, form, and circulation of such books transformed English gardening.

My concern with printed books is quite deliberate, for, indeed, while monks and scholars had composed manuscript herbals and gardening instructions for centuries,[2] the horticultural advice business took off in the era of the printed book. In his study of early modern "secrets" books William Eamon has argued that print technology influenced the organization and dissemination of all kinds of popular knowledge and instruction, since it was really printers "who created the how-to book. To the random assortments of recipes that had formerly circulated among craftsmen, printers added title pages, tables of contents, glossaries of technical terms, and prefaces, bringing them to the attention of a new public."[3] Title pages and prefaces of the new garden books show that they were aimed at markets with specialized tastes and needs: some books describe themselves as entertainment, while others are self-defined as sober scientific texts. Some writers were concerned to advertise their books' comprehensiveness, while others vaunted their selectivity or portability. In each case the apparatus of the printed book—title pages, prefaces, pagination, tables of contents, and indexes—guided the multiple uses of the text. Indexes and tables of contents, for example, allowed for experiencing the book both as a story and as a reference work. At the same time, alphabetical lists, dialogue,

[1] D. F. McKenzie, *Bibliography and the Sociology of Texts* (London: British Library, 1986), p. 8.

[2] Copies of the herbals of Dioscorides and Theophrastus would have been available in monastic libraries. Miles Hadfield mentions as the earliest known English treatise on gardening the manuscript by "Mayster Ion Gardener," in a copy dating from 1440, called "The Feate of Gardening" (*A History of British Gardening*, 2d ed. [London: John Murray, 1969], p. 31); in the thirteenth century, Walter of Henley wrote a treatise on husbandry in the form of a sermon (see Dorothea Oschinsky, *Walter of Henley and Other Treatises on Estate Management and Accounting* [Oxford: Clarendon Press, 1971]); for an example of a later manuscript, see Peter Aram, *A Practical Treatise of Flowers* (edited from Ingilby MS 3664 with introduction and notes by Frank Felsenstein), compiled by Aram in the late seventeenth century (Leeds: Leeds Philosophical and Literary Society, 1985).

[3] William Eamon, *Science and the Secrets of Nature: Books of Secrets in Medieval and Early Modern Culture* (Princeton: Princeton University Press, 1994), p. 125.

and calendar formats overtly and covertly invited different sorts of reading experiences, from memorization to reading out loud. Writers and printers also constantly changed their products, presenting their wares as "new and improved" in an effort to find new readers. (As a result, the bibliography of these books can be excruciatingly complex, since they were frequently reprinted with additions under new titles or represented as "enlarged" by new experiences and practices.)[4]

While it is hard to draw an even line of evolution because of this reprinting of old books under new titles, this chapter does map a change in the form of garden books from the random assemblage of "secrets" characteristic of the sixteenth-century manuals to the more structured and hierarchical format of the later seventeenth-century books. This transformation in book design accompanied the professionalization of gardening, as writers became more self-conscious about projecting an image of gardening as an orderly activity. But the evolving shape of the books also suggests a shift in how people found their pleasure in gardening and garden book reading. The earlier books let the gardener-readers delight in finding their own way through the book and the garden; the reader was the master of the book, just as he or she was meant to manage the disorder of nature. The later books, however, present readers with an ordered garden and book, rather than trusting them on their own. This order, it is implied, is "natural," mimicking nature's seasons and hierarchies, not requiring more than that the gentle reader see him- or herself in the text as lord of what he or she surveys. Both types of book thus quite differently invited readers to imagine themselves as in control, whether in gardening or reading.

In this sense, the garden manuals' form shows writers coping with the rampant development of garden practice described in chapter 1. There it was suggested that during the sixteenth and seventeenth centuries the diversification of gardeners, from nurserymen to virtuosi, reflected widespread social mobility in rural areas and cities. These changes provoked as much anxiety as they did enthusiasm about the

[4] For example, Thomas Hill's *A most brief and pleasaunte treatyse, teachynge how to dresse, sowe and set a garden* most likely first appeared in 1558, and a second edition was printed in 1563; it reappeared in 1568 as *The profitable arte of Gardening* with new appendixes on bees and planting and grafting fruit trees. The book was issued posthumously, completed by Hill's friend Henry Dethick in 1577 as *The Gardeners Labyrinth*, under the pseudonym Dydymus Mountain (i.e., Thomas Hill); four more editions appeared over the next seventy-five years.

improvement of English life and society. People like gardeners were exactly the problem: if the gardener's job was always to improve or better nature, whether in the soil or in himself, what threat did that pose to a society founded on respect for a traditional order grounded in nature? The garden manuals indeed impel the reader to find his or her pleasure in overcoming nature—but not without some ambivalence. In the earlier books, the confidence in the reader-gardener's technique and mastery over nature is palpable; the later books, however, attempt to bind together nature and culture, constructing a nature that imitates social order, with the better sort taking precedence.

Books for Housewives and Queens

As the gardening book took shape in the late sixteenth and early seventeenth centuries, writers, along with the printers, did not settle on a single model. The extremes are marked, at the one end, by William Lawson's *The Countrie Housewifes Garden* (1617), and, at the other, by John Parkinson's *Paradisi in Sole* (1629). Lawson's book is a slim quarto designed for use by the generic "country housewife"; Parkinson's is a compendious and amply illustrated folio volume, dedicated to Queen Henrietta Maria. While these books both express concern for the reader's enjoyment and profit, their disparities show how a garden book might be designed to please and influence different ranks of readers.

William Lawson's *The Countrie Housewifes Garden, containing rules for Herbes of Common use* contains only twenty-seven pages, and its tidy title page indicates without fanfare its modest contents (see figure 5). The book lacks a letter of dedication, epistle to the reader, and an index (a very short table of contents appears at the end of the book), and it is sparsely illustrated with ten patterns for elaborate knot gardens. The style is brisk and the rules of cultivation succinct. The advice on cultivating roses runs to two sentences: "Roses of all sorts (spoken of in the Orchard) must be Set. Some use to set slips and twine them, which sometimes, but seldom thrive all." Hollihocks, we are told, "riseth high, seedeth and dyeth; the chief use I know is ornament."[5]

---

[5] William Lawson, *The Countrie Housewifes Garden* (London, 1617; rpt., New York: Garland, 1982), p. 10 for roses, p. 14 for hollihocks.

THE
COVNTRIE
HOVSEWIFES
Garden.

Containing Rules for Hearbes of
common vse.

TOGETHER
With the Husbandry of Bees, Publiſhed
with ſecrets, very neceſſary for e-
uery Houſewife.

Together with diuers new knots for Gardens.

The Contents ſee at large in the laſt Page. *John Archer*

I haue giuen vnto you euery hearbe, and euery tree,
that ſhall be to you, for meate. GEN. 2. 29.

LONDON,
Printed by *Bar: Alſop,* for *Roger Iackſon.* 1617.

FIGURE 5. Title page of William Lawson, *The Countrie Housewifes Garden* (1617).
Reproduced by permission of the Folger Shakespeare Library.

Aware of the book's conspicuous brevity, Lawson did provide a short note of explanation: "I reckon these hearbes onely, because I teach my Country Housewife, not skilful Artists, and it should be an endles labour, and would make the matter tedious to reckon up, Landibeefe, Stocke-July Flowers, Charvall, Valerian, Go-to-bed-at nonne, Pyone, Licoras, Tansye, Garden-mints, Germander, Centauries, and a thousand such Physicke hearbes. Let her first grow cunning in this, and then she may inlarge her Garden, as her skill and ability increseth. And to helpe her the more, I have set downe these observations." The implication here is that in fact the country housewife hardly even needs or wants a book, since first she should learn by growing those things for which "skilful Artists" do not care. However, Lawson also apparently assumed that the housewife would be busy with her own practice and that she already knew what she liked. So he wrote that he first hesitated to waste paper in offering garden designs: "The number of formes, mazes and knots are so great, and men are so diversely delighted, that I leave everie housewife to her self, especially seeing to set down many had been but to fill much paper, yet lest I deprive her of all delight or direction, let her view these few, choyce, new formes." Again, the author betrayed some impatience with writing too much for this "country" reader, but he also revealed his trust in her instinctive taste and knowledge.

The book concludes the gardening section by emphasizing, once again, that a garden book is only as good as the housewife who uses it:

> Thus have I limned out a Garden to our Country Housewives and given
> them rules for common hearbes. If any of them (and sometime they are)
> be knotty, I refer them to other Writers. The skill and Paines of Weeding
> the garden with weeding knives or fingers, I refer to herselfe, and her
> maides, willing them to take the opportunity after a showre of raine;
> with all I advise the Mistress, either to be present herselfe or to teach her
> maides to know hearbes from weedes.[6]

For Lawson's housewife, the book supplemented her practice, and thus was as casual and unsystematic in form as that practice itself. It allowed the wife to consult other writers, if she wished, and it left her to herself, to find her own profit and delight in the text.

[6] Ibid., pp. 16–19.

Lawson's *Countrie Housewifes Garden* typifies the sixteenth-century gardening manual geared toward the "practical" gardener. When Thomas Hill came to write his first book on gardening, he was obviously thinking about how his text fit in with current expectations for other plant books and how-to books. The title-page description of his text as *A most brief and pleasaunte treatyse, teachynge howe to dress, sowe, and set a Garden, and what propertyes also these few hearbes heare spoken of, have to our comodytie: with the remedyes that may be used against such beasts, wormes, flies and such lyke* marks the pull of the herbal, a kind of book that focused on the medicinal uses of plants, as well as that of the "secrets" book, a manual that offered advice and "remedyes" for solving all sorts of human problems with nature. In his letter of dedication, Hill suggested that he hoped to promote his book as a kind of herbal when he claimed that it will reveal the "properties of sundry herbs right pleasent to be reade, and their commodities also to health." He also promised something not in the herbals: secrets of cultivation or "the necessarie remedies to such fautes as commonly happen in gardens."[7]

In *The Gardeners Labyrinth* (a later version of the same treatise), the reader is told that these "instructions are rare secretes, are part borrowed out of the worthie workes and treasures of the Greeke and Latin professors of husbandrie, and part purchased by friendship and earnest sute, of the skilfull observers and wittie searchers in our time of laudable secrets in Garden matters, serving as well for the use and singular comfort of mans life, as to a proper gaine and delight of the minde."[8] This language signals the important connection between gardening books and "secrets" books, which characteristically mixed, in no particular order, tips on alchemy, gardening, medicine, cookery, and cosmetics, throwing in some tales of marvels (Hill himself compiled one).[9] For example, in Thomas Lupton's *A Thousand Notable Things, of Sundry Sortes,* lurid stories like that of the Italian woman who

[7] Thomas Hill, *A most briefe and pleasaunte treatyse, teachynge howe to dresse, sowe, and set a garden* (London, [1563]), preface.

[8] Dydymus Mountain [Thomas Hill], *The Gardeners Labyrinth* (London, 1584), second part, p. 3.

[9] *Natural and artifial* [sic] *conclusions compiled first in Latin, by the worthiest and best authors both of the famous University of Padua in Italy, and divers other places, Englished since, and set forth by Thomas Hill, Londoner, whose own experiments in this kind were held most excellent and now again published, with a new addition of rarities for the practise of sundry artificers as also to recreate wits withal at vacant times* (London, 1670).

vomited nails jostle with recipes such as that "to preserve the teeth from rotting."[10] These books traded in technological fantasies of all kinds. They played to desires to transform, improve, or preserve what one had already, while, like modern advertising, they also tried to make people want to do unexpected things. For example, Thomas Hill's secrets book, *Natural and Artificial Conclusions*, reveals "how to make thy chamber appeare full of snakes and adders," and how "to make a light in the night time, that all thinges round about thy hall or parlour shall appear both black and greene,"[11] both accomplishments of doubtful pleasure or necessity.

William Eamon has explored in depth how in England and on the Continent, these books promised a kind of real and material power to the reader.[12] However, they also offered considerable entertainment, as they do today. In fact, in his book *Middle-Class Culture in Elizabethan England* Louis Wright discusses secrets books in the part titled "The Citizen's Literate Recreations," suggesting that they were often not taken quite seriously.[13] Some title-page advertisements do boast of the book's utility, such as Hugh Platt's *Jewell House of Art and Nature. Conteining divers rare and profitable Inventions, together with sundry new experimentes in the Art of Husbandry, Distillation, and Moulding*, and John Partridge's *The Treasurie of commodious Conceits, and hidden Secretes, Commonlie called The good huswives closet of provision, for the health of her Houshold, Meete and necessarie for the profitable use of all estates*. Others, however, dwell on the delights of the text: for example, Thomas Johnson's *Dainty Conceits, with a number of rare and witty inventions, never before printed, Made and invented for honest recreation, to passe away idle houres*, and John White's *A Rich Cabinet with a Variety of Inventions unlock'd and open'd for the Recreation of Ingenious spirits at their vacant hours*. Some offer a charming confusion of both, such as Thomas Johnson's *A new Booke of new Conceits, with a number of novelties annexed thereunto, Whereof some be profitable, some necessary, some strange, none hurtful, and all delectable*, or Thomas Lupton's *A thousand Notable things, of sundry*

[10] Thomas Lupton, *A thousand Notable things, of sundry sortes, whereof some are wonderfull, some straunge, some pleasant, divers necessary, a great sort profitable, and many very precious* (London, 1586).

[11] In Hill, *Natural and artificial conclusions*, pp. 22 and 29.

[12] Eamon, *Science and the Secrets of Nature*, p. 4.

[13] Louis B. Wright, *Middle-Class Culture in Elizabethan England* (Chapel Hill: University of North Carolina Press, 1935).

sortes, whereof some are wonderfull, some straunge, some pleasant, divers
necessary, a great sort profitable, and many very precious.

Lupton's *A Thousand Notable Things* exemplifies the breezy style of such texts, which recommended themselves to both rich and poor.[14] The "preface of the author to the reader" calls the book useful insofar as it brings together in one place and in English "notable, rare, pleasaunt, profitable and precious thinges": "For manye (I suppose) will buye this Booke for thinges whereto they are affectioned, that never coulde or would have bought, or looked on the bookes, wherein all they are." But rather than apologizing for the randomness with which he has assembled his secrets, Lupton justified the lack of order as a form of amusement:

> Perhappes you will mervell, that I have not placed them in better order,
> and that thinges of like matter are not joyned together. Truely there are
> so many of so diverse and sundry sortes and contrary effectes, that it
> could not be altogether observed. And in my judgment through the
> straungeness and varietie of matter, it will be more desirously and de-
> lightfully read: knowing we are made of such a moulde, that delicate
> Daintinesse delights us much: but we loathe to be fed too long with one
> foode.[15]

That is, Lupton appealed to an aesthetic of "variety" or diversity, where disorder and dissimilarity were agreeable. It was a pleasure that could coexist with use, because the printer provided an index and table of contents, which allowed a reader seeking "profit" to find exactly what he or she wanted.

The brevity and disarray of Lawson's *Countrie Housewifes Garden* may thus indicate some disregard for his country housewife, but they also reflect the general style of the practical garden book of the late sixteenth and early seventeenth centuries, which was, like the secrets book, meant to instruct *and* to delight. And the reading as well as the gardening was meant to please. In his *Floraes Paradise*, another wonderful collection of gardening secrets, great and small, Hugh Platt re-

---

[14] The poem on title page boasts that "It is not made to please some one degree, / no, no, nor yet to bring a gain to few: / For each therby, how ritch or poore they bee, / many reape much good, and michief great eschew" (Lupton, *A Thousand Notable Things*).

[15] Ibid., sig. a3–4.

lated how, out of his "owne particular experience" and conversations with "diverse gentlemen," he had gathered together "a pretty volume of observations" for the rich and poor. For this double audience, he avoided writing a "large and methodical Volume," choosing instead to "write briefly and confusedly," rather than "formally or largely," to reveal "the practicall and operative part of nature." This informality offered his reader an opportunity to find his or her own way through the jumble of secrets to what was needed.

Platt's final "pretty conceit," in which he tells how "that delicate knight, sir Francis Carew" produced cherries out of season for Queen Elizabeth, expresses the fine balance of the technical skill and imagination encouraged in these books. Platt's secret is that Carew,

> for the better accomplishment of his royall entertainement of our late Queene of happy memory, at his house at Beddington, led her Maiestie to a Cherrie tree, whose fruite hee had of purpose kept backe from ripening, at the least one month after all Cherries had taken their farewell of England. This secret he performed, by straining a Tent or cover of canvas over the whole tree, and wetting the same now & then with a scoope or horne, as the heate of the weather required; & so, by with-holding the sunne-beames from reflecting uppon the berries they grew both great, & were very long before they had gotten their perfect cherrie-colour; and when hee was assured of her Maiesties comming, he removed the Tent, & a few sunny daies brought them to their full maturitie.[16]

The recipe is precise, to be sure, offering the reader instructions for delaying the ripening of the cherries with shade and cold water, but the prose delicately unfolds a miniature narrative, conveying Carew's care for the queen, his anxious anticipation of her arrival at his house, and his pride in the secret's success. The combination of the "pretty" and the technical in the relation of this secret, which is also a story, encapsulates the pleasures of the sixteenth-century garden book, which lay in both reading the text and performing its works.

In contrast to Lawson's and Platt's books, Parkinson's *Paradisi in Sole: Paradisus Terrestris* is both formal and massive, running to 612 pages in folio exclusive of indexes. It begins with an elaborate, if somewhat crude, frontispiece depicting Adam and Eve in Paradise, sur-

---

[16] Hugh Platt, *Floraes Paradise* (London, 1608), pp. 174–75.

rounded by plants ranging from the gillyflower to the mythical "vegetable lamb" (figure 6). This frontispiece is followed by a dedication to Queen Henrietta Maria and Parkinson's own letter to "the courteous reader," explaining his intent. The book then presents numerous Latin letters and poems of commendation from physicians and colleagues and then a portrait of Parkinson himself. Only then do we get to the text, which is divided into three parts, covering the "garden of pleasant flowers," the kitchen garden, and the orchard. In all, it discusses almost a thousand plants, amply illustrated with 108 full-page woodcuts. The book ends with two indexes of plant names in Latin and English, "a Table of the Vertues and Properties of the hearbes contained in this Booke," and a list of errata. In comparison with *The Countrie Housewifes Garden*, Parkinson's book was thus meant to look immensely authoritative, bolstered by its sheer bulk, ties to royalty, commendations by professional experts, elaborate organization, expensive illustrations, and the apparatus of a major book, including frontispiece, indexes, and errata. It was ponderously delivered to men and women of means and sent the message that gardening is a serious business.

At first glance, the book thus resembles the folio herbals of its time, much more than the modest "secrets" books that are the *Countrie Housewifes'* cousins. In general, the herbal's format was highly conservative, organized around the encyclopedic description of plants for their human uses and detailing the "kinds," the places where they grow, the names, the "temperatures" for humoral medicine, and the "virtues" or uses. Their authors and printers differed only as to the right formats and groupings to convey this vast amount of information. As Gill Saunders reminds us, "there was no 'scientific' method of classification available to the herbalist. Plants in herbals were ordered according to a variety of principles (often within the same book), many of which relate to their medicinal properties. Some followed [the classical authors] Dioscorides, Theophrastus, and Pliny in distinguishing herbs according to taste, smell and edibility, or by those parts of the body which they were used to heal."[17] But the purpose and form remained the same.

In the printed books, writers claimed they were improving on models without altering anything: generally speaking, herbals just grew

[17] Gill Saunders, *Picturing Plants: An Analytical History of Botanical Illustration* (Berkeley: University of California Press, in association with the Victoria and Albert Museum, 1995), p. 24.

FIGURE 6. Title page of John Parkinson, *Paradisi in Sole* (1629). Reproduced by permission of the Annenberg Rare Book and Manuscript Library, University of Pennsylvania.

bigger. In his *New Herbal* (1551), William Turner knew he was doing something different in writing an English herbal, but he did not change the generic structure.[18] When John Gerard published his herbal in 1597, he saw himself as only following Turner, while improving and amplifying his approach.[19] Thomas Johnson's 1633 edition of Gerard's *Herbal* was also supposed to be the "latest word" in herbals. In his preface Johnson vigorously criticized every previous herbal. But all he really did to Gerard was put an overlay onto the earlier text, with the many additions and corrections marked by a double cross mark (++): for example, in the section on clove gillyflowers, Johnson retained Gerard's basic entry structure, including "the kindes, the description, the place, the names, the temperature, the vertues," and appended a note suggesting that the reader refer to Parkinson and also "at the time of the yeare repaire to the garden of Mistresse Tuggy (the wife of my late deceased friend Mr. Ralph Tuggy) in Westminster."[20] Thus, even when claiming to be new, herbals changed little over the years except in bulk.

Parkinson, however, imagined his reader as needing an entirely new sort of book, not only because it had more items, but because it redefined what the gardener should know and *think* about a plant. In Parkinson's *Paradisi in Sole,* we witness a writer recording his thoughts on what it meant to compose a gardening book as opposed to a herbal. He told the reader that he intended to "play the Gardiner," and not "the Empericke and give you receipts of medicines for all diseases." Nor would he offer "a treatise of cookery." Parkinson was concerned enough about generic conventions to include some "virtues" and "properties" of plants,[21] but he knew that many flowers have no medicinal uses, for they are, like the fritillaria, only "to be an ornament for the Gardens of the curious lovers of these delights, and to be worne of them abroad, which for the gallant beauty of many of them, deserveth their courteous entertainment, among many other the like pleasures."[22]

[18] William Turner, *A New Herbal* (London, 1551), dedication.
[19] *The Herball or Generall Historie of Plantes. Gathered by John Gerarde of London, Master in Chirurgerie* (London, 1597).
[20] *The Herball or Generall Historie of Plantes / Gathered by John Gerarde of London, Master in Chirurgerie. Very much Enlarged and Amended by Thomas Johnson* (London, 1633), p. 589.
[21] John Parkinson, *Paradisi in Sole: Paradisus Terrestris* (London, 1629; rpt., New York: Dover, 1991), epistle to the reader.
[22] Ibid., p. 45.

What he faced was inventing a book that orders its floral subject by principles other than uses.

In his epistle to the reader Parkinson judged that Latin herbals were out of date but he mostly complained that all the herbals, Latin and English, had said "little of flowers":

> First, having perused many Herbals in Latine, I observed that most of them have eyther neglected or not knowne the many diversities of the flower Plants, and rare fruits [that] are known to us at this time, and (except Clusius) have made mention but of a very few. In English likewise we have some extant, as Turner and Dodonaeus translated, who have said little of Flowers. Gerard who is last, hath no doubt given us the knowledge of as many as he attained unto in his time, but since his daies we have had many more varieties, then he or they ever heard of, as may be perceived by the store I have here produced.

Part of Parkinson's complaint here is conventional, where he claims that a new book is needed to record the new varieties and plants introduced into England. What was unprecedented was his writing a book about flowers, neglected by the Latin and English herbalists. Parkinson's book presented not just more or more diverse plants: it was meant to be a treasury of ornamental and rare species.

Parkinson also made the point in the epistle that the herbals were at once too inclusive and not inclusive enough, because they mixed ornamental flowers with common herbs:

> And none of them have particularly severed those that are beautifull flower plants, fit to store a garden of delight and pleasure, from the wilde and unfit: but have enterlaced many, one among another, whereby many that have desired to have faire flowers, have not known either what to choose, or what to desire. Divers Bookes of Flowers also have been set forth, some in our owne Countrey, and more in others, all which are as it were but handfuls snatched from the plentifull Treasury of Nature, none of them being willing or able to open all sorts, and declare them fully.

In this remarkable statement Parkinson showed his hand, revealing his intention to tell his gentle reader, once and for all, what is "fit" and "unfit," what belongs in the pleasure garden, and what is wild and thus disposable. Unlike Lawson, who relied on his housewife to create her own homely delights and to follow her own pleasure, Parkinson would *direct* his readers to their pleasure, so that now they would know what is truly delightful and what to desire.

So Parkinson proudly offered his readers a choice group of flowers, neatly ordered, as the means for gratifying and guiding them: "To satisfie therefore their desires that are lovers of such Delights, I took upon me this labour and charge, and have here selected and set forth a Garden of all the chiefest for choyce, and fairest for shew, from among all the severall Tribes and Kindreds of Natures beauty and have ranked them as neere as I could or as the worke would permit, in affinity one unto another."[23] Thus, for Parkinson his book's value lay in its selectivity and in its organization of nature into hierarchies and affinities. It would fashion a world in which you would know how pleasant and "choice" flowers were to be separated from the common herbs and "sallets" of the kitchen garden. Whereas Lawson allowed his housewife to wander, Parkinson led his reader in taking his or her pleasure in an orderly book, which represented the dream of an orderly world. There is irony, indeed, in the difference, when the housewife was left to her own devices while the better sort were told what to do.

It is not gender, then, that differentiates Parkinson's grand volume and Lawson's slim pamphlet, since both of them imagine an ideal female reader. But Parkinson's was a queen, who stood in for the gentle "lover of these delights," whereas Lawson's was a country housewife (albeit one equipped with servants), concerned with the productivity of her own plot of land. For Lawson's housewife, the book was to accompany her practice, and her pleasure was where she found it in reading. It was to be experienced like the "florilegium," a text much like a garden, to be browsed through and harvested according to each reader's needs.[24] For Parkinson's gentle reader, the garden book served as a treasury and a reflection of an ordered and ranked society of nature, defining garden desire.

---

[23] Ibid., epistle to the reader.
[24] See Saunders, *Picturing Plants*, p. 41, on "florilegia" as books of plates of flowers that began to appear for the most part in the early seventeenth century and on the Continent. On texts as "florilegia," see Mary A. Rouse and Richard H. Rouse, *Authentic Witnesses: Approaches to Medieval Texts and Manuscripts* (Notre Dame: University of Notre Dame Press, 1991). On the connections between gardens and texts in general, see Rebecca Bushnell, *A Culture of Teaching* (Ithaca: Cornell University Press, 1996), chap. 3; and Juliet Fleming, *Graffiti and the Writing Arts of Early Modern England* (Philadelphia: University of Pennsylvania Press, 2001).

Observing their intention to delight, the modern reader is often sur-
prised that most of these early gardening books lack pictures of flowers or fruits. The art of botanical illustration did not flourish in English
gardening books (as opposed to herbals) until the eighteenth century,
when copper engraving became common. Where there are illustrations in early gardening books, the crude figures mostly depict tools
and techniques (watering, grafting, or weeding) or designs for knot
gardens. Even John Evelyn hand-illustrated his *Elysium Britannicum*
manuscript with sketches of urns, machines, and garden tools, not
flowers.[25] What were these illustrations meant to do? What pleasure
could any reader who wanted a flower garden find in their stark out-
lines?

Some prefaces for the earlier husbandry books indicate that writers
hoped that illustrations might make their books more accessible.
Reynolde Scot's printer announced in Scot's book on growing hops
that he included pictures as an aid to the unlettered reader: "I also pray
you to take somewhat the more paines in conferring the wordes with
the figures, which will mutually give lyght one the other, and finallye
will assist the understanding of you the Reader, but chieflye of him that
cannot reade at all, for whose sake hee [Scot] devised and procured
these Figures to be made."[26] Such would also seem to be true of the
figures of tools in books like Gervase Markham's *English Husbandman*
and William Lawson's *New Orchard and Garden*. For example, Markham's book pictures the assembling of a plow, piece by piece (figure
7), apparently to help if one could not read the text. Writers certainly
appreciated the printers' efforts in producing new woodcuts (while
old ones were often reused). In his *New Orchard* Lawson praised the
woodcutter's art and cheerfully acknowledged the generosity of the
willing "stationer" who "(as being most desirous with me, to further
the common good) bestowed much cost and care in having the Knots
and Models by the best Artizan cutte in great varietie, that nothing may
be any way wanting to satisfie the curious desire of those, that would

[25] John Evelyn, *Elysium Britannicum,* ed. John E. Ingram (Philadelphia: University
of Pennsylvania Press, 2001).

[26] This note comes from the letter from the printer to the reader in the 1574 edition,
omitted from later editions (Reynolde Scot, *A Perfite platforme of a Hoppe Garden* [Lon-
don, 1574], sig. b3r).

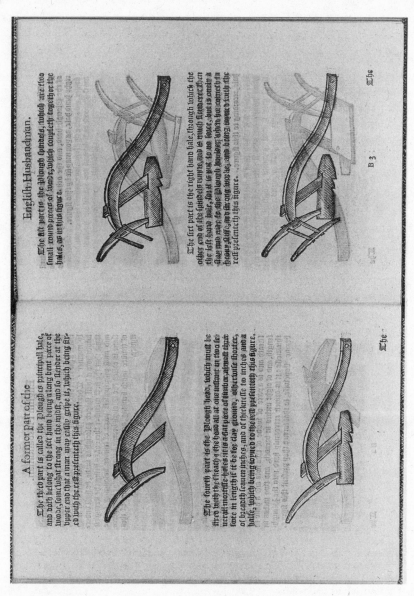

FIGURE 7. The parts of a plow, from Gervase Markham, *The English Husbandman* (1613). Reproduced by permission of the Folger Shakespeare Library.

make use of this booke."[27] In the latter part of the seventeenth century, however, and in the beginning of the eighteenth, the demand for the new style of copper engraving could add too much to the price of producing a book. Apparently the expense and the lack of a generous printer prevented John Rea from including engravings in his *Flora: seu, De Florum Cultura,* despite his own wishes.[28]

Certainly, when plants were represented, it was not because the pictures were pretty. John Rea excused his own lack of illustrations by complaining that John Parkinson's woodcuts were "such Artless things, being good for nothing, unless to raise the Price of the Book, serving neither for Ornament or Information, but rather to puzzle and affright the Spectators into an Aversion, than direct or invite their Affections; for did his Flowers appear no fairer on their stalks in the Garden, than they do on the leaves of his Book, few Ladies would be in love with them, much more than they are with his lovely pictures."[29] Even while these remarks are disingenuous, since Rea would have included engravings if he could have afforded them, his dismissing of Parkinson's "frightful" woodcuts indicates a new idea: that garden book illustrations should be attractive. Parkinson's pictures may be copious and even charming to us, but it is apparent that they do not show the "true beauty of flowers." For example, one of the many pages depicting that most exquisite of flowers, the tulip, has the stark black and white blooms cut off at the stem and crowded together in awkward rows (see figure 8). Such a figure could indeed do little more than identify species, and would hardly excite a lady's love.

However, Parkinson's illustrations may have functioned less to represent plants themselves than the *idea* of a plant set in the framework

[27] William Lawson, *New Orchard and Garden* (London, 1618; rpt., New York: Garland, 1982), preface to "all well minded."

[28] Apparently he *did* want to have illustrations in his book, but the prospect "so affrighted the stationers, that they offered him but thirty pounds for his pains. This displeased him so much that he brought home his manuscripts" (see Blanche Henrey, *British Botanical and Horticultural Literature before 1800,* 3 vols. [London: Oxford University Press, 1975], 1:195, quoting a letter to Samuel Hartlib repeated in one of Hartlib's letters to Boyle).

[29] John Rea, *Flora: seu, De Florum Cultura, or a Complete Florilege* (London, 1665), sig. b2r. See also William Coles's critique of the cuts in herbals of his time: "Though their Cutts do take up much roome and render their Books much more abundantly deare, yet they are so much inferior to those of Matthiolus and Dioscorides, in respect of the smallnesse of their Size, and the false placing of them, that the Botanick is as commonly puzzled as satisfied, and thereby disabled to give an ingenious account of them" (William Coles, *Adam in Eden: or Natures Paradise* [London, 1657], sig. a1v–2r).

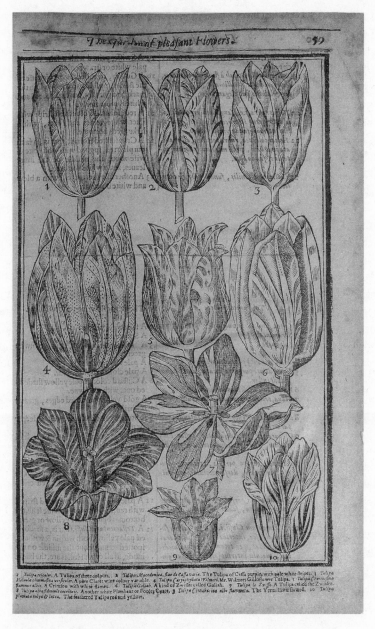

FIGURE 8. Pictures of tulips, from John Parkinson, *Paradisi in Sole* (1629). Reproduced by permission of the Annenberg Rare Book and Manuscript Library, University of Pennsylvania.

of a book. When plant images did occur in early books, as in the case of early herbals, rough and inaccurate woodcuts were used repeatedly with little concern for realism or even accuracy. While scholars of botanical illustration have mostly mocked them for their coarseness, Gill Saunders argues that the traditional herbal woodcuts were in fact intended to function as elements of a book's design or "decorative motifs breaking up the blocks of text: the *Grete Herbal* (1526) with its images contained within a framing line, is printed to look like a manuscript, including illuminated initials. The strongly symmetrical illustrations resemble printers' devices, decorative motifs, ciphers or pictograms of the plants they 'represent.'"[30] In line with this function, then, the image of the plant was made to fit into the woodblock shape, rather than the page of the book designed to suit the image.[31]

Even though the continental illustrators Hans Weiditz in Otto Brunfels's *Herbarum Vivae Eicones* (1530–36) and Leonhart Fuchs in his *De Historia Stirpium* (1542) had already broken new ground in representing plants as drawn from life, English herbals (and some gardening books) continued to use this kind of patterned illustration of plants throughout the seventeenth century. Saunders notes of Parkinson's *Paradisi* that the illustrations also have a kind of "geometric regularity."[32] In this case, not only would they fit in with the look of the book itself; this regularity would also have suited the purposes of the text. As Rea suggested, they might not have aroused longing in the ladies; what they could do, however, was further Parkinson's aim of representing the natural world as defined by place, order, and rank, when the flowers were gathered into the frame of a book.

Recognizing that such flower images expressed more the order of the book and the beauty of order than the random delights of nature helps to explain the abundant pictures of gardening tools and practices. Like the geometric images of flowers, illustrations of pruning knives or garden knots celebrate the gardener's technical mastery over nature and not the appeal of plants. Thomas Hill's *Gardeners Labyrinth* set the example by depicting appropriate tools used in a garden setting, including the second part's title-page image that shows men working in an enclosed garden (figure 9). In this image, some of the

[30] Saunders, *Picturing Plants,* p. 28.
[31] Ibid., p. 32: "The obsessive impulse towards symmetry and rectangularization was disrupted by Brunfels and Fuchs."
[32] Ibid., pp. 103–4.

THE SECOND PART OF THE

Gardeners Labyrinth, vttering such skilfull experiences and worthie secretes, about the particular sowing and re-
moouing of the most Kitchin Hearbes, with the wittie ordering
of other daintie Hearbes, delectable Floures, pleasant Fruites,
and fine Roots, as the like hath not heretofore been vttered
of anie. Besides the Phisicke benefits of each Hearbe
annexed, with the commoditie of waters
distilled out of them, right ne-
nessarie to be knowen.

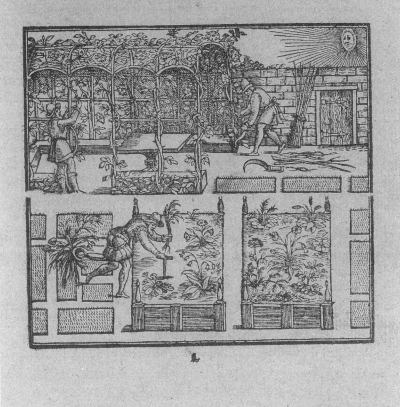

FIGURE 9. Men working in the garden, from Dydymus Mountain [Thomas Hill], *The Gardeners Labyrinth* (1594). Reproduced by permission of the Folger Shakespeare Library.

plants might be identifiable, including what looks like a single gilly-flower or dianthus in the bed on the right. However, the woodcut fore-grounds the gardeners' technique rather than the plants themselves, showing their methods of pruning or setting slips in a neat rectangular plot. In Markham's *English Husbandman*, even where pictures of plants do appear, they are there to show the uses of tools. For example, the book includes figures to guide grafting, where the plant bends to the will of the illustrator as it would to the gardener's hand. In such figures the plant itself is generic and cut to fit the size of the woodblock, and in one case, marked itself with the image of the letter "H," the cut for grafting (see figure 10).[33] This regularity in turn replicated the geometric design of flower plots themselves. Markham included, along with all his tools and diagrams, models of "the fashion of the garden-plot for pleasure": "the plain square, the square triangular or circular, the square of eight diamonds" (see figure 11).[34] It was, after all, a world in which the organic was subdued at every level by the knife and the surveyor's rod, and the books both directed and advertised this subjection.[35]

These illustrations of tools, practices, and knot gardens thus encourage the gardener to take pleasure in his or her mastery of nature. William Lawson's entire *New Orchard and Garden* can be read as a cheerful guide to regulation as much as nurture. Lawson boasted that he "can bring any tree (beginning by time) to any forme. The Peare and Holly may bee made to spread, and the Oake to close."[36] This claim is accompanied by a block print of the "perfect form of an apple tree," where the tree's "perfect form" is made to conform to the rectangular shape of the wood block itself (figure 12). In the text Lawson did apologize for what he calls the "deformity" of the drawing, but only "because I am nothing skillful either in painting or carving," and not because it might be a "deformed" tree. There was symmetry, then, to be found between the body of the book and the shape of the plant, meeting in the "perfect form" of a rectangular tree.

[33] See also Gervase Markham, *The English Husbandman* (London, 1613; rpt., New York: Garland, 1982), p. 68, on sets for vines; more tools on pp. 97–98; and an abstract model of a garden fence, p. 113.

[34] Ibid., pp. 112–15.

[35] I am grateful to Crystal Bartolovich for sharing with me her work on the subject of surveying. See also Andrew McRae, *God Speed the Plough: The Representation of Agrarian England, 1500–1660* (Cambridge: Cambridge University Press, 1996), chap. 6.

[36] Lawson, *New Orchard*, p. 35.

Then goe to the body, arme, or branch of that tree which
you intend to graft, which is to be presupposed must euer
haue a smooth and tender barke, and with a very sharpe
knife slit the barke, two slits at least, two inches long a
peece, and about halfe an inch or more distance betweene
the two slits : then make another slit crosse-wise ouer-
thwart, from long slit to long slit, the figure whereof will
be thus :

Then with your knife raise the barke gently from the
tree,

FIGURE 10. Grafting a tree, from Gervase Markham, *The English Husbandman* (1613).
Reproduced by permission of the Folger Shakespeare Library.

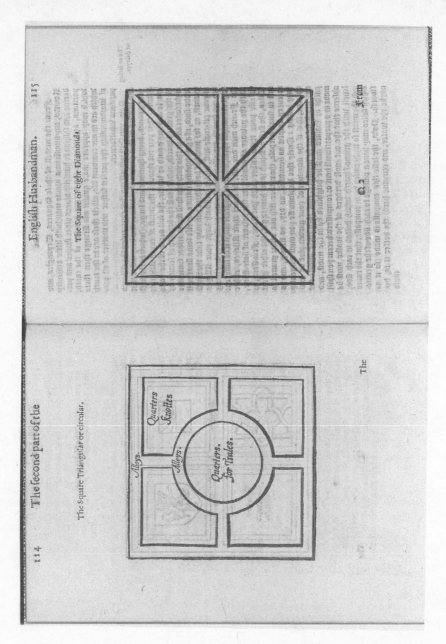

FIGURE 11. Garden plots, from Gervase Markham, *The English Husbandman* (1613). Reproduced by permission of the Folger Shakespeare Library.

The perfect forme of an Apple tree.

If any thinke a trǽ cannot well be bꝛought to this foꝛme: *Experto crede Roberto.* I can ſhew diuers of them vnder 20, yeates of age.

Time beſt for proining. ☞ The fitteſt time of the Moone foꝛ pꝛoyning is as of grafting,when the ſappe is ready to ſtirre (not pꝛoudly ſtirring) and ſo to couer the wound,and of the yeat a month before(oꝛ at leaſt when) you graffe. Dꝛeſſe Peares,Apꝛicocks,Peaches, Cheries,and Bullyes ſooner. And old trǽs befoꝛe yong plants,you may dꝛeſſe at any time betwirt Leafe and Leafe. And note, that where you take any thing away,the ſapp the next ſummer will be putting:beſure therefoꝛe when he puts a bud in any place where you would not haue him, rub it off with your finger.

Dreſſe betime. ☞ And here you muſt remember the common homely Pꝛouerbe : Soone crookes the tree that good Camell muſt be. Begiane betime with trǽs, and doe what you liſt: but if you let them grow great and ſtubboꝛne, you muſt do as the trees liſt. They will not bend but bꝛeake, noꝛ be woundewith

FIGURE 12. The perfect form of an apple tree, from William Lawson, *New Orchard and Garden* (1618). Reproduced by permission of the Folger Shakespeare Library.

While the pleasant disarray of the sixteenth- and early seventeenth-century garden book might invite the gardener's pleasure in finding his or her own way randomly through it, the illustrations thus advocate the reader's and gardener's taking control of his or her environment. They remind us that the book means to teach the reader to shape an order in nature, whether through pruning, design, or grafting, just as the book itself subdues plants' images to its own ends. The absence of such illustrations in most of the later seventeenth-century garden manuals is telling, insofar as, as we shall see in chapter 5, those books expressed more ambivalence about the balance of art and nature in gardening practice. These later books relied more on metaphor and rhetoric to convey their belief in a natural order.

Natural Form

Parkinson's *Paradisi in Sole* set the pattern for a half-century's worth of garden books that also sought to construct hierarchy and order in the plant world. For example, Leonard Meager's *The English Gardener: or a Sure Guide to young Planters and Gardeners, in Three Parts* imitated but reversed Parkinson's design, beginning with the "order of Planting and raising all sorts of Stocks, Fruit-trees and Shrubs," then coming to the kitchen garden, and ending with "the ordering of the Garden of Pleasure . . . also the choicest and most approved ways for the raising all sorts of Flowers and their Seasons."[37] *Paradisi in Sole* clearly inspired John Rea's *Flora*, first published in 1665, even though Rea judged that Parkinson's book was out of date because it lacked both "many noble things of newer discovery," and what was included was "by Time grown stale and for Unworthiness turned out of every good Garden." He wrote that he thought about revising *Paradisi in Sole* but then decided to write an entirely new book, "to be fashioned into the form of a Florilege, furnished with all requisites belonging to a Florist, [rather] than continued in the old method of an Herbal: and instead of old names, uncertain places, and little or no virtues, to insert some other things much more considerable."[38] But Rea's real innovation was to convert Parkinson's ranks into an explicit seasonal order.

[37] Leonard Meager, *The English Gardener: or a Sure Guide to young Planters and Gardeners, in Three Parts* (London, 1670).
[38] Rea, *Flora*, "To the reader."

In Rea's text, Flora, the goddess of spring flowers, is the undisputed monarch. The elaborate engraved frontispiece displays Flora, Ceres, and Pomona, accompanied by an explanatory poem that names Flora as queen (figure 13). This frontispiece, with Flora situated at the apex of a triangle anchored by Ceres and Pomona, makes Parkinson's title page, with its random display of plants crowded into an oval frame, look positively unruly (figure 6). Flora's plants are elevated over those of Ceres, "Goddess of Seeds and Tillage," which are also the flowers of summer, as well as over those of Pomona or the orchard, the autumn plants. This order is at once hierarchical, where Flora and the valued spring bulbs rule, and also seasonal and thus seen as natural. Of course, there was nothing natural about it: the spring bulbs, which Parkinson had called "out-landish" or foreign flowers, were still the height of fashion, and that is why they came first. (Parkinson had reported that, despite their defects, these flowers "are almost in all places with all persons, especially with the better sort of the Gentry of the Land, as greatly desired and accepted as any other the most choicest.")[39] While the form might suggest an immutable aristocratic order in nature, reproduced in the book, this hierarchy was still a matter of fashion and desire that the book was meant to define.

Before Rea, books of seasonal advice were mostly produced for the common reader. The omnipresent printed almanacs of the period often contained agricultural wisdom along with their myriad prognostications, proverbs, and miscellaneous information. In England, the idea of seasonal garden books goes back to Thomas Tusser's very popular *A hundreth pointes of husbandries* (1557). This nifty item offered helpful hints on both husbandry and housewifery, organized by consecutive months starting in August. *A hundreth pointes* were followed up in 1573 by *Five hundreth points of good husbandry, united to as many of good huswiferie, first devised, and nowe lately augmented with diverse approved lessons concerning hopps and gardening, and other needful matters, together with an abstract before every moneth, conteining the whole effect of the sayd moneth with a table and a preface in the beginning both necessary to be reade for the better understanding of the booke.* As this title-page advertisement suggests, the later book is a much more systematic and elaborate production than the 1557 volume (while not five times as long),

[39] Parkinson, *Paradisi in Sole*, p. 8.

FIGURE 13. Frontispiece of John Rea, *Flora: seu, De Florum Cultura* (1665). Reproduced by permission of the Huntington Library, San Marino, California.

adding a table of contents and a system of abstracts preceding each month. The reader is told to follow a monthly program:

> In every month, or in aught be begonne
> Read over that month, what dayles to be donne,
> So neyther this travell, shall seeme to be lost:
> Nor thou to repent, of this trifeling cost.[40]

Andrew McRae argues that this format implies an effort "to fix information in the minds of the illiterate or semi-literate," anticipating a reader who was a "small farmer" rather than a gentleman.[41] It would also have been a comfortable format for those wont to use almanacs to guide daily experience.[42]

Later versions of seasonal gardening manuals still presented themselves as suited to the inexperienced or even "unlettered" reader. John Evelyn is credited with producing the first "garden calendar" book in English (as opposed to Tusser's hints for husbandry), the *Kalendarium Hortense* appended to his *Sylva* and published in 1664.[43] Evelyn explained to his readers that he wrote this calendar, listing what should be done in the garden every month, because "the order in which they shall find each particular to be dispos'd, may not only render the Work more facile and delightsome; but redeem it from that extreame confusion, which for want of a constant, and uniform Method, we find does so universally distract our ordinary sort of Garden'rs" (in the 1666 edition of the *Kalendarium*, published separately, "our ordinary sort" became the "vulgar sort of them"). Evelyn did take pains here to distance himself from any astrological method of gardening advice, which might be implied by his using a monthly scheme. For him, the purpose of this formal "Oeconomy and Discipline" was to assist the common gardener's understanding and memory.[44]

However, Evelyn's calendar was imitated by several garden writers who implicitly or explicitly expanded the calendar's audience to include the gentry. Samuel Gilbert's *Florist's Vade-Mecum* described this

[40] Thomas Tusser, *Five Hundreth Points of Good Husbandry* (London, 1573), front matter.

[41] McRae, *God Speed*, p. 147.

[42] See Bernard Capp, *English Almanacs, 1500–1800: Astrology and the Popular Press* (Ithaca: Cornell University Press, 1979).

[43] See Henrey, *British Botanical and Horticultural Literature*, 1:187.

[44] John Evelyn, *Kalendarium Hortense*, in *Sylva* (London, 1664), p. 56.

monthly format as the more "natural" order, appropriate for common, professional, and elite readers alike. He proclaimed that "I follow not the method, most Authors have, in Writing of all Bulbous rooted flowers by themselves and all Tuberous and Grummous rooted flowers so too, &c, but as more natural, you will find the flowers treated on successively as they blow one after another, and as they appear in each month." While he professed that his tract was designed for the "meanest florist," it also had an alphabetical index, which allowed it to be consulted by the professional florist. Further, as Gilbert put it in his dedicatory poem to Lady Margaret Packington, the book's natural order mimicked social order, pleasing for the aristocratic reader. He promised that Lady Margaret would find the book's flowers

> all in their Orders rankt, as they appear
> In your rich Livery, they yearly wear.
> And therefore bound to wait you in your Bow'rs,
> To be divertisement for vacant hours.[45]

Thus, the calendar form was supposedly useful for the "mean florist," but it is also fashioned as a diverting array where a gentle reader could see the garden world laid out and ready to serve.

In his *Fruit-Garden Kalendar* (1718) John Laurence explicitly connected the social and seasonal orders as represented in the calendar book. He began his calendar, unexpectedly, with the statement that "it is on all Hands granted, and, with great Reason agreed on, that good Laws are necessary and essential to the Being of Good Government," for without law, there is only "anarchy and disorder." It is as if he were beginning a rational political treatise of the period, arguing for the rule of law as the guarantor of social and political order. But Laurence went on to remark that the same is true of the vegetable kingdom, which would decay without "the seasonable Execution of good Laws." So, he confessed, it is thus "with a View of restoring and establishing a true and exact Order and Oeconomy in a garden: that we composed this calendar," with "a due regard to the order of Nature, resolving to make every Thing plain and intelligible, even to young beginners, by a *natural* Method of Proceeding." "Law," allied with the gardener's control,

---

[45] Samuel Gilbert, *Florist's Vade-Mecum*, second edition (London, 1682), epistle to the reader.

was not seen as antithetical to nature, if practiced in accordance with her ways.

However, Laurence's "natural Method" is not a free method. Rather, to follow the "Order of Time" is "to be led, as it were, by the Hand; to be directed and pointed to something to be done, not only each successive year, but if possible every day, at least every Month of the Year, toward forwarding the natural Hopes of being rewarded with Fruit and plenty. Such a Sort of Manuduction as this must needs be very desirable and easy to the Mind: and every true Lover of a Garden should me thinks entertain such a Guide with Kindness and Candor; especially whilst nothing is offered to him choaking or unnatural."[46] In the calendar form, the reader experiences the order of nature, which reflects the social order of a well-governed polity. The gardener reader is subject to the book's governance as much as he or she is thought to be a willing subject to English law. That governance is not supposed to be seen as "choaking or unnatural" because, aligned with natural law, it is as inevitable as the passing of the seasons. The book leads the reader "by the hand," with parental "kindness and candor," exacting a loving submission to nature's rule.

When reading these calendars, however, one cannot forget that the gardener's year is as much a matter of culture as nature. The calendars rarely concur on when the gardener's year begins, partly because different kinds of gardeners care for different plants. In Evelyn's *Kalendarium* and Laurence's *Fruit-Garden Kalendar,* the year begins in January; but in *The Retir'd Gardener* the florist's year begins in September. One could hark back to Tusser's book, which was geared to the tenant farmer's agricultural year. The 1573 *Five Hundreth Points* starts the calendar in September, whereas *A Hundreth Good Pointes* begins in August. (McRae thinks that this change suggests a new focus on an audience of tenant farmers and the changes of land tenure that took place in September.)[47] The "natural order" of the gardener's calendar year is not transcendent; it is ultimately an order of decorum, corresponding to the gardener's task and his social role.

As we shall see in chapter 5, gardeners also knew only too well that they themselves had an influence over the "natural order," when they came to quarrel over methods for meddling in natural processes and

[46] John Laurence, *The Fruit-Garden Kalendar* (London, 1718), pp. 1–4.
[47] McRae, *God Speed*, p. 147.

the timing of the seasons of fruits and flowers. As Platt's secret for bringing cherries out of season indicates, many gardeners did everything they could to fight the cycle of nature. The Italian "secrets" writer Giambattista Della Porta told his readers that they could control the influence of the seasons: "when [a gardener] is disposed to hinder the ripening of any thing, or else to help it forward, that it may be more rare and of better worth, he effects it by Counterfeiting the times and seasons of the year, making the Winter to be as the Summer, and the Springtime as the Winter."[48] Others, however, protested at what they saw as such ungodly arrogance, for, as John Parkinson worried, "if any man can forme plants at his will and pleasure, he can do as much as God himself that created them."[49] There was much to be gained in exerting mastery over the ways of nature, counterfeiting the seasons, but there was also much to be lost, from the point of view of those who feared interfering in what they saw as God's given order of creation.

Books as Tools

Samuel Gilbert thus thought that his *Florist's Vade-Mecum* was to be valued for its natural method, but he also liked it because it was a small and neat book, "the whole fitted as a pocket companion to all Lovers of Flowers and their propagation." It was designed, he insisted, not like recent overblown or "bumbastick" works made for pedants in their studies, but "for the benefit of the meanest Florist, that perhaps understands not how, or hath not the conveniency of searching a Dictionary to know the meaning of *Esculent, Horti culture, Sterilize, . . . irrigate*" (thus forgetting Lady Margaret Packington for the moment).[50] That is, the *Florist's Vade-Mecum* was seen as simple and sufficient unto itself; it was not to be consulted in a library with the aid of a dictionary.

[48] "Amongst other means, engraffing is not a little helpful hereunto. Wherefore let us see, how we may by engraffing, produce grapes in the Spring Time. If we see a Cherry tree bring forth her fruit in the Spring-time, and we desire to have Grapes about that time, there is fit opportunity of attaining our desire, as Tarentinus writeth. If you engraff a black Vine into the Cherry-tree, you shall have Grapes growing in the spring-time. For the tree will bring forth Grapes the very same season, wherein it would bring forth her own fruit" (John Baptista [della] Porta, *Natural Magick* [London, 1658], p. 74).
[49] Parkinson, *Paradisi in Sole*, p. 24.
[50] Gilbert, *Florist's Vade-Mecum*, preface.

Instead, its format as a pocket companion meant that it might be literally carried into the garden, like a pruning knife or shears.

Gilbert's conception of his book as a tool for the "meanest florist," inexpert in technical terms yet a specialist in flowers, occurs elsewhere in gardening books of the late seventeenth century. For example, in *The Flower Garden* William Hughes insisted that he did not "intend this first part to Flowrists, Gardeners, or others who have experience in the recreation, though to them also it may be useful, but chiefly for more plain and ordinary Country men and women as a perpetual Almanack or Remembrancer of them, when and which way, most of their Flowers are to be ordered." On this basis, he justified his book's brevity, for "the price thereof is small, and therefore within the most ordinary reach which larger books are not."[51] This rhetoric justifying the smaller, pocket volume and its accessibility was hardly new in how-to and garden books, although here it echoed the theme of "scientific" education for the common gardener, a concept reaching back to the Hartlib circle's proposals to develop public programs in agricultural reform.[52] As early as the late sixteenth century, the claim of public service was common in herbals and garden books, even if these books were unlikely ever to reach a "country" reader. One must wonder how often Hughes's book fell into the hands of plain and ordinary country folk.

It is true that, in this time of greater literacy, smaller garden books did sell more copies than larger ones. John Evelyn's impressive translation of Jean de la Quintinie's *The Compleat Gard'ner* appeared in 1693; at the time, it cost twenty shillings.[53] A few years later, in 1699, the enterprising nurserymen George London and Henry Wise decided to publish an abridgment. London and Wise explained to the reader how they had taken their "learned author . . . abstracting out of each Title or general Head, all that is useful; and have reduc'd into a proper method, that which in the original was so prolix and interwoven, that the reader was rather tir'd than informed."[54] Evelyn's folio was never reprinted, whereas London and Wise's book went into seven edi-

51 William Hughes, *The Flower Garden* (London, 1672), preface to the reader.
52 See Charles Webster, *The Great Instauration: Science, Medicine, and Reform, 1626–1660* (New York: Holmes and Meier, 1975), pp. 465–83.
53 Henrey, *British Botanical and Horticultural Literature*, 1:190.
54 Jean de La Quintinie, *The Compleat Gard'ner . . . Now compendiously Abridg'd and made of more Use, with very Considerable Improvements, by George London and Henry Wise* (London, 1699).

tions.[55] As Blanche Henrey has observed, the folio garden book thus gradually went out of fashion by the end of the seventeenth century, giving way to smaller quarto and octavo volumes.[56]

But it is probable that more than just poor people were buying these smaller, cheaper books. In his conclusion to his epistle to the reader in *Adam in Eden: or, Natures Paradise,* William Coles deliberately defined his herbal's readership as professionals ("Physicians, Chirurgions & Apothecaries") and the "Nobility and Gentry." When he then commended *his* own book for its brevity and low cost, in this case, he was not trying to increase its accessibility to the unlearned. Rather he saw the format as a part of its professional value.[57] By the middle of the seventeenth century, economy of size was less a mark of a class distinction than an emerging standard for a book meant to be kept for use.

Partly such books must have appealed to professionals and the gentry because they suited the new image of a science book. John Worlidge offered his *Systema Horti-culturae* to both "such [men] that have fair estates and pleasant Seats in the Country" and "the honest and plain Countreyman in the improvement of his Ville, by enlarging the bounds and limits of his Gardens."[58] He told the reader that he composed his books for this broad audience according to the guidelines set by Ralph Austen in his book *A Treatise of Fruit Trees* (from the second edition of Austen's treatise's epistle dedicatory to Robert Boyle, replacing an earlier letter to Samuel Hartlib). In that letter, Austen cited the following requirements for books that would serve the new science of husbandry: "First, That they be of small Bulk and Price; Because great Volumns (as many are upon this Subject) are of too great a Price for mean Husbandmen to buy, as also take up more time to peruse then they can spare from other Labours. Secondly, That the Stile and Expressions be plaine, and suited to the Vulgar (even to the Capacities of the meanest, for these (Generally) must be the Workmen and Labourers thereabout [)]."[59] The curious point is that such cheap, plain books

[55] Henrey, *British Botanical and Horticultural Literature,* 1:214.

[56] Ibid. Henrey also notes there that only a few works were still published in folio: "The majority were duodecimo, octavo, or small quarto volumes." This was true of most books: on the change in the format of Bibles, see Ian Green, *Print and Protestantism* (Oxford: Oxford University Press, 2000), pp. 60–64.

[57] Coles, *Adam in Eden,* epistle to the reader.

[58] John Worlidge, *Systema Horti-culturae or, The art of gardening* (London, 1677; rpt., New York: Garland, 1982), preface to the reader.

[59] Ralph Austen, *A Treatise of Fruit-Trees . . . The Third Impression, Revised, with Additions* (Oxford: 1665), sig. a4v–a5r.

would have been seen as suitable to both the estate owner and the poor man. There was clearly something pleasing to the better sort in this utilitarian image.

Writers must have seen that the small size and neat format, ostensibly to serve the "mean husbandman," could appeal to the country gentlemen as well. As field companions designed for work, these books would have provided their owners a self-image as sensible men. As the next chapter will suggest, the culture of fruit and flowers was unique in inviting the gentleman to labor in the garden, and the "vademecum" surely helped to foster that culture. The companion book was a tool in the hand of both gentleman and countryman, part of the apparatus of the craft. And like expensive tools that are bought and polished but never used, the book could provide one with the comforting illusion that one was a practical person, even if someone else did the work.

For all these garden books, from the first printed books of the sixteenth century on, were meant to be read, and it may have mattered less that their advice never became practice. Just as in today's books the full-color illustrations evoke cravings for a garden that one cannot ever hope to produce, so the early books, too, stimulated a fantasy of achieving control over nature. In these earlier days, the reader's pleasure did not come from lush images of fruits and flowers: instead, it was to be found in tools and designs, in browsing or in orderly display, when the deepest delight in gardening came from a sense of mastery conveyed by the book itself. It is no matter, in the end, if many of those who consulted these books may just have been "armchair" gardeners, or masters of others who actually toiled in the dirt. The illusion they project is of a book as a working tool, both an instrument of the gardener's technique and a reflection of his or her place in nature. Perhaps the best sign of a book's success would be its ability to persuade the reader that reading about gardening was close to the act of working in the garden, and that such experience was easier to come by. The claims of the books to shape garden practice thus stem less from the content of their advice and more from their capacity to create the aura of power.

❦ 3 ❦

Labor, Pleasure, and Art

Gardening books are indeed prescriptions for back-breaking work, no matter how much the armchair gardener would like to ignore it. However seemingly artless the garden might be, to make it come to life someone must bend, cut, and dig. Some books leave unsaid who actually does this work. In the modern *America's Garden Book*, for example, James and Louise Bush-Brown instruct the reader:

> In preparing soil for the planting of large deciduous trees, the top-soil should be removed, sub-soil excavated to a depth of 18 inches or 2 feet below the final grade, and the hole filled with additional top-soil. . . . The planting bed should be round and 3 feet wider than the diameter of the ball of earth that will come with the roots. . . . But if a tree must be planted at a certain position where rock is near the surface, the rock will have to be removed. Blasting a hole in the rock, removing the pieces, and filling the place with soil is the best method.[1]

The unsentimental prose fails to specify who does this crushing labor of digging, blasting, and filling; we find passive constructions and gerunds, but no explicit mention of You, the reader and gardener, who must delve and sweat.

The Bush-Browns' unending descriptions of heaving and raking, pounding and slashing, are hardly forecast by the manual's first lines,

[1] James Bush-Brown and Louise Bush-Brown, *America's Garden Book* (New York: Charles Scribner's Sons, 1965), pp. 209–10.

which paint a far more refined image of the gardener's work: "Gardening," they tell us, "is an art, science and a craft. In order to obtain the most rewarding satisfactions from this many-jeweled occupation the gardener should possess something of the creative, buoyant spirit of the artist, the eager, inquiring mind of the scientist, and the skillful hands and diligent zeal of the craftsman." Only in their reference to the garden itself as "a loving taskmaster, demanding of the gardener the careful planning of seasonal work and daily diligence" do we see what is to come, the garden's tyranny over its faithful servant.[2]

Why would any respectable middle-class person want to spend a weekend digging in the dirt? An answer would come quickly to the lips of most suburban gardeners, for whom gardening is a passion and not a chore: because it is deeply pleasurable—and a pleasure that is hard to describe. You might not get this answer if you asked a day worker for a landscape contractor, who spends his days mowing other people's lawns or pulling out their weeds: digging in other people's gardens hardly provides the same satisfaction, either because it is not done by choice or because one does not own the fruit of one's labor. Garden work and pleasure have thus never been absolute in value: their meaning has always been tied to who you are and why you garden.

Much ink has been spilled in recent cultural criticism on the representation of upper- and lower-class garden labor in early modern English culture and especially in literary texts. Most of the scholarship builds on Raymond Williams's influential book, *The Country and the City*, which analyzed the "extraction of just this curse [of labor], by the power of art" in rural literature. This feat, Williams argued, was "achieved by a simple extraction of the existence of laborers."[3] Following Williams, in *The Politics of Landscape: Rural Scenery and Society in English Poetry 1630–1660*, James Turner described how, in seven-

---

[2] Ibid., p. 1; see further, on the wages this "rewarding master" pays the servant as "through the years it creates in the heart of the gardener an awareness of beauty which becomes a deeply enriching experience in his life; it imparts to him a reverence for Nature and her immutable laws; it teaches patience and humility" (p. 1). Cf. *The English Husbandman*, where Gervase Markham identified as the "perfect gard'ner's" three virtues "Diligence, Industry and Art," where "Industry" is understood as "labour, pain, and study" and "Art" as the gardener's "skill, habit and understanding in what he professeth" (London, 1613; rpt., New York: Garland, 1982), second part, p. 105.

[3] Raymond Williams, *The Country and the City* (London: Chatto and Windus, 1973), p. 32.

teenth-century painting and literature, agricultural labor was displaced either to nature itself, where "Nature, instead of man, 'labours hard,'" or credited to the landlord's beneficent presence, an ideology that (in Marx's words in the *1844 Manuscripts*) "'turns the fertility of the land into an attribute of the landlord.'"[4] In *The Georgic Revolution*, however, Anthony Low offered an opposite view, by putting poetry in the context of seventeenth-century husbandry discourse. Low focused instead on the fortunes of the georgic, the literary genre that redeems labor for the gentry (as opposed to the pastoral, which displays a rural world at leisure).[5] In contrast to Turner and Williams, Low argued that many seventeenth-century writers valued the gentleman who worked for himself and for the benefit of England.

Seeing work as a virtue for all classes of men was hardly a new idea in the seventeenth century. Influenced by reformist theology, a tract published in 1532 entitled *Here Begynneth a newe tracte or treatyse moost profytable for all husbande men: and very frutefull for all other persons to rede* cited with uncompromising severity "the apostles'" words that "he that laboureth nat shuld nat ete. . . . The which is an harde text after the literall sence. For by that letter the kynge, the queen, nor all other lordes spirituall and temporall should nat ete without they should labour."[6] As Andrew McRae notes, even in the sixteenth century, the early "country house" husbandry manuals defined for the gentleman farmer at least a "vicarious involvement in labour [which] permits an equation of the landlord with Virgil's 'happy husbandman.'"[7] Such in-

---

[4] James Turner, *The Politics of Landscape: Rural Scenery and Society in English Poetry, 1630–1660* (Cambridge: Harvard University Press, 1979), chap. 6, "The Vanishing Swain: Literary Depictions of Rural Labor," pp. 161–62 (citing Marx, *1844 Manuscripts*). See also p. 165, on the ways in which "almost everything which anybody *does* in the countryside is taboo."

[5] Anthony Low, *The Georgic Revolution* (Princeton: Princeton University Press, 1985). On pastoral, see Louis Adrian Montrose, "'Of Gentlemen and Shepherds': The Politics of Elizabethan Pastoral Form," *ELH* 50 (1983): 415–59; and Andrew McRae, *God Speed the Plough: The Representation of Agrarian England, 1500–1660* (Cambridge: Cambridge University Press, 1996): "In accordance with the imperatives of *otium*, the typical landscape of Elizabethan pastoral was an arena of recreation and rejuvenation. Considerations of labour, complaint, and rural business, by comparison were left to the contemporary preacher, satirist, and agrarian improver" (p. 269).

[6] [John] Fitzherbert, *Here Begynneth a newe tracte or treatyse moost profytable for all husbande men: and very frutefull for all other persons to rede* (London, 1532). See McRae, *God Speed*, p. 269: "It thus becomes apparent that throughout the Tudor years a tradition of religious, social, and political discourse consistently upheld the value of labour . . . albeit that labor which accorded with orthodox notions of degree."

[7] McRae, *God Speed*, p. 206.

junctions to work did multiply in seventeenth-century husbandry manuals and rural literature that invoked "the classical ethos of 'profit and pleasure'" as well as a Protestant work ethic.[8] Of course, most of this work was indeed either "vicarious" or more along the lines of supervising the workers and surveying the land. As Steven Shapin has noted, in the end "the gentleman was a master for whom others labored. He could be recognized by his idleness, and the practical equation between leisure and gentility was acknowledged even by commentators who argued in favor of vocation and virtue."[9]

The difference between Turner's and Low's arguments about agricultural labor in fact collapses in the case of the horticultural manuals that set a delicate balance between labor and pleasure in cultivating fruits and flowers. The previous chapter explored how reading about flower and fruit gardening might itself delight as well as instruct, whether in browsing, dreaming of mastery, or contemplating the elegance of nature's order. Profit and pleasure, use and entertainment, were thus intimately connected in reading. This chapter considers how these books justified the pleasures of garden work itself for very different sorts of gardeners, and in particular, for the gentleman gardener of the later seventeenth century.

Today the typical upper-class flower gardener, who would never think of cleaning a toilet, cheerfully hefts shovels full of manure in the flower garden. Even in the case of gardeners long ago, we cannot too easily divide flower and fruit gardening roles between a gentleman who may have designed and enjoyed the garden and the laborers who executed and maintained it. Gentlemen and women would indeed cultivate flowers and fruit themselves rather than just leaving it to hired help, if only because it was relatively easy work. In 1653, Ralph Austen encouraged men to do their own orchard work, noting that "men will labour hard, and a long time in some labours full of hazard and danger, and perhaps unjust too, and all for a little profit: but here, in this employment, men may with a little labour, in a short time, without hazard or danger, and that justly, obtaine great, and many profits, and those with Pleasures superadded."[10] William Lawson imagined his

    [8] Ibid., p. 283.
    [9] Steven Shapin, *A Social History of Truth: Civility and Science in Seventeenth-Century England* (Chicago: University of Chicago Press, 1994), p. 51.
    [10] R. A. Austen, *A Treatise of Fruit-Trees* (Oxford, 1653; rpt., New York: Garland, 1982), preface to the reader.

gardener viewing the fruits of his own orchard labor and pausing to view its end: "unspeakeable pleasure, and infinite commoditie." Indeed, for Lawson, it was labor itself that brought pleasure *after* the tedious business of one's "lawfull calling":

> For it is not to be doubted: but as God hath given man things profitable, so hath he allowed him honest comfort, delight, and recreation in all the works of his hands. Nay, all his labours under the Sunne without this are troubles, and vexation of minde: For what is greedy gaine, without delight? but moyling, and turmoyling in slavery? . . . And who can deny, but the principall end of an Orchard is the honest delight of one wearied with the works of his lawfull calling? The very works of, and in an Orchard and Garden, are better than the ease and rest of and [*sic*] from other laboures.[11]

The argument for pleasure here goes beyond simply savoring apples or contemplating cherry blossoms to suggest that the work itself pleases, and partly because it is indeed "unnecessary" labor, done not serving one's "lawfull calling."

This chapter follows the shifts in those values according to which these pleasures of the flower garden and fruit orchard were managed and the work made suitable for different ranks of men over the course of two centuries. For gentlemen, in particular, pleasure became tied to work of different kinds and thus understood as virtuous. In some cases, the pleasure was compared with the delights of the imagination; in others, it was construed as physical refreshment from "business" or as the play of experimentation with nature. As Lawson saw acutely, however, it was delightful work and suited to gentlemen, precisely because it was not necessary.

Art and Craft

The value of garden labor cannot be separated from the question of who worked in the garden, which was rarely the product of a single pair of hands. In the sixteenth- and early seventeenth-century books,

---

[11] William Lawson, *A New Orchard and Garden* (London, 1618; rpt., New York: Garland, 1982), pp. 54–56.

descriptions of gardening are often vague about who does what, and the ambiguity may surface syntactically in a shift of pronouns and verb moods: is the gardener "you" or "he" who works? Is the mood imperative, declaratory, or hortatory? In the following passage from William Lawson's *A New Orchard and Garden,* the picture of the gardener's unrelenting toil is brutally honest, yet from the first it is unclear exactly who *is* this gardener—an employee, or someone who could be a master-reader?

> The Gardiner had not need to be an idle, or lazie Lubber, for so your Orchard being a matter of such moment will not prosper. There will ever bee some thing to doe. Weedes are always growing. . . . But at Michaelltide is the best gardening, when or some what before your Bees would bee taken, & fruict gathered, with your Saffron, and at Martin-tide, is the best planting, or transplanting. About the beginning of November, set your bees in their Winter seates, and see they stand warm, drie, cleane, close, and sweete. . . . In Winter your young trees and hearbs would be lightened of snow, and your Allyes clensed. . . . After December, gather your grafts, prune your trees: Graft in the latter end of February, or beginning of March, as the spring growes in forwardnesse.

Up to this point the prose moves back and forth between the imperative and the passive moods: the reader is directed to "set your bees," "gather your grafts," and "prune your trees," but elsewhere he merely accepts its gifts, as "your bees would bee taken" and your fruit "gathered."

As the passage proceeds, however, the syntax moves into the third person, with the reemergence of "your gardiner":

> When Summer cloathes your borders with green and peckled colours, Your Gardiner must dresse his hedges, and antike Workes. Watch his Bees, and hive them: distill his Roses, and other hearbes. After Midsommer, every third yeare remove your Saffron, and now begins Sommer Fruict, to ripe and crave your hand, to pull them. If he have a garden (as hee must need) to keepe, you must needs allow him good helpe, to ende his labours which are endlesse. . . . Such a Gardner as will conscionably, quietly and patiently travell in your Orchard, God shall crowne the labors of his hands with joyfulnesse, and make the cloudes droppe fatnesse upon your Trees, hee will provoke your love, and earne his Wages,

and fees belonging to his place: The house being served, fallen fruict, superfluity of hearbes, and floures, seedes, grasses, sets, and besides other
offal, that fruict which your bountifull hand shall award him withall:
will much augment his Wages, and the profite of your bees will pay you
backe againe. If you bee not able, nor willing to hyre a Gardener, keepe
your profites to your selfe, but then you must take all the paines.

When the text mentions "your gardener," it appears that all the work
may be meant to be done by the surrogate gardener-employee. This
gardener curiously enough dresses "his hedges" rather than "your
hedges" and watches "his" bees, which just a few sentences earlier
were "your" bees. The next part clearly distinguishes between you the
reader and your gardener-employee, in the discussion of wages, but
then the final section pulls back, as if to explain the earlier pronoun
confusion. It is careful to note that if you cannot afford to pay a gardener, then you will have to "take all the paines."[12] The impression the
passage gives at first is that of course you have someone to labor for
you, but it allows room for the master-reader to do the work himself,
whether by choice or by necessity.

If even in the sixteenth and early seventeenth centuries, gentlemen
and women might use their hands in the garden—to tie, cut, and bend
as well as pluck and gather—on what terms might they do so, and
when was such labor appropriate? In his *Boke named the Governour*,
Thomas Elyot recommended instructing his young "governor" in selected manual arts (gardening was not among them at the time). When
he considered painting, he was at pains to justify it as training for military functions (for example, in map-making). He also cautioned that,
even so, "I intende not, by these examples, to make of a prince or noble mannes sonne a commune painter or kerver, which shall present
him selfe openly stained or embrued with sondry colours, or poudered
over with the duste of stones that he cutteth or perfumed with tedious
savours of the metalies by him yoten."[13] If the governor was to do ar-
tisanal labor of this kind, he must never appear in public stained by
work.

What was true of painting at the time held for other kinds of artful

[12] Ibid., p. 2.
[13] Thomas Elyot, *The Boke named the Governour* (London, 1531), ed. H. H. S. Croft, 2
vols. (1883; rpt., New York: Burt Franklin, 1967), 1:48.

work—including literary labor. In his essay on the Elizabethan pastoral, in discussing Puttenham's *Arte of English Poesie*, Louis Montrose detects a similar dissembling of work in the art of writing. If a poet is a "maker" and an artificer, then he is also potentially a kind of laborer; but if so, then he must never be seen to take pains, in order to preserve the courtier's pose of leisure. In Montrose's words, "it is precisely the expenditure of labor for profit that Puttenham teaches the courtly poets to perfect—and to dissemble. . . . What the courtier must dissemble above all else is his investment of time and labor in learning and performance."[14] Whether in painting, poetry, or gardening, the gentleman could work, but he must not appear to be making an effort; neither, more critically, should he be seen as needing to work.

Puttenham's own sustained comparison between horticulture and poesy helps to clarify how gardening might be seen at this time as a kind of aesthetic labor, lesser than the work of poetry but better than a common craft like carpentry. As Mara Miller notes in *The Garden as an Art*, gardens have always enjoyed "an ambiguous status in a number of different respects—between poles of 'art' and/or the 'artificial' on the one hand and 'Nature' on the other, between art and craft, and between fine and applied art."[15] In the section in Puttenham's *The Arte of English Poesie* entitled "that the good poet or maker ought to dissemble his arte, and in what cases the artificiall is more to be commended than the naturall, and contrariwise," the argument uses gardening to explain the interactions of art and nature. In some cases, Puttenham wrote, "we say arte is an ayde and coadiutor to nature . . . as the good gardiner seasons his soyle by sundrie sorts of compost . . . and waters his plants, and weedes his herbes or floures, and prunes his branches, and unleaves his boughes to let in the sunne, and twentie other waies cherisheth them and cureth their infirmities, and so makes that never or seldome any of them miscarry but bring foorth their flours and fruites in season." The same is true of the poet who improves "natural" language.

However, in turning again to horticulture, Puttenham argued further that art—horticultural and poetical—may also "surmount" and "alter nature's skill, so as by meanes of it her owne effects shall appeare

[14] Montrose, "Of Gentlemen and Shepherds," pp. 445–46.
[15] Mara Miller, *The Garden as an Art* (Albany: State University of New York Press, 1993), p. 72.

more beautifull or straunge and miraculous." So the "Gardiner by his arte . . . will embellish the same in virtue, shape, odour, and taste, that nature of her selfe woulde never have done, as to make the single gillifloure, or marigold, or daisie, double, and the white rose redde, yellow, or carnation, a bitter mellon sweete; a sweete apple soure; a plumme or cherrie without a stone; a peare without core or kernell, a goord or coucumber like to a horne or any other figure he will: any of which things nature could not doe without mans helpe and arte." The gardener resembles the poet in producing what is "strange" and "miraculous," just as the poet may create words and things that never existed in nature. Gardening not only produces greater fruit; it is an art capable of fashioning what is singular and unnatural or alien ("strange"), fruits and flowers existing before only in the gardener's imagination.

Yet, while Puttenham's gardener is thus an artist, he is inferior to the greatest poets, whose art comes from imagination alone and is thus paradoxically more "natural." The poet, like "nature her selfe working by her owne peculiar vertue and proper instinct and not by example or meditation or exercise as all other artificers do, is then most admired when he is most natural and least artificial."[16] If we read Puttenham against the grain, to find what he tells us about gardening (as opposed to poetry), we see that gardening joins poetry as "art" and carpentry as a "craft" but falls a little behind poetry because the gardener must labor, in the end, and use the stuff of nature. Poetry is best when its effects issue directly from instinct or inspiration (one must forget, for a moment, that this is a poetics how-to manual), and when it is less tied to the limits of the material world.[17] Thus, while both poetry and gardening produce "art objects," the poet's product is superior when it is produced more freely and thus with less labor.[18]

[16] George Puttenham, *The Arte of English Poesie* (London, 1589), ed. Gladys Doidge Willcock and Alice Walker (Cambridge: Cambridge University Press, 1936), pp. 303–7.

[17] See Miller, *Garden as an Art*, p. 84, on the issue of skill: "Where art tries to conceal the hand of the artist and the effort required, craft revels in their revelation. If we take this lack of interest in the evidence of skill as our guide, then gardens are an art, not a craft. At least by the time of the 'great' gardens tradition, it had become customary to conceal evidence of toil and skill." But she does note that the sixteenth-century garden books "delineate a new fascination with skills and knowledge."

[18] For an overview of the notion of "three natures," in connection with gardening, see John Dixon Hunt, *Greater Perfections: The Practice of Garden Theory* (Philadelphia: University of Pennsylvania Press, 2000), pp. 32–75.

Puttenham's careful distinction thus lets us see what might have been at stake, in the late sixteenth century, in allowing gentlemen to work in their own gardens. For ordinary gardeners, of course, the end was producing the material stuff, for oneself or for the market. But gentlemen should not be compelled by necessity (though Lawson bluntly confronted that possibility). Some gardeners (and Puttenham implied they are the lower sort) might merely aid nature's ways, cherishing and protecting the blooms and cultivating the fruit. But the greater art of gardening and the work of gentlemen lay in fashioning something closer to the poet's free works of the imagination. These works were imagined as paradoxically most spontaneous and most artificial, creating not what is needed, but only what is desired.

Managing Garden Pleasure

These social aesthetics of gardening, thus suspended between art and craft, also mixed "profit and delight," terms most familiar to us from the language of Renaissance poetics yet also omnipresent in garden manuals. In *The Profitable Arte of Gardening*, Thomas Hill mentions as the two great "commodities" of a garden "profit, which ryseth through the increase of herbes and flowers: the other is pleasure, very delectable through the delight of walking in the same . . . by the commodities of taking the freshe ayer and sweete smell of flowers in the same."[19] Hill's text mixes pleasure and profit, even when it separates them syntactically, by speaking of the "commodities" of sensual pleasure (where "commodity" would appear to carry both its obsolete sense of occasion and the better-known one of profit or utility).[20]

This happy balance, however, was not always so easy to strike. In his deadly serious book *Certaine experiments concerning fish and fruit*, John Taverner expressed his distrust of garden pleasure unless it was closely linked to profit: so, in speaking of ponds, he was at pains to distinguish their English uses from the abuses of the Romans, who "imployed incredible wealth in making of ponds, in which with sea water, they kept diverse kind of sea fish, for delicacie and wantonnesse,

[19] Thomas Hill, *The Profitable Arte of Gardening* (London, 1568), fol. 1 (verso).
[20] On the "pleasure and profit" balance in husbandry literature and poetry, see McRae, *God Speed*, chap. 9.

rather then profit."[21] For the good Protestant Taverner, the "honest recreation" of a nice English garden pond differed from the "wanton" pleasure of the Roman kind, precisely because the English one avoided gratuitous superfluity, vanity, and delicacy and served the common wealth. Such anxiety about pleasure intensified when it came to the question of flowers propagated for their beauty or rarity as opposed to uses in cosmetics, cookery, or medicine.

Flower and fruit gardening has always brought a special kind of gratification. Georgic poetry may celebrate the rural life free from the pressures of court and city, the freshness of the air and water, and the views of "every Mountaine, Forrest, River and Valley: . . . their loves, delights and naturall situations."[22] But cultivating flowers and fruit is acutely sensual and direct; we experience flowers and fruit individually, and we touch, taste, and smell as well as see them. In his *Florist's Vade-Mecum,* Samuel Gilbert defended the raising of flowers as a more healthful "divertissement" for our bodies than those kinds of pleasures than gentlemen characteristically seek, "being attended with much more (nay all) innocency, fewer (nay no) evil circumstances, than either that one which is too much lavished away in Hunting, Hawking, Bowling, Drinking, Drabbing, Dicing, &c, wherein is much pain taken, if not more, without refunding pleasure."[23] Growing flowers produces more economical pleasure than typical gentlemanly pursuits, but Gilbert knew that life among flowers was still recreation for the senses, and garden writers were all too aware of how one could overindulge in such delights.[24]

When we witness Adam and Eve's gardening in *Paradise Lost,* we can see how Milton's representation of their flower and fruit gardening—which is not quite work—managed sensual pleasure and moral risk.

---

[21] John Taverner, *Certaine experiments concerning fish and fruite, practiced by John Taverner gentleman, and by him published for the benefit of others* (London, 1600), p. 1.

[22] Michael Drayton, *Poly-Olbion,* in *The Works of Michael Drayton: Tercentenary Edition,* vol. 4, ed. J. William Hebel (Oxford: Basil Blackwell, 1961), p. vi.

[23] Samuel Gilbert, *The Florist's Vade-Mecum* (London, 1683), epistle to the reader.

[24] See Marcia Vale, *The Gentleman's Recreations: Accomplishments and Pastimes of the English Gentleman, 1580–1630* (Cambridge: D. S. Brewer; Totowa, N.J.: Rowman and Littlefield, 1977), on the characterization of pleasures for an earlier generation of gentlemen, falling into categories of exercise (horsemanship, hunting, coursing, hawking, fowling, fishing, archery, fencing and dueling, tennis, bowling, football, swimming), aesthetic practices (music, dancing, and visual arts), and then more morally vexed areas of travel, going to the theater, gaming, and love.

At first, their gardening pursuits look like genteel recreation, when after

> no more toil
> Of thir sweet Gard'ning labor than suffic'd
> To recommend cool Zephyr and made ease
> More easy, wholesome thirst and appetite
> More grateful, to their Supper fruits they fell . . .
>   (book 4, ll. 325–31)[25]

Here they imitate the country gentry whose innocent garden exercise promotes good health and enjoyment of life. Elsewhere in book 4, however, the language of "reformation" is applied to their gardening, lending it a Protestant moral odor.[26] When Adam advises Eve that it is time to retire to bed, he reminds her that tomorrow

> we must be risen
> And at our pleasant labor, to reform
> Yon flowery Arbours, yonder Alleys green
> Our walk at noon, with branches overgrown,
> That mock our scant manuring, and require
> More hands than ours to lop their wanton growth.
>   (book 4, ll. 624–29)[27]

These lines fashion a proleptic association of Edenic gardening with "reformation," that is, an image of garden labor that can redeem a fallen

---

[25] All citations from *Paradise Lost* are from John Milton, *Complete Poems and Major Prose*, ed. Merritt Y. Hughes (Indianapolis: Bobbs-Merrill, 1957).

[26] William Lawson saw pruning as equivalent to spiritual reformation: "Such is the condition of all earthly things, whereby a man receaveth profit or pleasure, that they degenerate presently without good ordering. Man himselfe left to himselfe, growes from his heavenly and spirituall generation, and becommeth beastly, yea develish to his owne kinde, unlesse he be regenerate. No marvaile then, if trees make their shootes, and put their sprayes disorderly. And truely (if I were worthy to judge) there is not a mischiefe that breedeth greater and more generall harme to all the Orchard, (especially if they be of any continuance) that ever I saw . . . than the want of the skilfull dressing of trees" (*New Orchard*, pp. 32–33).

[27] In book 5, we hear about the purpose of their garden work, which is to prevent both excess and unfruitful growing "where any row / Of Fruit-trees overwoody reach'd too far / Their pamper'd boughs, and needed hands to check / Fruitless imbraces" (ll. 212–15).

world that would otherwise revert to chaos.[28] Gardening is necessary to control the "wantonness" of Eden and its rampant sensuality.

Eve more urgently requires that they try harder to control their garden, wishing for helpers (children, that is) and insisting that she and Adam work apart, because their pleasure in each other's company keeps them from stemming the "luxury" of the garden:

> Adam, well may we labour still to dress
> This Garden, still to tend Plant, Herb and Flow'r,
> Our pleasant task enjoined, but till more hands
> Aid us, the work under our labour grows,
> Luxurious by restraint; what we by day
> Lop overgrown, or prune, or prop, or bind,
> One night or two with wanton growth derides
> Tending to wild.
>
> (book 9, ll. 205–12)

Adam and Eve's mutual sexual pleasure, which interrupts their work, is shadowed in the image of the garden's luxurious plant life that "with wanton growth derides / Tending to wild." Eve shrewdly recognizes that the more she cuts, the more it grows, but she wants to contain it.[29] Naïve Adam, however, persists with his gentlemanly insistence that, while he admires Eve's desire to work,

> not so strictly hath our Lord impos'd
> Labour, as to debar us when we need
> Refreshment . . .
> For not to irksome toil, but to delight
> He made us, and delight to Reason join'd.
>
> (book 9, ll. 235–44)

[28] On the notions of work and labor in Eden in *Paradise Lost*, see Maureen Quilligan, "Freedom, Service, and the Trade in Slaves: The Problem of Labor in *Paradise Lost*," in *Subject and Object in Renaissance Culture*, ed. Margreta De Grazia, Maureen Quilligan, and Peter Stallybrass (Cambridge: Cambridge University Press, 1996), pp. 213–34. Quilligan analyzes this scene in the context of the growing use of slave labor in the New World, as well as domestic ideology. On this passage from *Paradise Lost*, also see Low, *Georgic Revolution*, pp. 316–17.

[29] In this language the passage also echoes the Puritan "reformist" spirit of the new agriculture associated with the Hartlib circle: see Charles Webster, *The Great Instauration: Science, Medicine, and Reform, 1626–1660* (New York: Holmes and Meier, 1976), pp. 465–83.

For Adam, the pleasures of gardening take precedence over the need to work, or concern for any kind of "profit," but Eve sees danger in the garden's wild delights.

For real gardeners, one way of expressing and resolving this tension between profit and delight was in garden design. In the sixteenth and early seventeenth centuries, the ideal for the common gardener was the garden that served both ends. In *The English Husbandman*, Markham insisted that only the English knew how to blend beauty and productivity in the orchard: he chastised the Italians, the French, and the Dutch "who doe make a diversitie and distinguishment of Orchardes, as namely, one for profit, which they fashion rudely and without forme, the other for delight, which they make comely, decent, and with all good proportion." But for the English, for the ends of both "commoditie" and "comlinesse" Markham proposed to "joyne them both together, and make them onely but one Orchard."[30] Similarly, William Lawson thought his country housewife might want to "sever" the flower and kitchen gardens but only on practical grounds, for example, to avoid onions' ill effects on flowers or the gaps created by harvesting. He allowed that he did not "mean so perfect a distinction that the Garden for flowres should or can be without hearbs good for the kitchen, or the kitchen Garden should want flowres."[31] However, by the end of the seventeenth century the flower and kitchen gardens were in fact rigidly separated in the grounds of the gentry.[32] In his *Paradisi in Sole*, John Parkinson banished the unsightly and smelly kitchen garden to the back of the house: "For the many different scents that arise from the herbes, such as Cabbage, Onions, &c., are scarce well pleasing to perfume the lodgings of any house; and the many overtures and breaches as it were of many of the beds thereof, which most necessarily bee, are also as little pleasant to the sight."[33] He did want to ensure that you could see the flower garden from the "fairest" rooms

---

[30] Markham, *English Husbandman*, book 1, second part, p. 33.

[31] William Lawson, *The Countrie Housewifes Garden* (London, 1617), p. 10.

[32] See Andrew McRae, "Husbandry Manuals and the Language of Agrarian Improvement," in *Culture and Cultivation in Early Modern England: Writing and the Land*, ed. Michael Leslie and Timothy Raylor (Leicester: Leicester University Press, 1992), pp. 48–89.

[33] John Parkinson, *Paradisi in Sole: Paradisus Terristris* (London, 1629; rpt., New York: Dover, 1991), p. 461. See Ellen C. Eyler, *Early English Gardens and Garden Books* (published for the Folger Shakespeare Library; Charlottesville: University Press of Virginia, 1963), pp. 19–20.

of the house.[34] The pleasure garden's beauty lay in its formal design, which could not be maintained in the useful herb or vegetable garden, which is constantly subject to harvesting.[35] Literal use or profit there was incompatible with aesthetic form.

In the sixteenth century pleasure and profit might be more evenly allocated across the ranks of men. For Leonard Mascall in 1572, in gardening "the poor man may with pleasure finde, / Some thing to help his meede," the rich man would find fruit, and "the noble man that needeth naught" might find such "pleasant fruit to serve his use, / And give eche man his fill." Thus pleasure and use were spread across social ranks.[36] Thomas Hill imagined the common gardener's "diligently view[ing] the prosperity of his hearbes and flowers ... for the delight and comfort of his wearied mind, which he may by himselfe, or fellowship of his friends conceive, in the delectable sights, and fragrant smelles of the flowers, by walking up and downe, and about the garden in them": the "commodity" of the garden is the herbs and flowers but also the pleasure of experiencing them after the day's work.[37] But by 1606 Hugh Platt believed more strictly that his garden advice would profit the lower ranks, "who by their manuall works, may gain a greater imployment, then heeretofore in their usual callings"; and it would bring pleasure to others, "who delight to see a raritie spring out of their own labours, and to provoke Nature to play."[38] Manual workers required profit and employment, but others needed only work to play. In his *Adam in Eden* (1657) William Coles emphatically declared that the vulgar "profit" motive for reading his book and cultivating flowers and herbs should be secondary, whereas it is pleasure and "melting inducements" that entice gentlemen to the garden:

[34] Parkinson, *Paradisi in Sole*, p. 1.

[35] "As our former Garden of pleasure is wholly formable in every part with squares, trayles, and knots, and to bee still maintained in their due form and beautie: so on the contrary side this Garden cannot long conserve any forme, for that every part thereof is subject to mutation and alteration" (ibid., p. 462).

[36] Leonard Mascall, *A Booke of the Arte and maner, howe to plant and graffe all sortes of trees* (London, 1572), "The book unto the Reader."

[37] Dydymus Mountain [Thomas Hill], *The Gardeners Labyrinth* (London, 1594; rpt., New York: Garland, 1982), p. 24. See also pp. 3–4: "The person which shall enjoy or have in a readiness these three, and will purposedly or with diligence frame to him a well dressed garden, shal after obtain these ii commodities, as utilitie and delight: the utilitie, yeeldeth the plentie of herbs, floures, and fruits right dilectable: but the pleasure of the same procureth a delight, and (as Varro writeth) a iucunditie of minde."

[38] Hugh Platt, *Floraes Paradise, beautified with sundry sorts of delicate fruits and flowers* (London, 1608), sig. a3v.

If pleasures may invite him, what fairer objects are there for the sight then these painted Braveries? what Odours can ravish the sense of smelling more than those of flowers? If the sensuality of the Taste hath delighted him, what can be more acceptable than the luxurious deliciousnesse of Fruit. . . . If none of these melting inducements carry force enough with them, the Reader must give me leave to descend to the great argument of the World, Profit, which above the general good, hath been a Bait, that hath caught the vulgar.[39]

Turning away from the insistence on profit (what Gervase Markham called "the whole aime of our lives in this world"),[40] Coles implied that the higher motivation—or at least the more persuasive one—for gardening is the pursuit of "sensuality" and "luxury."

Coles's emphasis on the pleasures of gardening, as opposed to vulgar profit, returns us to the distinction that Puttenham created in describing the higher art of gardening, which produces what is "beautifull or straunge and miraculous," as opposed to that sort of gardening that helps plants prosper, that "cherisheth them and cureth their infirmities, and so makes that never or seldome any of them miscarry but bring foorth their flours and fruites in season." Even though seventeenth-century husbandry books stalwartly continued to preach that profit and pleasure awaited the gardener, whether country gentleman or farmer, those books that dwelled on fruits and flowers for cultivation by gentlemen and ladies were less shy about encouraging their gentle reader to pursue delight in the garden without concern for gain.

Knowledge, Imagination, and Play

Pleasure, however, had to be managed, even for gentlemen. In his 1597 *Herbal*, John Gerard had also spoken rapturously of the sensual appeal of flowers. But he mixed this with the appeal of "knowing" them. In his dedication to William Cecil, he considered how we value plants for knowledge or delight, since of all God's creatures "that have all in all ages diversely entertained many excellent wits, and drawn them to the contemplation of the divine wisdome, none have provoked mens stud-

---

39 William Coles, *Adam in Eden* (London, 1657), epistle to the reader.
40 Markham, *English Husbandman*, "former part," sig. a3v.

ies more, or satisfied their desire so much, as plants have done." The delights of sight and smell may come first, since they are the inducement to work, whether in the study or the field:

> For if delight may provoke mens labor, what greater delight is there than to behold the earth apparelled with plants, as with a robe of embroidered worke, set with orient pearles, and garnished with great diversitie of rare and costly jewels? If this varietie and perfection of colours may affect the eye, it is such in herbs and flowers, that no Apelles, no Zeuxis, ever could by any art expresse the like: if odours, or if taste may worke satisfaction, they are so soveraigne in plants, and so comfortable, that no confection of the Apothecaries can equall their excellent vertue.

However, having set up the primacy of these sensual "delights" comparable to luxury items such as jewels, costly fabrics, and sweet confections, the passage then proceeds to undercut such pleasure as secondary when compared with intellectual pleasure, for "these delights are in the outward sences: the principall delight is in the minde, singularly enriched with the knowledge of these visible things, setting foorth to us the invisible wisdome and admirable workmanship of almighty God. The delight is great, but the use greater, and joyned often with necessity." Gerard's rhetoric thus nervously backs off from sensual allurement to put forward the "delight" of the mind, which consists in knowing these visible things that lead the beholder to God. Then, in an odd turn at the end, this pleasure gives way to the familiar appeal to use and necessity.

This fine oscillation in Gerard's prefatory rhetoric between delight, knowledge, and use signals the author's concern for his immediate audience, William Cecil, whose extraordinary garden at Theobolds Gerard superintended. While the preface returns to the theme of use and necessity in observing how much men work to ornament and supply their households, when addressing Cecil the text quickly turns, once again, "beside the fruit, to speake again in a word of delight: gardens, especially sich as your Honor hath, furnished with many rare simples, do singularly delight, when in them a man doth behold a flourishing shew of summer beauties in the middest of winter's force, and a goodly spring of flowers, where abroad a leafe is not to be seene."[41]

---

[41] John Gerard, *The Herball or Generall Historie of Plants* (London, 1597), dedication to Cecil.

them, "before the over-bearing Power of Sensual Delights hath taken place."[50]

Laurence did see gardening as part of a program of moral and educational reform, but he appreciated it most as an "exercise" of retreat or retirement from the worlds of politics and business where all "conversation" endangers a man of "honor and probity."[51] Instead, the civil conversation of a garden offers solitary "Entertainment": "There a Man may converse with his God, by contemplating his works of wonder in each flower and in every plant. . . . There a man may converse with himselfe and consider, that whilst he is uncorrupted by vain Conversation, whilst he is busie and innocent, his Garden is his paradise."[52] Laurence's image of solitary "conversation" in the garden finds its most exquisite expression in Andrew Marvell's poem "The Garden," from half a century earlier, where the speaker praises the "Innocence" and "Quiet" he has found in the "delicious solitude" of a garden. In conjunction with this isolation from the "busy companies of men" and the cruelties of sexual love, the garden experience can be at once sensual and spiritual: the poet mouths "the luscious clusters of the vine" and accepts the garden's gift of ripe apples, melons, nectarines, and the "curious peach," until he falls on the grass "ensnared with flowers." Yet this is no mere orgy, for "meanwhile the mind, from

---

[50] Laurence, *The Gentleman's Recreation*, in *Gardening Improv'd*, preface, sig. a4v–a5r. The passage continues: "And therefore I question not, but we might soon see a more virtuous and enlightened Age, if it were but rescued from the intolerable Trammels of Logick and Rhetorick, the Aversion and Bane of Youth, and some of the easy Parts of Natural Philosophy, Practical Mathematicks, and Gardening Operations substituted in their Place: By which means, young persons may be discreetly tol'd by easy and familiar Methods, in all such innocent Exercises of the Mind and Entertainments of Life, as may probably lay a Foundation for contemplative Genius, and produce a virtuous and useful old Age."

[51] Laurence, *The Gentleman's Recreation*, sig. a7r–v. On "retirement," which was understood at this time in its meaning of being withdrawn or secluded, see also George London and Henry Wise's *The Retir'd Gard'ner* (2 vols.), the first "being a translation of *Le Jardinier Solitaire*, or Dialogues between a Gentleman and a Gard'ner" (London, 1706). See Milton's "Il Penseroso," l. 49, where the speaker bids that "pensive Nun" to "add to these retired Leisure, / That in trim Gardens takes his pleasure."

[52] Laurence, *The Gentleman's Recreation*, sig. a7r–v. But in this solitude, a man was not seen to be less than manly. Working in the garden, "Man is Lord of All," disposing at his will, and thus he can afford to abandon politics properly speaking. Gardening was not only the best model for government; it surpassed any other form of government, for "in short, whatever Government even the Fancy can paint to him to be either better or more beautiful, that form is presently submitted to. This is no imaginary Pleasure, neither, but real and personal."

pleasure less, / Withdraws into its happiness," releasing the soul from the "body's vest." In this "paradise of one," the poet's mind retires, while it fashions a new world:

> yet it creates, transcending these,
> Far other worlds, and other seas,
> Annihilating all that's made,
> To a green thought in a green shade.

The poem achieves the highest sublimation of the garden experience: this speaker need not lift a finger there, even to gather the fruit, because the apples "drop about his head," the grapes "crush their wine" on his mouth, and the nectarine and peach "into my hands themselves do reach," for his work lies purely in creating "green thoughts," the pattern of the garden of the mind.[53] In effect, it returns us to Puttenham's analogy between the poet and the gardener, who produce the fruits of the imagination.

The idea of gardening as physical and spiritual recreation, whereby body and mind are refreshed and freed to contemplate God and self, is linked with the other way of thinking about the gentleman gardener's work, what Hugh Platt had described as the "pleasuring" of men, "who delight to see a raritie spring out of their own labours, and to provoke Nature to play, and to shew some of her pleasing varieties, when she hath met with a stirring workman," that is, in experimenting with natural "curiosities." At the beginning of the century, Francis Bacon had redefined the quest for knowledge as a form of work.[54] This revision allowed men like Stephen Blake to proclaim in his own garden book in 1664, "let all degrees of men know, whether they be high or low, rich or poor, they ought to labour either in body or mind, that

[53] Text from *Andrew Marvell*, ed. Frank Kermode and Keith Walter (Oxford: Oxford University Press, 1990). Compare here Marvell's "Upon Appleton House," which criticizes how Lord Fairfax "retired" and "laid these gardens out in sport / In the just figure of a fort" (ll. 285–86).

[54] See Low, *Georgic Revolution*, pp. 139–41: "For Bacon, however, the fall was less a permanent curse than an opportunity: a chance for man, with God's help and approval, to take matters into his own hands, and by his labors to regain the control over nature that he lost in the garden of Eden." He notes how Francis Bacon in particular "emphasized hard practical work and experimentation, insisted that humanity (under God's benevolent eye) take its destiny into its own hands, stressed the material benefits and fruitfulness of all useful endeavors, [and] praised invention and discovery. . . ."

they may some way or other cooperate and contribute to the common good, or else they are unworthy of the blessings of this life."[55] Thanks to Bacon, thinking was working, and thus a gentleman's experimenting with nature could be moral as well.[56]

Many sixteenth- and early seventeenth-century garden books had argued that labor creates knowledge of nature as much as knowledge governs labor, when hand and mind join to make art. Thus Thomas Hill observed in *The Gardeners Labyrinth* that "yet not sufficient is it to a gardener, that he knoweth . . . without any cost bestowed, which the works & labours of the same require: nor the will again of the workman . . . shall smally availe, without he have both art & skill in the same."[57] Many of the gardening books published in the second half of the seventeenth century continue this theme and reflect the general spirit of the mid-century agricultural reform movement, which advocated moral and intellectual self-improvement, the furthering of human knowledge, and the service of "necessity." But when Stephen Blake revived the notion of our being born to work, he contrasted his own form of garden toil with the work of "carnal men" for whom "the god of this world hath so blinded their eyes that they cannot see the reasons of the working of the course of nature, nor how they labor for that which they do not enjoy." He would "prove why man should labour for wisdome and reason, which is to understand the working of the course of nature."[58] In the gardening books of the sixteenth and early seventeenth century, "knowledge" or "skill" was always essential to becoming a good gardener; to Blake, however, it was now more important that being a good gardener would lead to knowledge or "wisdome and reason." It was an end in itself, as the physical toil of gardening was subsumed into intellectual work.[59]

---

[55] Stephen Blake, *The Compleat Gardeners Practice, Directing the Exact Way of Gardening in Three Parts* (London, 1664), sig. a3.

[56] As Montrose notes, the new "labor" praised in the seventeenth century is not the "punitive post-lapsarian labor but . . . the unalienated labor of Edenic cultivation"; further, in the works of a writer like Milton, "the validation of agricultural labor goes hand in hand with a radical critique of aristocratic values and styles—a critique that is, of course, not proletarian in character but rather religious, intellectual and bourgeois," as opposed to the character of pastoral, which was "dominantly aristocratic in values and style" ("Of Gentlemen and Shepherds," p. 426).

[57] Dydymus Mountain [Thomas Hill], *The Gardeners Labyrinth*, p. 3.

[58] Blake, *Compleat Gardeners Practice*, sig. a3.

[59] On writing as work, see John Ozell's translation of Boileau's "Epistle to my Gardener," from *The Works of Monsieur Boileau*. In this epistle, the poet directly compares

This notion of genteel garden work that leads to knowledge is the legacy of Bacon's transformation of labor's value in the service of a new science. Here the gardener might also find his place between the worlds of art and science, in the curious work of experiment and invention.[60] Anthony Low and Andrew McRae, among other scholars, have described how a fundamentally Protestant and "idealistic conception of human labor underpinned the practical aims of the Baconian programme in its pursuit of scientific knowledge as a mean to national prosperity."[61] But the other side of this "program" of virtuous research was the notion of experimentation that did not necessarily result in profit, but, rather, in the pleasure of seeing nature betray her secrets. For all the language of serious "reformation" and public service that we see in the writing of men associated with the Royal Society, we frequently glimpse what Thomas Sprat called, in his *History of the Royal Society*, "the pleasure and enjoyments of present discoveries" for those not concerned with "petty profit."[62] As we saw in chapter 1, the distaste for "popular" uses or gain was a hallmark of their practice. Sprat insisted that his men of science were immune to the idle pleasures of the old natural philosophy and its marvels: "It [the old natural philosophy of marvels] is like Romances, in respect to True History which by multiplying varieties of extraordinary Events, and surprising circumstances, makes that seem dull and tasteless. And to say no more, the very delight which it raises, is nothing so solid: but as the satisfaction of Fancy, it affects us a little, in the beginning, but soon wearies, and surfeits." Yet he did not deny these men of science their own pleasure,

---

the gardener's and the poet's labor: he wonders what the gardener thinks of him, seeing him muse, while he (the gardener) is working. The poet imagines that his gardener might think that he (the gardener) has "more employment here than I / And that my labour's lighter here than thine; / But sure you wouldst not change thy work for mine. / Couldst thou a day or two, from gardening free / Try how my work would with thy head agree." After a description of his own mental labors he envisions his gardener declaring: "I'd rather in this garden spend my time / In digging, than be forced to pump for rhyme" (in *The Oxford Book of Garden Verse*, ed. John Dixon Hunt [Oxford: Oxford University Press, 1994], pp. 83–84).

[60] More specifically, Low, in turn, has examined the influence of new georgic ideology on the construing of writing as labor, in particular in Ben Jonson's writings, where he notes the exhortations to intellectual labor in Jonson's ode to Shakespeare and in a passage from *Timber* (*Georgic Revolution*, pp. 105–6).

[61] McRae, *God Speed*, p. 216.

[62] Thomas Sprat, *The History of the Royal Society of London, for the Improving of Natural Knowledge* (London, 1667), ed. Jackson L. Cope and Harold Whitmore Jones (St. Louis: Washington University Press, 1958), p. 110.

for "a just History of Nature, like the pleasure of Reason, would not be, perhaps, so quick and violent, but of far longer continuance, in its contentment."[63]

The culture of fruits and flowers thus resolved the tension about gentlemanly labor in a way quite different from either the moralization of labor that Low describes or the displacement or erasure of work seen by Williams and Turner in seventeenth-century literature. Raising fruits and flowers is in fact described not in terms of the morality of work but more in accordance with the virtues of retirement, recreation, and the pleasures of knowledge. Unlike the case posed by the sixteenth- and early seventeenth-century writers, who drew on the formula of "profit and delight" in justifying garden work, when addressing horticulture for gentlemen the later books suppressed the value of use in its justification. The very vanity of the work lent it its highest value insofar as the path to knowledge of God, self, or nature's secrets remained uncontaminated by the vulgarity of "petty profit." Thus one can not say work was seen as "useless" or unproductive—it was uncompelled. The gentleman was still the master of his own pleasure in the garden.

[63] Ibid., pp. 90–91.

❧4❧

The Ladies' Part

Andrew Marvell's fantasy of a garden as a "paradise of one," without male and especially female companionship, says much about the motives of masculine green desire. The man who luxuriates in that garden is the sole master there, imagining Eden as a place where women are not needed. The accounts of labor and pleasure that fill the pages of early English gardening books indeed beg the question: where were women in the early modern garden?

Women were certainly not publishing garden books at this time, though they may have scribbled ideas in the margins of books or recorded them in their diaries. Archival evidence is scanty, since in most cases women's work was unpaid labor.[1] Some garden images from the medieval and early modern periods include all sorts of women working there, with varying degrees of realism. A manuscript illustration accompanying a French translation of Pietro de Crescenzi's *Liber Ruralium Commodorum* depicts a patrician woman decorously tending a flower in the midst of an enclosed garden, while other fine gentlemen and women linger near by (figure 14). Dutch art of a later period depicts laboring women as well as men weeding, sowing, and watering, while their mistress looks on, directing their work (see figure 1). But only a few sixteenth- and seventeenth-century books were explicitly

---

[1] See Sara Mendelson and Patricia Crawford, *Women in Early Modern England: 1550–1720* (Oxford: Oxford University Press, 1998), pp. 257–59, on the "invisibility" of women's work in general in this period. For the eighteenth century, see Bridget Hill, *Women, Work, and Sexual Politics in Eighteenth-Century England* (Oxford: Basil Blackwell, 1989), chap. 9.

FIGURE 14. Patrician woman tending a flower, a manuscript illustration from *Le Livre Rustican des prouffiz ruralaux*, translation of Pietro de Crescenzi, *Liber Ruralium Commodorum*, Book VIII, MSS. additional 19.720. f. 214. Reproduced by permission of the British Library.

addressed to the woman gardener, and even these texts can be misleading. If how-to books often suggest how authors *wish* their readers would behave, rather than what they can or will do, their remarks about women should be distrusted. Such books tend to be particularly evasive when defining how and where women worked, being more concerned about what they ought to be than with what they actually were. At this time women of almost all ranks were surely to be found in the kitchen, stillroom, and the flower, fruit, and vegetable garden, although only the poor worked in the fields, but what were they doing, and how was it valued?[2]

Much of what we think we know about women gardeners in this period comes from a literary culture that painted women both as flower

[2] For a general overview of women's agricultural labor in early modern Europe, see Olwen Hufton, *The Prospect before Her: A History of Women in Western Europe*, vol. 1: *1500–1800* (New York: Knopf, 1996), pp. 155–64.

gatherers and "flowers" themselves. This chapter explores the complex relationship between the images of women in the garden manuals and the literary female gardener, a relationship far more vexed than the case of the image of male gardeners, literary or otherwise. In poems and prose, women were seen contemplating, maintaining, gathering, and bestowing flowers and fruit but not producing them, no matter how hard they may have been working at the time. In the late seventeenth century, this literary culture appears to have seeped into garden manuals where, while women were addressed as readers who enjoy flowers, the art of breeding and cultivating all plants became a masculine activity, whether done for leisure or professionally. As Andrew McRae has argued, when the new "georgic economics" of the seventeenth century characterized masculine labor as combining spiritual improvement, "delight," and material profit, it "efface[d] the labours of women, whether in the fields, in the household or in childbirth. If the curse was Adam's, so shall be the reward."[3] Gardening books from the seventeenth and early eighteenth centuries may have addressed and depicted the gentle female reader as the goddess Flora or her garden's titular deity, but it was the male reader who was seen to manage that garden, whether for use or pleasure. While women were certainly still working, they became almost invisible as designers, propagators, and cultivators.

The question of women's garden labor is inextricably tied to the general history of women's work in the early modern period, which has been debated since the appearance of Alice Clark's *Working Life of Women in the Seventeenth Century*, first published in 1919. Clark argued that a transition to capitalism in the late seventeenth and early eighteenth centuries transformed middle-class women from productive housewives who contributed to the household economy into idle bourgeois consumers. Clark's account has been criticized from many viewpoints, both for a misplaced nostalgia for a medieval working culture that included women and for her backdating of the effects of industrialization. She has also been taken to task because "to advance her thesis of the serial decline from healthy activity to idleness or exploitation (depending on class) she had recourse to prescriptive literature and assumed that the ideology was strong enough to produce

---

[3] Andrew McRae, *God Speed the Plough: The Representation of Agrarian England, 1500–1660* (Cambridge: Cambridge University Press, 1996), p. 217.

the reality."[4] This chapter cannot answer the question of what women really did in the garden or the field in this period, which is ultimately a task for the social historian, but it does assume that they were indeed working in many ways. What this chapter can do is track a shift in the ideology of gardening from the sixteenth- and early seventeenth-century manuals concerned with the housewife's practical work to the culture of the early eighteenth-century garden books, where women's garden practice was marginalized and, when it was displayed, was purely metaphorical. While this rhetoric may have not realistically depicted women's garden work, it does reveal how the idea of the feminine culture of fruit and flowers changed from the sixteenth to the early eighteenth century, just as it did in the world of masculine gardening.

Housewives in the Garden

William Lawson's *Countrie Housewifes Garden* (1617) was the first English printed book explicitly addressed to the female gardener. However, earlier books such as Thomas Tusser's *Five Hundreth Points of Good Husbandry* had already recognized women's role in horticulture. As Tusser's doggerel directs:

> In March, May, and Aprill, from morning to night,
> In sowing and setting, good huswives delight;
> To have in a garden, or other like plot:
> To trim up their house and furnish their pot.
> The nature of flowers dame physick doth sheaw
> She teacheth them all, to be knowne to a feawe.
> To set or to sow, or els sowne to remove:
> How that should be practiced, learn if ye love.[5]

---

[4] Hufton, *Prospect before Her*, p. 25. See also Alice Clark, *Working Life of Women in the Seventeenth Century* (first published 1919), ed. Amy Louise Erickson (London: Routledge, 1992). Erickson's introduction summarizes the critiques of Clark and the work on women's history that puts Clark in context: most important, the evidence to suggest the continuity of women's work and working conditions. Erickson also remarks on the difficulty of reconstructing the history of women's unpaid or domestic agricultural labor.

[5] Thomas Tusser, *Five hundreth points of good husbandry, united to as many of good huswiferie* (London, 1573), fol. 43.

In his lists of "what warkes a wife shulde do in a generalitie," Fitzherbert also listed gardening: so the text recommends that "in the beginnyng of March, or a lytell before: is tyme for a wyfe to make her garden; and to get as many good sedes and herbes as she can gette and specially suche as be good for the potte and for to eate: And as oft as nede shall require it must be wedded, for else the wede woll over-growe the hearbs."[6]

Before immediately accepting such directions as a reflection of what women were doing at home, we should remember that this notion of the domestic garden as the housewife's responsibility derived as much from classical texts on husbandry as from reality.[7] Chapter 1 showed how both Conrad Heresbach's and Thomas Hill's telling of garden-ing's "prehistory" eventually placed gardening in women's hands, when explaining the role gardening played in "meaner" households. For both, the common garden's being "out of order" should be blamed on the housewife. The distinction between Heresbach's and Hill's his-tories is a small but telling one, insofar as Herebach's story focuses solely on growing food for the household's own use, whereas Hill's implies that women became involved after the emergence of a market in garden produce.[8] In Hill's logic, the housewife's function was tied to the spread of gardening across social ranks and growing stuff for the marketplace. Both histories implied that gardening's increasing "low-ness" should be linked with its supervision by the "huswife," but Hill also suggested that the housewife contributed to the garden's "com-modity," when gardening was valued for producing both beauty ("the procreation and delight of minds") and profit for the household ("proper gain").[9] The value of women's garden work thus remained ambiguous: it was "low" and practical to be sure, but there did not seem to be anything inherently wrong with that.

Behind this kind of storytelling about a domestic and commercial

[6] [John] Fitzherbert, *Here begynneth a newe tracte or treatise moost profytable for all hus-bandemen: and very frutefull for all other persons to rede* (London, 1532), fol. xlix.

[7] Joan Thirsk, "Making a Fresh Start: Sixteenth-Century Agriculture and the Clas-sical Inspiration," in *Culture and Cultivation in Early Modern England: Writing and the Land*, ed. Michael Leslie and Timothy Raylor (Leicester: Leicester University Press, 1992), pp. 1–20.

[8] Dydymus Mountain [Thomas Hill], *The Gardeners Labyrinth* (London, 1594; rpt., New York: Garland, 1982), pp. 2–3.

[9] On the contribution of women's domestic labor to the household economy, see Er-ickson, introduction to Clark, *Working Life*, pp. xviii–xix.

garden economy is an uncertain history. In England and on the Continent, country housewives did indeed bring their surplus produce to towns and cities or to surrounding manors, and poor women culled herbs from the open fields and peddled them in the street.[10] Contemporary drawings of London's markets represent women, poor and prosperous, engaged in market business and "crying" their fruits and herbs, which could be either their own or the products of market gardens (see figure 15 for a contemporary drawing of Grace Church market in London, with male and female vendors).[11] Many household accounts record payments to women for weeding as well as for incidental work. The stewards of Hampton Court employed women for threepence a day to pull out "charlock, nettles, convolvulus, dodder, thistles, dandelions and groundsel,"[12] and other household accounts list payments to women for cultivating strawberries and collecting seeds.[13] As for women of the middling sort, we do know that in the 1540s Sabine Saunders in Northamptonshire asked her brother-in-law in London to send her seeds every spring for her garden.[14] The herbals occasionally mention ordinary women gardeners as independent workers or innovators. The best-known example is the note Thomas Johnson added to his edition of Gerard's *Herbal* in the section on clove gillyflowers, where he recommends that the reader "at thet time of the yeare repaire to the garden of Mistresse Tuggy (the wife of my late deceased friend Mr. Ralph Tuggy) in Westminster, which in the excellencie and varitie of these delights exceedeth all that I have seene)."[15] Even aristocratic women occupied themselves with the garden: the diary of Lady Margaret Hoby indicates that garden activities, including the supervision of harvesting, were part of her daily routine; she anxiously recorded for April 6, 1605, that "this day I bestoed to much time

[10] See Mendelson and Crawford, *Women in Early Modern England:* "The 1678 domestic accounts of the family of Seymour of Berry Pomeroy in Devon included payments from 5s. 6d to around 1 pound to the herb-woman, to the milkwoman for 3s. 7d, and to Mrs. Gardner for two pecks of peas" (p. 270).

[11] See Sean Shesgreen, ed., *The Criers and Hawkers of London: Engravings and Drawings by Marcellus Laroon* (Stanford: Stanford University Press, 1990).

[12] Martin Hoyles, *The Story of Gardening* (London: Journeyman Press, 1991), p. 194.

[13] Mendelson and Crawford, *Women in Early Modern England*, pp. 273–74.

[14] Miles Hadfield, *A History of British Gardening* (London: John Murray, 1969), p. 46.

[15] Thomas Johnson, *The Herball or Generall Historie of Plantes gathered by John Gerarde of London Master in Chirurgerie Very much Enlarged and Amended by Thomas Johnson Citizen and Apothecarye of London* (London, 1633), p. 589.

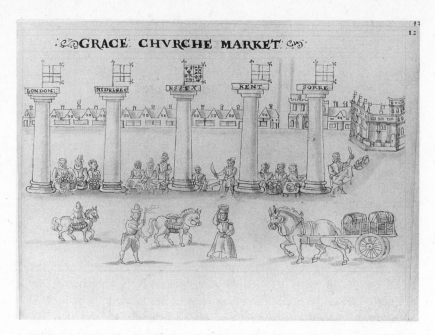

FIGURE 15. Men and women selling their garden produce in Grace Church Market, drawing by Hugh Alley for *A Caveatt for the Citty of London*. Reproduced by permission of the Folger Shakespeare Library.

in the Garden and therby was worse able to performe spirituall duties."[16] On the highest end of the social scale, Lucy, Countess of Bedford is often cited as exemplary for overseeing the creation of magnificent gardens at Twickenham and Moor Park in the early seventeenth century, and Charles Evelyn and Stephen Switzer spoke with admiration of the "female horticulture" of the Duchess Dowager of Beaufort and her garden at Badminton.[17] Switzer noted with approval that "what progress [the Duchess] made in Exoticks, and how much of her time she virtuously and busily employed in the garden, is easily observable from the Thousands of those foreign plants . . . there regi-

[16] Joanna Moody, ed., *The Private Life of an Elizabethan Lady: The Diary of Lady Margaret Hoby, 1599–1605* (Stroud, Gloucestershire: Sutton, 1998), p. 211.

[17] See Roy Strong, *The Renaissance Garden in England* (London: Thames and Hudson, 1979), p. 120 and pp. 145–47. Charles Evelyn, *The Lady's Recreation*, part 3 of John Laurence, *Gardening Improv'd* (London, 1718; rpt., New York: Garland, 1982), pp. 2–3.

mented together."[18] But for the most part, such evidence is anecdotal. Gardens and flowers are, after all, ephemeral things, not recorded in wills and deeds, and for the most part, women's gardening, like much domestic labor, went unnoticed or unrecorded. What we have left, instead, is prescription rather than description of women's garden labor.

The gardening instructions directed specifically to women are relatively brief. Gervase Markham devoted a tiny part of his fat book of instructions titled *The English Housewife* (1631) to the wife's function as a gardener. Further, Markham's gardening section is located at the beginning of a long chapter on cookery, so that his housewife's knowledge of herbs and plants is presented as her first step to providing food for her family and not as producing goods for the market:

> To proceed then to this knowledge of cookery, you shall understand, that the first steppe thereunto is, to have Knowledge of all sorts of hearbs belonging to the Kuchin, whether they be for the Pot, for sallets, for sauces, for servings, or for any other Seasoning, or adorning; which skill of Knowledge of Hearbs she must get by her own true labour and experience, and not by my relation, which would be much too tedious. . . . She shall also know the time of yeare, Month and Moone, in which all Hearbs are to be sowne; and when they are in their best flourishing, that gathering all Hearbs in their height of goodnesse, shee may have the prime use of the same. And because I will enable, and not burden her memory, I will here give her a short epitome of all that knowledge.[19]

A few pages follow on the times of sowing, the transplanting of herbs, and the choice, "prosperity," and gathering of seeds; this brevity contrasts significantly with the extensive account of the cultivation of herbs, flowers, and vegetables in *The English Husbandman*. Markham's comment that he does not want to "burden" the housewife's memory with too many "tedious" written rules, because she must learn from experience, would seem to echo the value he places on experience in *The English Husbandman*. But in *The English Housewife* garden experience does not appear to carry a comparable value, because it is confined to household service.

[18] Stephen Switzer, *Ichnographia Rustica, or, The Nobleman, Gentleman, and Gardener's Recreation* (London, 1718; rpt., New York: Garland, 1982), p. 72.

[19] Gervase Markham, *The English Housewife* (London, 1631), p. 61.

In his similarly concise *Countrie Housewifes Garden*, William Lawson justified his own brevity on the grounds that the field is limited for women who are not "skillful artists." Chapter 2 describes some of the ambivalence expressed in Lawson's little book, which at once suggests his lack of concern for this reader and yet that he trusts her to know what she likes and allows her to follow her pleasure in both reading and gardening. Like Markham's instruction, Lawson's direction implies that the country housewife was not what he would call an "artist" and that it would take "endless labor" of writing on his behalf to make her into one. Instead, she needed to learn through working. But then Lawson did seem to allow some literal space for her to enlarge both herself and her garden, if she indeed had the space (and Lawson did assume that she had maids to help her weed).

Lawson confessed that he was happy to leave the design of the garden to the housewife—especially since it would save him some paper—and he recognized her interest in the garden's beauty by providing some choice examples of garden knots. He advised her to attend to her flowers while not neglecting the vegetables, for "though your Garden for flowers doth in a sort peculiarly challenge to it selfe a profite, and exquisite forme to the eyes, yet you may not altogether neglect this, where your hearbes for the pot doe grow." The housewife's attention was thus drawn to the garden's form as well as to its uses (a concern visible in the alphabetical list of plants, which notes both medicinal and ornamental virtues). The text never explicitly marks this kind of garden as specifically feminine. In this section, it is not in fact clear to whom the garden ultimately belongs, for the text speaks of men's as well as women's "delight" and in an ambiguous way of the "owner." When it comes to the "scope of the ground" of the garden and the orchard, the text determines "we must leave the quantity to every man's ability and will."[20] Lawson's flower and herb garden is thus not clearly gendered feminine, echoing his other book, *A New Orchard and Garden*, where both are masculine domains. But the wife does play an important part there.

The sixteenth- and early seventeenth-century prescriptions for women thus defined a role for them in the garden mostly in association with cooking, growing food, and producing materials for home

[20] William Lawson, *The Countrie Housewifes Garden* (London, 1617; rpt., New York: Garland, 1982), pp. 9–11.

FIGURE 16. Frontispiece image of Elizabeth I, from Henry Lyte, *The Light of Britaine* (1588). Reproduced by permission of the Folger Shakespeare Library.

tion into something sinister (1.5.83). In this case, the gathering of flowers reflects the housewife's role in family physic: in her closet the housewife prepared cosmetics and medicines from plants, and books of recipes were often given titles that suggested the association.[29] It is odd that in this play this housewifely function of gathering flowers for use evokes a sense of danger.

But at least the Queen collects flowers for some purpose, unlike Ophelia, who does it only for art—or for no reason at all. In the first quarto of *Hamlet* (but not the Folio) Ophelia enters, quite mad, muttering, "Well, God a mercy, I a bin a gathering of floures,"[30] flowers that she then bestows upon her audience (although it is not specified in any early text which goes to whom):

> *Ophelia:* There's rosemary, that's for remembrance: pray you love, remember. And there is pansies, that's for thoughts.
> *Laertes:* A document in madness: thoughts and remembrance fitted.
> *Ophelia:* There's fennel for you, and columbines. There's rue for you,
> And here's some for me. We may call it herb a grace a Sundays. You may wear your rue with a difference. There's a daisy. I would give you some violets, but they wither'd all when my father died.
>
> (4.5.174–85)

This scene replaces the notion of women gathering flowers for physic with their "emblematic usages."[31] Ophelia has no real use for flowers, only a symbolic relationship with them. Indeed, Laertes comments on her distribution as an art form: he laments, "Thought and afflictions, passion, hell itself / She turns to favour and prettiness" (4.5.188–89). In this act of bestowing flowers, she herself is as "pretty" as the blossoms she offers.

Although in *The Winter's Tale* the disguised princess Perdita is called

[29] For example, *A Closet for Ladies and Gentlemen, Or, the Art of Preserving, Conserving and Candying . . . Also Divers Sovereigne Medicines and Salves for Sundry diseases* (London, 1608), or John Partridge's *The Treasury of Hidden Secrets, Commonlie Called, The good-Huswives Closet of Provision* (London, 1653). See Lena Cowen Orlin, *Elizabethan Households: An Anthology* (Washington, D.C.: Folger Shakespeare Library, 1995); also her article "Gertrude's Closet," *Shakespeare Jahrbuch* 134 (1998): 44–67, on the pharmaceutical closet (p. 62).

[30] *The tragicall historie of Hamlet, Prince of Denmarke by William Shakespeare* (London, 1603), sig. h1v.

[31] Goody, *Culture of Flowers*, p. 180.

a gardener and she talks about horticulture, we really do not see her garden at all. In this she offers a marked contrast to "Old Adam," the emblematic gardener of *Richard II*'s gardening scene, where cultivation is a preeminently masculine activity of violent binding, lopping, and digging out: Old Adam's gardeners "bind up young dangling apricocks," "cut off the heads of [too] fast growing sprays," and "root away / The noisome weeds" (3.4.29–39). Like Ophelia, Perdita gathers and bestows flowers according to the quality of the recipient, so that even in her role as the shepherdess she plays the part of the aristocrat who dabbles in the garden, rather than that of the housewife who grubs in the earth. Correspondingly, she chooses her flowers for their symbolic qualities.

While Perdita offers her flowers, the others view her as an *objet d'art*, just as Laertes could not help admiring the mad Ophelia's "prettiness." When Camillo watches Perdita play her part, he sighs, "I should leave grazing, were I of your flock, / And only live by gazing" (4.4.108–9). Perdita is introduced by Florizel as the goddess Flora herself "peering in April's front" (4.4.2–3), and Polixenes comments after her flower scene that she is "the prettiest low-born lass that ever / Ran on the green-sord" (4.4.156–57). Even when criticizing the cultivation of gillyflowers, Perdita herself acknowledges that she, like a flower, is an object of desire: she declares that

> I'll not put
> The dibble in the earth to set one slip of them;
> No more than were I painted I would wish
> This youth should say 'twere well, and only therefore
> Desire to breed by me.
>
> (4.4.99–103)

If, as Frances Dolan has concluded, Perdita's rejection of cosmetics signals her rejection of "illegitimate female agency and creativity,"[32] her aligning herself with the uncultivated flower also suggests her passivity (see chap. 5 for a further discussion of Perdita's objections to

---

[32] Frances E. Dolan, "'Taking the Pencil out of God's Hand': Art, Nature, and the Face-Painting Debate in Early Modern England," *PMLA* 108 (1993): 224–39: "Most anticosmetics treatises emphasize that a woman who paints herself refuses to submit to her passive role as a creature, a being with no legitimate capacity for self-transformation or self-determination, and insists on herself as a creator" (pp. 229–30).

grafting). While it is implied that she works, the audience sees Perdita as a consumer of pleasure and a pleasure to be consumed. As Elizabeth Hyde remarks, in early modern culture to be Flora was to embody "the powers of beauty, fertility, and seduction believed to be inherent in both women and flowers."[33] As the Flora of the sheep-shearing feast, Perdita embodies a notion of gardening as bringing to fruition what is already present, elegant, and delightful.

When Milton came to fashion his Eve as a gardener in Eden in *Paradise Lost*, he did draw on the image of the domestic housewife who dutifully tends her plants and prepares their fruits for an innocent meal. But to prepare her for the fall, he transformed her into a flower woman, who is desirable and vulnerable. When Satan prepares his final assault on humanity in book 9, he sees Eve surrounded by the flowers of Eden. She is the queen of the flowers, both their stay and their symbol:

> Veil'd in a Cloud of Fragrance, where she stood,
> [Satan] Half spi'd, so thick the Roses bushing round
> About her glow'd, oft stooping to support
> Each Flow'r of slender stalk, whose head though gay,
> Carnation, Purple, Azure, or speckt with Gold,
> Hung drooping unsustain'd, they she upstays
> Gentle with Myrtle band, mindless the while,
> Herself, though fairest unsupport'ed Flow'r
> From her best prop so far, and storm so nigh.[34]
>
> (book 9, ll. 425–33)

Eve's mistake, the text implies, is to imagine herself the gardener rather than the flower (so she is also blamed for wanting to make Adam's and her work more efficient). In this arbor where she is the object of Satan's lust, she is the flower to be plucked, even while she persists in thinking that she is the one who can manage the garden. With the Fall, Eve is defaced and "deflowered," and she withers, like the roses of the crown Adam had woven for her as his "harvest queen" (book 9, ll. 840–42).

[33] Hyde, "Gender, Flowers, and the Baroque Nature of Kingship," p. 238.
[34] All citations from *Paradise Lost* are from John Milton, *Complete Poems and Major Prose*, ed. Merritt Y. Hughes (Indianapolis: Bobbs-Merrill, 1957).

The Lady's Recreation

This deeply embedded literary image of the woman as the giver of flowers and the flower to be gathered appears infrequently, if at all, in the gardening prescriptions for women written in the late sixteenth and early seventeenth centuries, which are focused on the country housewife in her domestic garden. When gardening spread over class boundaries in the later seventeenth century, however, this image of the "flower woman" came to dominate the picture of women in gardening books. Two potentially contradictory factors, in particular, influenced the gendering of gardening in this later period. On the one hand, in manuals women were located in flower gardens rather than kitchen ones, even while the texts distinguished between the aristocratic woman who embodied the garden and the country housewife whose practices and plants were not worth even discussing. On the other hand, the sophisticated culture and hybridization of flowers became the province of male "florists," both amateurs and professional, who grew special flowers for ornamental purposes and for profit.[35] As we saw in chapter 1, the professional nursery trade prospered in the seventeenth century, when men saw the profit to be made in growing plants to supply the gardens of the rich. Further, new flowers were streaming into England from Europe as well as India, Africa, and the New World as men voyaged in search of horticultural novelties to add to their own collections of rarities or on behalf of wealthy patrons who wished to establish grand gardens. The Dutch craze of "tulipmania" was only the most extreme version of a competitive market that drove the business of horticultural experiment and the writing of garden books.

Sometimes it was women who were seen as craving these exotic fruits and flowers. Even in the early seventeenth century, several of the horticultural recipes in secrets books were directed toward satisfying feminine desire, whether the hunger of Queen Elizabeth gratified by the cherries of that delicate knight Francis Carew (see chap. 2) or the modest wishes of Lawson's country housewife. For example, in his recipes for "sundry new and artificial wayes for the keeping of fruits and flowers, in their fresh hew, as they are gathered from their stalks

---

[35] Ruth Duthie, *Florists' Flowers and Societies* (Haverfordwest, Dyfed: C. I. Thomas and Sons, 1988).

and branches," Hugh Platt boasted of how he could satisfy feminine desire with a simple secret for prolonging the cherry season: "Now me-thinkes I see a whole troupe of gallant dames attending with their list-ning eares, or rather longing with their great bellies, to learne some new found skill, how they may play at chopcherrie, when cherrie time is past. Wel, to give these Ladies some content, I will unfolde a scroule. . . . Then receive it Ladies with plain termes into your open lappes."[36] Like Faustus bringing grapes out of season for the pregnant Duchess of Vanholt, whether through this secret or many others prof-fered in his own *Delights for Ladies,*[37] Platt claimed (with a leer) to sat-isfy all women's longings for luxuries, horticultural or otherwise.

Whereas the sixteenth- and early seventeenth-century gardening manuals such as Markham's *English Husbandman,* Platt's *Floraes Par-adise,* and Lawson's *New Orchard and Garden* did indeed describe cul-tivating flowers as either masculine or gender-neutral work, by the mid-seventeenth century several garden manuals betrayed a sense that flower gardening was a particularly feminine activity. In his herbal, *Theatrum Botanicum,* John Parkinson distinguished this "mas-culine" volume from his earlier "feminine" book of flowers, *Paradisi in Sole:* "Having by long paines and endeavours, composed this Manlike Worke of Herbes and Plants, Most gracious Soveraigne (as I formerly did a Feminine of Flowers, and presented it to the Queenes most ex-cellent Majesty), I could do no less than submissively lay it at your Majesties feet."[38] Parkinson had indeed dedicated his garden book, *Paradisi in Sole,* to Henrietta Maria in 1629 on the grounds that he knows "your Majestie [is] so much delighted with all the faire Flowers of a garden, and furnished with them as farre beyond others, as you are eminent before them," as if she were the epitome of all "Florists."[39] William Temple demurred in his essay "Upon the Gardens of Epicu-rus: or Gardening in the Year 1685," "I will not enter upon any account of flowers, having only pleased myself with seeing or smelling them, and not troubled myself with the Care, which is more the Ladies part than the Mens."[40] We might take this as a commonplace that women

[36] Hugh Platt, *Jewell House of Art and Nature* (London, 1594), p. 3.

[37] Hugh Platt, *Delights for Ladies* (London, 1609).

[38] John Parkinson, *Theatrum Botanicum* (London, 1640), dedication.

[39] John Parkinson, *Paradisi in Sole: Paradisus Terristris* (London, 1629; rpt., New York: Dover, 1991), dedication.

[40] Sir William Temple, *Miscellanea: The Second Part in Four Essays* (London, 1690), p. 120.

were entrusted with flowers if we had not already seen in Lawson's, Platt's, and Markham's earlier books for men such an intense interest in cultivating flowers as well as cereals, salad crops, and fruits.

If women were thus associated with the culture of flowers, especially for gentle audiences, we still need to account for the fact that the flower gardening books of the late sixteenth and early seventeenth century were written by men and, for the most part, for men. The art of growing flowers now extended beyond the home. The "florists' societies" that were formed in England as early as the seventeenth century were in fact all male,[41] and the nurseries and seed-shops were overwhelmingly run by men. Late in the seventeenth century, in his *Florist's Vade-Mecum* (a guide to cultivating flowers alone), Samuel Gilbert rather defensively invited the professional masculine reader: "he is welcome to enter, that is the least lover of Flowers; but those that think the Divertisement too easie or effeminate. . . . is welcomer (if possible) to stay out; and indeed is forbid Reading or Censuring what he understandeth not, or hath no affection for."[42] Gilbert responded here to the implication that flower gardening might seem "effeminate" as opposed to practical kitchen gardening or medical herbal practice. Instead, Gilbert saw flower gardening as appropriate for two different kinds of men: the professional "florist" and the gentleman enthusiast, who, as we saw in chapter 3, enjoyed flower gardening as an act of contemplation, experimentation, or recreation.[43] When Jean de la Quintinie came to describe the birth of floriculture, he attributed it to "Persons with . . . Curiosity" who "begun to gather together some of all those Beautiful Plants which they observ'd so curiously to enamel, and so admirably to perfume the Fields, where they were before confusedly dispersed."[44] While the gender of these "persons" is unclear, the tenor of the descriptions suggests that housewives have no place in this story—nor do any women. The focus instead is on the "curious" man and his "gard'ner," who cultivate floral rarities.

La Quintinie's history was not in this respect an isolated phenomenon. Even those few garden books that appear to be directed to women

[41] Duthie, *Florists' Flowers*, pp. 13–17.

[42] Samuel Gilbert, *The Florist's Vade-Mecum* (London, 1682), epistle to the reader.

[43] See Hyde, "Gender, Flowers, and the Baroque Nature of Kingship," and Duthie, *Florists' Flowers*.

[44] Jean de la Quintinie, *The Compleat Gard'ner*, trans. John Evelyn (translation of *Instruction pour les jardins fruitiers et potagers*) (London, 1693; rpt., New York: Garland, 1982), preface.

in fact also assume a male—and gentlemanly—readership. While dedicated to Henrietta Maria, the text of Parkinson's *Paradisi in Sole* assumes men *and* women were involved in the flower garden, since both men and women are addressed in the instructions that follow. When Parkinson wrote about setting up a flower garden border, for example, he addressed his readers as "gentlemen," while in the following section on flowers he spoke about the delights of ladies and gentlewomen. On the matter of planting bulbs he instructed "all gentlemen and gentlewomen" to be careful as to "whom they trust with the planting and replanting of these fine flowers."[45] In 1717, Charles Evelyn entitled his book on flower gardening *The Lady's Recreation*, and wrote in the preface:

> As the curious Part of Gardening in general, has been always an
> Amusement chosen by the greatest of Men, for the unbending of their
> Thoughts, and to retire from the World; so the Management of the
> Flower-Garden in particular, is oftentime the Diversion of the Ladies,
> where the Gardens are not very extensive, and the Inspection thereof
> doth not take up too much of their time. And as an Encouragement to
> the fair Sex, in this most pleasant and agreeable Employment, a certain
> Lady of the first Quality, who had a Soul above her Title, Sense beyond
> what is common in her Sex, and Greatness and good Nature so agreeably
> mix'd, as to leave few Equals behind her [the late Duchess Dowager of
> Beaufort], thought it no Diminution to concern herself in the directing
> part of her Gardens; wherein, by her Knowledge and Management, she
> has given the greatest example of Female Horticulture, perhaps, that any
> Nation can produce.[46]

However, while it refers to the reader as "you," the text itself apparently expects a male as much as a female reader: it refers to male flower experts such as John Worlidge and consistently cautions or advises the "gentleman" reader, not any lady. For example, the author declared, "I presume I have no Occasion to put the Gentleman in Mind of fixing his Garden near some River or plenteous Springs of Water"; as for the matter of design and form of the garden, he concluded that in these matters "every Builder is most capable of pleasing himself."[47]

---

[45] Parkinson, *Paradisi in Sole*, pp. 7–13.
[46] Evelyn, *The Lady's Recreation*, pp. 1–2.
[47] Ibid., pp. 8–9.

In fact, after the preface, the only women mentioned in *The Lady's Recreation* are country housewives and kitchen maids, when the narrative pauses to note the plants that the author did not care to discuss, "the other Flowers and Plants more common and therefore not worthy particular notice":

The Fox-Glove, Garden-Mallows, Toad-Flax, Scabious, Snail-Flowers, Blue-Bottles, Fennel Flower, double Pellitory, Fatherfew, double Lady's Smock, Gentianella, Caterpillars, Grove-Thistles, Apple of Love, Canterbury Bells, Thorny Apple, Oak of Jerusalem, Wolf-Bane, Batchelor's Button, Bell-Flower, Rockets, Monk's Hood, Campions, Moth Mulleins, Garden Lupines, &c. These almost every Country Dame has in her Garden, and knows how to sow, plant, and propagate them. Then, for your sweet Herbs, there's Marjoram, Basil, Penny-Royal, Mastick, Lavender, Thyme, Sage Gold and Silver, and double-flowered Rosemary, which every Kitchin-Maid is so well acquainted with, that I need make no farther Mention of them.[48]

Not only was the "gentleman" florist asked to avoid these kitchen-maid flowers: as Samuel Gilbert put it in *The Florist's Vade-Mecum*, the professional florist reader should also neglect such common flowers, "trifles adored amongst Country women in their Gardens, but of no esteem to a Florist, who is taken up with things of more value."[49] The country housewife and her plants were recognized only to be discarded from the printed record, because they and their gardens were without "value."

Thus in the framework and the text of the book itself, women at either end of the social ladder are excluded. The lady, like the Duchess of Beaufort, is the pretext for a book on the flowers, but she is represented only in the book's front matter. On the lower end we find the country dame and the kitchen maid; their province is "common" flowers and herbs (mostly grown from seed) about which a gentleman need not bother to write or read. They stand outside the realm of serious cultivation, and so they stand outside the text. Thus the flower books made it clear that women did work in gardens, but they and their work ceased to be represented except in the images of the aristocratic lady diverted in her bower and arbor.

[48] Ibid., pp. 78–79.
[49] Gilbert, *Florist's Vade-Mecum*, p. 215.

The front matter of John Rea's compendious *Flora* (1665) elaborately details this image of the lady of flowers. The engraved frontispiece represents the goddesses Flora, Ceres, and Pomona as the guiding spirits of the book (see figure 13). In the explanatory poem called "The Mind of the Front" Rea pictured his Flora as a queen generously bestowing her jewels on the reader:

> Meanwhile the Queen calls for her Cabinet,
> And all her Jewells doth expose,
> Shews what they are, and by what artist set,
> Then kindly bids you pick and choose;
> Come boldly on, and your collection make,
> Tis a free gift, pray wear them for her sake.[50]

The goddess Flora here evokes the earlier images of Elizabeth I; she also recalls Parkinson's dedication to Henrietta Maria, since Rea very self-consciously presented his book as a replacement for *Paradisi in Sole.* (Henrietta Maria had appeared as the goddess Chloris or Flora in Ben Jonson's masque *Chloridia.*)[51] Rea's Flora may be a jeweler who displays her wares, but she gives them freely and not for profit, for the reader's adornment and "collection." The realm of Flora is therefore exclusive: her part of the book covers "the choicest Plants, Flowers, and Fruits, that will endure the extremity of our long Winters: describing all such as are not vulgarly known."[52]

When in his prefatory remarks he addressed his compliments to both men and women, as well the upper and the lower gentry, Rea intricately sorted out the gendering of flower gardening. In his first letter, to Lord Gerard, he spoke of his hopes for Gerard's gardens at Bromley, and his wish that Gerard would find this "florilege"

> aiming at the advancement of an Art, as laudable as delightful, and able to acquaint you with all the glories of our best Gardens, as also how to instruct your own Gardeners, not only in the names, but likewise in the natures, kinds, and qualities, of every Plant, Fruit, and Flower, fit to be

---

[50] John Rea, *Flora: seu, De Florum Cultura, or a Complete Florilege* (London, 1665), frontispiece.

[51] See Strong, *Artist and the Garden*, pp. 103–21, on Henrietta Maria and her masque gardens of "sensual desire" and "love and beauty," where the queen herself reigned as a chaste Neo-Platonic love goddess.

[52] Rea, *Flora*, sig. b1v.

collected by the best Florists; together with the order to be used in their Cultivation, Planting, Propagation and Improvement: a knowledge rarely found among those of that profession, and never until now (in so plain a method) made publick.

This presentation identifies the practice of gardening as an art and a knowledge that Rea offered to make "publick" to those who are of the "profession" of florist. It is knowledge that he would impart to the aristocrat, who would then instruct his own gardeners. Rea's second letter of dedication, to Sir Thomas Hanmer, presents the book in a slightly more humble and "English" way to a fellow gardener (who is still his social superior), insofar as he offers it as "a rude Draught of a Rustick Garden, Planted with such Flowers and Fruits as will prosper in our cold Countrey." Here Rea enacted a different kind of humility and invoked values of the local and the "rustick" world in framing the book's "garden." With both of these letters, he linked flower and fruit gardening with the desires of the aristocracy, the acts of the skillful professional, and the interests of the country gentleman.

These two prose dedications to Hanmer and Lord Gerard are set off, in turn, by two poems to the ladies. One is a poem of dedication to Gerard's wife, which depicts the garden being at the lady's command, and the other is directed to Mistress Trever Hanmer, "now wife to Sir John Warner, knight," describing her as a spectator of flowers. In the poem to Lady Gerard, the conceit is that when she walks in the garden, "coy Adonis" will "yield to Your Beauties greater pow'r. / For you may pluck his Virgin flower. . . . Thus your rich Beauty and rare Parts / Excell all Flow'rs, exceed all Arts." In the garden, the lady moves the flowers simply by her own beauty. The poem to Hanmer's daughter is only slightly less hyperbolic, when it calls on her to bring her loveliness to the garden and "bless with your sweeter breath the Myrtle bow'rs / And be the Genius of these Plants and Flow'rs." These women are styled as affecting the flower garden through their mere presence, not with their hands.

The sequence of dedications ends with Rea's poem titled "Flora to the Ladies," in which the goddess Flora invites the ladies into the garden—not, however, to do anything other than look and fashion chaplets for their hair. In seeing the flowers the ladies glimpse great beauty, while they also view themselves. In turn, they make the garden thrive just by being there:

And now behold as you pass by
The White, the Purple, and blush Paeony.
With some fair Lillies that invite,
The double Red, and double White:
Who now their beauties do disclose,
To entertain the lovely Rose,
The White, and Red, together meet
To match their mixture by your Cheek; . . .
See how your presence makes to shine
The Damask and the Crystalline.

Like Andrew Marvell's mower's fairies, in "The Mower Against Gardens," who "till more by their presence than their skill," or his Mary Fairfax in "Upon Appleton House," the woman does nothing even as she *is* everything in the flower garden.[53] Even though the poem renders her extraordinary powers, it is because she is the flower of nature itself, while it is the man who has the art.

Women worked in the garden, without question, throughout this time: poor women as weeders for a few pennies a day; country and urban housewives as providers for their own families and producers for the market; and women of higher ranks as planners of great gardens. But many factors came to block the image of that effort. An increasing emphasis on the status of gardening as both a profession and an occupation inevitably excluded the discussion of women's domestic garden labor. As Michael Roberts observes, in a culture concerned with occupational identity and "the pursuit of an occupation as the regular, daily undertaking of the same kind of work, exercising skills learnt and rights to trade obtained through a lengthy apprenticeship, there is no doubt that we should have to conclude that a great majority of the women of early modern England were not, in this sense 'occupied'" (while he notes that this would also be true for many men).[54] And so, very few women could be said to serve in the gardening occupation or profession.

[53] See Andrew Marvell, "The Mower Against Gardens," and "Upon Appleton House," in *Andrew Marvell*, ed. Frank Kermode and Keith Walker (Oxford: Oxford University Press, 1990).

[54] Michael Roberts, "'Words they are Women, and Deeds They are Men': Images of Work and Gender in Early Modern England," in *Women and Work in Pre-industrial England*, ed. Lindsey Charles and Lorna Duffin (Kent: Croom Helm, 1985), p. 138.

Further, both literary culture and a burgeoning scientific culture were based on conventions and imperatives that precluded recognizing the work of country housewives or the efforts of women of rank. From the second half of the century on, the culture of the botanical collector and virtuoso was predominately male. Women did attend some public lectures in science (for example, Robert Boyle invited women to his lectures on the air pump and his research on colors),[55] and the first journal devoted to scientific subjects for a female readership, *The Ladies' Diary, or the Woman's Almanac*, first appeared in 1704.[56] But the culture surrounding both the collection and the production of flowers and specimens for display was overwhelmingly invested in masculine social status.[57] All of these circumstances combined to paint women as flowers, the object of green desire, rather than to depict them as those who cultivate them.

[55] See Patricia Phillips, *The Scientific Lady: A Social History of Women's Scientific Interests, 1520–1918* (New York: St. Martin's Press, 1990), pp. 122–24.

[56] Ibid., pp. 98–101.

[57] See Marjorie Swann, *Curiosities and Texts: The Culture of Collecting in Early Modern England* (Philadelphia: University of Pennsylvania Press, 2001).

❦ 5 ❦

Garden Society

In her 1981 collection *Green Thoughts: A Writer in the Garden*, Eleanor Perényi warns her reader about one of the pitfalls of gardening: beware of what your choice of flowers might say about you. Color tells all, when "the preferred color of the unsophisticated is firehouse red. . . . Orange and yellow come next, then pink, with blue and white, both comparatively rare in nature, last on the list. . . . It follows that blue and white are the choice of the discriminating. . . . White has perhaps the higher status. White flowers have always had an aura of luxury and expense, partly because so many of them are imported from warmer climates and must be grown under glass." Perényi then confesses that "this may be as good a place as any to admit that there is such a thing [as class distinction] in gardening. When, for example, I say that gladiolas are beyond the pale, I am not making a strictly aesthetic judgment." What she means is that they are not upper-class.[1]

As Perényi's opinion of white flowers suggests, if we now value white blossoms for their rarity and delicacy we are implicitly using social standards, by which the "rare" or expensive thing is elevated over the "common." Early modern garden writers would have understood such an entanglement of the social worlds of plants and people, when the world was still caught up in what Michel Foucault has called "the age of resemblance." In Foucault's account it was not until the seventeenth century that scientists and philosophers began to detach the

---

[1] Eleanor Perényi, *Green Thoughts: A Writer in the Garden* (New York: Random House, 1981), p. 31.

natural order from its "similitudes" to people and to sort it out instead in rational taxonomies.[2] Plants came to be perceived less according to their human analogues and uses and more in terms of the form of their leaves, fruits, and flowers. But, as Keith Thomas has noted, discarding taxonomies of resemblance and function did not mean abandoning hierarchies of value: all the new systems of classification, he claims, "had inescapably hierarchical implications; and there was an obvious parallel between the descending categories of scientific taxonomy and the diminishing units of human society."[3]

The artificiality of such structures is in fact betrayed by Perényi's comments about white flowers. For what she says is not true in one regard: white flowers have not always been prized. In the early modern period, a dramatically or multicolored flower was always valued over the white flower, as was the double over the single bloom, and much effort was expended on transforming white and single flowers into something rich and strange. As Charles Evelyn reported of "gillyflowers" or carnations, "the single Colours are but little esteem'd, the strip'd, fleak'd [sic] or powder'd upon White and Blush, with darker or lighter Red, the Crimson, sadder or brighter Purple, deeper or paler Scarlet, are accounted the finest Colours."[4] Francis Bacon thought that the color white was often a sign of the flower's degeneration, or a lack of culture, since "it is observed by some that gilly-flowers, sweet-williams, violets, that are coloured, if they be neglected, and neither watered, nor new moulded, nor transplanted, will turn white. And it is probable that the white with much culture may turn coloured."[5] White, it appears, was thought of as "common," while variegation was rare and beautiful. The only constant in the story of flowers is thus that their value is always changing.

[2] Michel Foucault, *Les mots et les choses* (Paris: Gallimard, 1960), translated as *The Order of Things* (New York: Random House, 1970).

[3] Keith Thomas, *Man and the Natural World: A History of the Modern Sensibility* (New York: Pantheon, 1983), p. 66. See also Allen J. Grieco, "The Social Politics of Pre-Linnaean Botanical Classification," *I Tatti Studies: Essays in the Renaissance* 4 (1991): 131–49: "The values attributed to the hierarchy of the plant world were, of course, based on the presupposition that plants at the top of the ladder were closer to God and those at the bottom were farther away . . ."; in turn, this order was translated into strictures about diet, whereby it was considered appropriate for the better orders to eat fruits and for the lower orders to consume root vegetables (p. 146).

[4] Charles Evelyn, *The Lady's Recreation* (London, 1717), part 3 of John Laurence, *Gardening Improv'd* (London, 1718; rpt., New York: Garland, 1982), p. 25.

[5] Francis Bacon, *Sylva Sylvarum* (London, 1627), in *The Works of Francis Bacon*, ed. James Spedding, Robert L. Ellis, and Douglas D. Heath, 14 vols. (London, 1859), 2:502–3.

While writers and printers of early English printed garden books and herbals tried hard to rank and classify plants, they could not agree on how to do it. Chapter 2 explored how authors and printers collaborated in creating order in the plant world in the form of a book—whether through alphabetical listings, categories of uses, or seasons of the year. The efforts of John Parkinson, John Rea, and many others to sort out plants into their "ranks" and "tribes" responded to what they saw as disorder both in the human representation of nature and in nature itself. Yet, at the time, most human interaction with the plant world in fact undermined rather than sustained any impression of order or hierarchy in nature. In England, as elsewhere, the still highly local nature of plant lore and nomenclature resisted any systemizing.[6] Parkinson explained irritably that in England primroses and cowslips

> have . . . divers names, according to severall Countries, as Primroses, Cowslips, Oxeslips, Palsieworts and Petty Mulleins. The first kindes, which are lower than the rest, are generally called by the name of Primroses (as I thinke) throughout England. The other are diversely named; in some countries they call them Paigles, or Palsieworts, or Petty Mulleins, which are called Cowslips in other. . . . The Franticke, Fantasticke, or Foolish Cowslip, in some places is called by the Country people, Jacke an Apes on horse-backe, which is a usuall name with them given to many other plants, as Daisies, Marigolds, &c., if they be strange or fantasticall, differing in forme from the ordinary kinde of the single ones.[7]

If one cannot even find the right name for these plants, how can one set their places?

But it was not only local lore that destabilized the botanical order. In the burgeoning commercial market in flowers and plants, values changed rapidly according to fashion and scarcity of supply. Eager to cash in on the market, gardeners worked hard to transform what Parkinson called an "unfit" plant into a "fit" one. Horticultural manuals mark a concern with keeping up to date on the changing fashions in flowers. Samuel Gilbert's book on flowers is riddled with evaluative

[6] See Thomas, *Man and the Natural World*, p. 83.
[7] John Parkinson, *Paradisi in Sole: Paradisus Terristris* (London, 1629; rpt., New York: Dover, 1991), p. 247.

judgments: for example, he remarked of the double white hepatica that it is as "thick and double as the Peach or blue coloured, but more rarely met withal and therefore more regarded."[8] Parkinson promoted his services in steering his readers toward the "choicest" plants, since he felt that they did not know "what to desire." But toward the end of the seventeenth century, John Rea felt that he needed to revise Parkinson not only because so many new plants had been discovered but also because Parkinson had included many things "by time grown stale and for unworthiness turned out of every good garden."[9] John Worlidge insisted in his *Systema Horti-culturae* that gardeners needed *his* book because plants did not mean what they used to mean: "It was not long since . . . that our best Gardens were only worthy of those natural beauties that now flourish in every ordinary Partir, [and] many of our now vulgar dishes of Tillage also were but lately esteem'd as rarities."[10] So many of the plants that Parkinson had included as ornaments to his garden of pleasant flowers Worlidge relegated to a short chapter "of some more Vulgar flowers," which "either for scent or shew are raised in the more ordinary Country gardens."[11] For Worlidge, Parkinson's most esteemed flower, the crown imperial lily, was but a "dull flower"[12] (although Gilbert later came to its defense). Gilbert and Worlidge both extravagantly praised the auricula, which Gilbert noted was "so much now in esteem,"[13] whereas for Parkinson, auriculas or "bear's ears" had been just another kind of cowslip.[14]

This chapter investigates the difficulties inherent in aligning human and garden society, that is, the social order and natural order, when neither had a stable hierarchy of value. The relationship became more complicated when people were not only defining the natural order but also interfering with what they themselves had created by creating

[8] Samuel Gilbert, *The Florist's Vade-Mecum* (London, 1682), p. 29.

[9] John Rea, *Flora: seu, De Florum Cultura, or a Complete Florilege* (London, 1665), epistle to the reader.

[10] *Systema Horti-culturae, or The Arts of Gardening, by J.W. Gent* [John Worlidge] (London, 1677; rpt., New York: Garland, 1982), preface to the reader.

[11] Ibid., p. 146.

[12] Ibid., p. 118.

[13] Gilbert, *Florist's Vade-Mecum*, p. 43.

[14] As Thomas describes the changes, "Flowers thus followed fashions as much as did clothes. Until the 1620s the most prized were the gillyflowers and carnations. They were overtaken first by tulips and then from the 1680s by auriculas. . . . As each flower went out of fashion it lost its commercial value and descended the social scale" (*Man and the Natural World*, p. 231).

new marvels out of common plants, threatening the notion of a "given" or natural order. This was, after all, as we saw in chapter 1, a world in which gardening offered a way to social advancement; in this context, offering people ways to create rarities in their gardens was not only a metaphor for social climbing—it was also a means to do so. This chapter begins by exploring how a literary text might create a natural order that matches a conservative social order, drawing on Shakespeare's *Winter's Tale*, where Perdita, as "Flora," bestows flowers on her audience at the sheep-shearing festival. The second section then turns to examine what—despite whatever you might see in plays and poems—people were really doing with flowers in the sixteenth and early seventeenth century in valuing "curiosities" and supplying the appetite for horticultural marvels. The chapter concludes by analyzing the later reaction against such ambitious gardeners, who were criticized as being presumptuous and writing for gain. The end of the seventeenth century saw a turn in the rhetoric of the gentleman gardener, who wanted to believe both in garden art and in a God-given nature, which cannot be manipulated for profit.

Human Order/Flower Order

More than any other type of early modern writing, literary texts compared people to plants in their common experience of growing, flourishing, and fading. As we have seen in chapter 4, women from the Virgin Mary and the Virgin Queen down to the country maid were imagined as flowers. But such analogies were not confined to literary texts or depictions of women; gardeners, too, saw the connections. Parkinson began his *Paradisi in Sole* with an elaborate comparison of the lives of plants and people: some people might look virtuous but have little substance, just as "many flowers have a glorious shew of beauty and bravery, yet stinking in smell, or else of no other use"; "Some also rise up and appear like a Lilly among Thornes, or as a goodly Flower among many Weedes or Grasse, either by their honourable authoritie, or eminence of learning or riches, whereby they excell others, and thereby may doe good to many." Our life, too, is like a flower, easily cropped, and so the world of states and kings is also mutable, "as where many goodly flowers & fruits did grow this yeare and age, in another they are quite pulled or digged up, and either weedes and grasse grow in their place, or some building erected thereon, and their place is no more known."[15]

In particular the humanist educational treatises of the early modern period are full of such comparisons. In an earlier book, *A Culture of Teaching*, I wrote at length on the relationship between rules for cultivating plants and the humanist practices of cultivating people, and thus I will not dwell in detail on the evidence here. Critical to this chapter's argument, however, is the overwhelming evidence from early modern humanist educational literature that people were divided in their thinking about how much both a plant's and a person's nature could be altered or improved by cultivation. On the one hand, humanist teachers, like contemporary gardeners, were confident that they could shape any child's will and mind though careful culture. On the other hand, they recognized that each child has a unique and inborn nature that cannot be changed. This recognition of the power of nature had two consequences: it acknowledged a child's capacity for resistance, yet it also justified the creation of a hierarchy of natural difference, in both gender and social status.[16]

This chapter extends the argument made in *A Culture of Teaching* in another direction to consider closely how "garden society" was connected to human society, so that any claim to transform the innate nature or value of plants was controversial. In Shakespeare's *Winter's Tale*, we witness the disguised princess Perdita categorizing people in relationship to plants, according to time of life, gender, and rank. In the midst of this scene arises her testy conversation with Polixenes about the grafting of gillyflowers, in which she declares herself as opposing any altering of a plant's nature. We thus see her exercising her own art in ordering plants and people, in the name of natural hierarchy, even while she herself decries the effects of art.

This Shakespearean scene of the lady bestowing flowers enacts what Jack Goody has called the "emblematic usage of flowers" in literary culture. What we do know about the "language of flowers" in early modern English culture comes mostly from literary texts, emblem

---

[15] Parkinson, *Paradisi in Sole*, epistle to the reader.
[16] See Rebecca Bushnell, *A Culture of Teaching: Early Modern Humanism in Theory and Practice* (Ithaca: Cornell University Press, 1996), chap. 3.

books, and herbals, the products of written culture and not local lore. But this was hardly a stable or fixed sort of language.[17] Even the herbal books record a wide variety of meanings of flowers, rather than one set of standardized beliefs. Thus, when in *Hamlet* mad Ophelia bestows columbines, fennel, rue, daisies, pansies, and rosemary on the members of the Danish court, she appears to be performing a significant act: she declares that rosemary is "for remembrance" and pansies are for "thoughts" (from the French "pensée"), but for the rest, we can hardly say what she means. Readers and, in particular, editors still seek to impose a meaning on these flowers: for example, the editor of the Arden Shakespeare *Hamlet*, Harold Jenkins, driven by the need to make the columbine signify something, suggests a reference to its horned shape and thus "marital infidelity." As for daisies, as Jenkins says: "the daisy has proved baffling."[18] The effect of the scene, in the end, is to mystify the meanings of flowers: Ophelia is mad, after all, and the flowers' failure to signify is in keeping with that play's other failures of meaning.[19]

Perdita's flower scene in *The Winter's Tale* much more explicitly invokes social categories and the interlaced world of people and plants. Perdita's distribution of flowers draws on traditional notions of their uses and yet ultimately transforms them, when she matches plants to the status of the recipients. She offers to fit each of the men with the flowers she says symbolize their ages. The old men receive rosemary and rue for their "evergreen" nature (for "these keep / Seeming and savor all the winter long"), and Polixenes comments pointedly that "well you fit our ages / With flow'rs of winter."[20] She gives the flowers of "middle summer" to "men of middle age"; this partly marks the season of their lives, but it also suggests their "heat" or humoral "temperature." These are all "hot" herbs: mint stirs lust; savory quickens lethargy; marjoram is "a ready agent in cold diseases of the brain and head,"[21] and "hot" lavender also helps diseases caused by cold. This

---

[17] Jack Goody, *The Culture of Flowers* (Cambridge: Cambridge University Press, 1993), pp. 179–82.

[18] Harold Jenkins, ed., *Hamlet* (London: Methuen, 1982), pp. 539–40.

[19] I am indebted to Peter Stallybrass for this point.

[20] All citations from Shakespeare are from *The Riverside Shakespeare*, ed. G. Blakemore Evans (Boston: Houghton Mifflin, 1974).

[21] Thomas Johnson, *The Herball or Generall Historie of Plantes gathered by John Gerarde of London Master in Chirurgerie Very much Enlarged and Amended by Thomas Johnson Citizen and Apothecarye of London* (London, 1633), p. 665.

group of flowers, then, characterizes the "heat" of middle-aged men (or is perhaps meant to make them hot again).

When Perdita turns to the young folk—Florizel and the unnamed maidens—she maintains the seasonal framework but also divides it according to gender and rank. If it were the right season, she says, they would all get spring flowers: daffodils, violets, primroses; then bold oxlips and the crown imperial; and lilies and the "flow'r-de-luce." At first, it would seem that all the young people are gathered together in this imaginary spring bouquet of plants that are primarily cool and moist, but there is a difference between them. When addressing the maidens she cites the daffodils that "take / The winds of March with beauty"; then "violets, dim / but sweeter than the lids of Juno's eyes," and finally the "pale primroses / That die unmarried" (4.4.73–129). All these flowers are implicitly feminized: dim (because they hang their heads), seductive, sweet, pale, and virginal. Turning, it appears, to Florizel, she then speaks of "bold oxlips and / The crown imperial; lilies of all kinds / (The flow'r-de-luce being one)": the latter three flowers are more clearly masculine. In fact, the "oxlip" and the "primrose," along with the cowslip, were varieties of the same flower: Parkinson noted that primroses have but one flower on a stem, while cowslips have several, and "those are usually called Oxelips, whose flowers are naked, or bare without huskes to containe them, being not so sweet as the Cowslip."[22] But Perdita names Florizel the "bold oxlip," not the shy primrose.

Florizel is not only like the masculine oxlip: he also earns those aristocratic flowers, the flower-de-luce and the crown imperial lily. Parkinson called the lily "the more stately flower," and declared that "the Crowne Imperiall for his stately beautifulness, deserveth the first place in this our Garden of delight, to be here entreated of before all other Lillies."[23] This lily is not the virgin lily of sacred tradition: it is the masculine lily that bears the "crown imperial." Finally, Florizel is also the flower-de-luce (the Dutch iris and the bearded iris), familiar to us now as the symbol of French royalty (see, for example, in Shakespeare's *1 and 2 Henry VI*).[24]

---

[22] Parkinson, *Paradisi in Sole*, p. 247.

[23] Ibid., p. 27.

[24] Thomas notes of hierarchy in plants that "it was customary to name new flowers after kings and queens, aristocrats and other notabililties, so that the very nomenclature of these flowers reflected their social pretensions" (*Man and the Natural World*, p. 233).

Perdita's distribution of plants thus rises up a ladder of both gender and rank. By beginning with a seasonal listing, her ordering intimates a natural correspondence between the worlds of plants and people, first according to the seasons of the year and the ages of man, and then according to gender and status: both would seem to be equally a "state of nature." Like the seasonal design of John Rea's book *Flora* (see chap. 2)—and Perdita is after all the Flora of the sheep-shearing feast—the world of *The Winter's Tale* thus sustains, even until the end, the image of a natural ranking of flowers and people. Of course, it also makes Perdita instrumental in fashioning that order, through her inventing a language of flowers.

Manufacturing Curiosities

While Shakespeare was staging his ladies inventing a flower language, in the real market for plants the norm was disorder rather than order. Not only did taste and market values construct and deconstruct social hierarchy in plants, but gardeners intent on profit also tried to work the system to their advantage. As early as 1587, William Harrison commented in his *Description of England*, with mixed admiration and disapproval, how in English gardens "art also helpeth nature in the daily coloring, doubling and enlarging the proportion of our flowers, it is incredible to report: for so curious and cunning are our gardeners now in these days that they do presume to do in manner what they list with nature, and moderate her course in things as if they were her superiors."[25] Gardeners pursued the cultivation of "curious" or rare plants as part of a broader culture of collecting. The aristocrat's and gentleman's obsession with assembling "cabinets of curiosities" often extended to flowers and fruit, and gardeners and nurserymen were ready to serve them for a price.[26] Some collections were supplied by

[25] William Harrison, *Description of England* (Ithaca: Cornell University Press, for the Folger Shakespeare Library, 1968; rpt., New York: Dover, 1994), chap. 20, p. 265.

[26] On curiosities and collecting see Horst Bredekamp, *The Lure of Antiquity and the Cult of the Machine: The Kunstkammer and the Evolution of Nature, Art, and Technology,* trans. Allison Brown (Princeton: Markus Wiener, 1995); Steven Mullaney, "Strange Things, Gross Terms, Curious Customs: The Rehearsal of Cultures in the Late Renaissance," in *Representing the English Renaissance,* ed. Stephen Greenblatt (Berkeley: University of California Press, 1988), pp. 65–92; Marjorie Swann, *Curiosities and Texts: The Cultures of Collecting in Early Modern England* (Philadelphia: University of Pennsylva-

travel: the John Tradescants became famous for their "ark" of marvels—herbaceous and otherwise—at Lambeth, built as they worked for others by fetching exotic plants from Europe and the New World.[27] By the time Tradescant the Elder printed the catalogue of his plants in 1634, he could list more than 750 items that made up his own collection of horticultural rarities.[28]

Responding to this market, breeders also experimented with techniques that would produce such plants. Gardeners might want the plants for themselves or for their masters and mistresses, but, with the growth of the nursery and seed business, they were also interested in making money.[29] It is not surprising that this kind of experimentation also led to abuse and corruption: by the late seventeenth century we find Samuel Gilbert complaining of "the Mercenary Flower Catchers about London, or some that are of the same stamp scatter'd up and down the Countrey, Fathering new names on Old Flowers to enhance their price; and if a Plant of value and a rarity, tho' you pay dear for it, until you receive it in Flower you will to your cost and disappointment, Experience, their unfaithfulness."[30] Not only (as we saw in chapter 1) were new gardeners flooding the markets and misrepresenting themselves as experts, they were also peddling common flowers as rarities.

From the end of the sixteenth century on, long before the biological process of plant hybridization was understood, stunning experiments filled the horticultural manuals, where we find recipes—some of them preposterous—for changing the scent, taste, and shape, and the very nature of all sorts of fruits and flowers.[31] Many of these recipes were derived from Italian and German books of secrets, which celebrated the human power to alter just about anything in nature. In horticul-

---

nia Press, 2001); and Barbara M. Benedict, *Curiosity: A Cultural History of Early Modern Inquiry* (Chicago: University of Chicago Press, 2001).

[27] See Swann, *Curiosities,* chap. 1; also Prudence Leith-Ross, *The John Tradescants: Gardeners to the Rose and Lily Queen* (London: Peter Owen, 1984).

[28] Leith-Ross, *The John Tradescants,* p. 92; see appendix for the catalogue.

[29] See Thomas, *Man and the Natural World,* p. 233: "The constant desire to keep ahead of the fashion (or at least to profit by selling to those who wished to keep ahead) was one of the chief stimuli to horticultural innovation. It underlay the preoccupation with rarity, novelty, and hybridization. . . . It also led to the proliferation of an infinite number of new varieties of every fashionable plant."

[30] Gilbert, *Florist's Vade-Mecum,* epistle to the reader.

[31] On the history of plant hybridization before Mendel, see Conway Zirkle, *The Beginnings of Plant Hybridization* (Philadelphia: University of Pennsylvania Press, 1935).

tural circles, the secrets of Giambattista Della Porta's wildly popular *Natural Magic* commanded considerable attention.[32] As William Eamon puts it, Della Porta's "natural magic" was a way of "making marvels naturally,"[33] working within nature's rules by exploiting its systems of attractions and antipathies. So Della Porta himself proclaimed that magic is nothing unnatural but rather "the survey of the whole course of Nature," even when it surpasses nature.[34] When he wrote of the art of bringing fruit to ripen before its time, he explained how this "art being as it were Natures Ape, even in her imitation of Nature, effects greater matters then nature does. Hence it is that a Magician being furnished with Art, as it were another Nature, searching thoroughly in those works which Nature does accomplish by many secret means and close operations, does work upon Nature . . . takes his sundry advantages of Nature's instruments, and thereby either hastens or hinders her work, making things ripe before or after their natural season, and so indeed makes nature to be his instrument."[35] He is the counterpart of Puttenham's gardener who surpasses nature in making something strange and miraculous (see chapter 3).

Della Porta's "third book of Natural Magick" "delivers certain precepts of Husbandry, and shows how to intermingle sundry kinds of plants and how to produce new kinds." It is a marvelous compendium of every possible thing you might—or might not—want to do with fruit or flowers: to generate a plant from "putrefaction," "to make one fruit compounded of many," to have fruits and flowers "at all time[s] of the year," to grow fruit that is unusually big or without a stone, kernel, rind, or shell, to make fruits and flowers "to be of diverse colors, such as are not naturally incident to their kind" or sweeter, or to see that "fruits that are in their growing, may be made to receive and resemble all figures and impressions whatsoever." The principle behind many of these recipes is that of "copulation" or fusion through grafting of disparate things on fertile ground. These methods cannot fail to

---

[32] See William Eamon, *Science and the Secrets of Nature: Books of Secrets in Medieval and Early Modern Culture* (Princeton: Princeton University Press, 1994), p. 206. While first published in Latin and not intended for a popular audience, *Natural Magic* appeared in five different vernacular languages and fifty editions in the sixteenth and seventeenth centuries.

[33] Ibid., p. 218.

[34] Giambattista Della Porta, *Magia naturalis* (1558), translated as *Natural Magick* (London, 1658), book 1, chap. 2, p. 2.

[35] Ibid., book 3, chap. 8, pp. 73–74.

work, Della Porta wrote, because "the ground never grows old or barren, but is everywhere naturally rank to receive new seed, and to produce new, and is ever unsatisfied fruitfulness, and brings perpetual increase. And if nature be always admirable, she will seem more wonderful in plants. Copulation was but of one kind, here it is almost infinite, and not only every tree can be engrafted into every tree, but one tree may be adulterated with them all." And so it is daily, "by chance, by nature or new experience, new plants are made." Without the intervention of men, Della Porta believed, nature would be dull: nature "brought forth but one kind of Pear tree" but men have made myriad kinds; the clove gillyflower was once ordinary "that the gardeners art has made so dainty and sweet scented."[36] This work thus celebrates the infinite variety of nature and human taste for change, and it expresses bold confidence in the power of the human hand and imagination.

In the sixteenth and early seventeenth centuries, English garden books and books of secrets delivered similar recipes to improve fruits and flowers in taste or color, make them ripen or bloom off season, mark them with a human imprint, and even produce entirely new kinds. Thomas Hill's *Natural and Artificial Conclusions* instructed the reader "how to make sundrie devises or Armes or suche like, in a Rose, Carnation, or Flower de luce or Lily," and "how to make an hearb to growe, which shall have many savors and taste" (should you wish to do so, plant lettuce and endive so that the seeds touch one another).[37] Leonard Mascall gave directions how to mold fruit in bizarre shapes: "To make an Apple growe within a glasse, take a glasse what fashion ye list, and put your Apple therein when he is but small, and bind him fast to the Glasse, and the Glasse also to the tree, and let him growe, thus ye may have Apples of divers proportions, according to the fashion of your glasse, thus may ye make of Coucombers, Gourdes, or pome citrons, the like fashion."[38] Gervase Markham advised that "if you would have your Lillyes of a purple colour, you shall steep your seedes in the Lees of read wine, and that will change their complexion,

[36] Ibid., "Table and Proeme to the Third Book," p. 58.
[37] Thomas Hill, *A brief and pleasaunt treatise on natural and artificial conclusions* (London, 1581), sig. b5v.
[38] Leonard Mascall, *A booke of the Arte and maner, howe to plant and graffe all sortes of trees, howe to set stones, and sowe Pepines to make wylde trees to graffe on* (London, 1572), p. 77.

and also you shall water the plants with the same Lees likewise; if you will have them scarlet red, you shall put vermillion or cynaber between the rinde and the small heads growing about the roote."[39]

Reaching beyond merely altering a fruit's or flower's "complexion" and shape, the writers ventured to recommend ways to make entirely new kinds of plants. Markham wrote of the

> effects, wonders, and strange issues which do proceede from many quaint motions and helpes in grafting, as thus: if you will have Peaches, Cherryes, Apples, Quinces, Medlars, Damson, or any Plumbe whatsoever to ripen early . . . you shall then graft them on the Mulberry stocke; . . . if you graft Apples, Peares or any fruit upon a Figge-tree stock, they will beare fruit without blooming; if you take an apple graft, a peare graft of like bignesse, and having cloven them, joyne them as one body in grafting, the fruit they bring forth will be halfe Apple and halfe Peare, and so likewise of all other fruits which are of contrary tastes and natures.[40]

Like Della Porta's recipes, these gardening secrets convey the belief that bringing any two disparate things in nature into close conjunction or "copulation" will always result in something extraordinary. They betray a delight in artificiality; it was clearly admirable that a plant should look like something it was not meant to be.

Remarkable in such compendia of recipes is the indiscriminate mixture of what could and could not work, except by accident. Their promulgators did not seem know how or care to draw any line between the practical and the fantastic, proud as they were of their own technique. As Eamon observes, through revealing the "correct techniques" all secrets books similarly "promised to give readers access to 'secrets of nature' that might be exploited for material gain or used for the betterment of humanity." Occult magic treatises painted a murky picture of hidden forces, but secrets books claimed to deal in the stuff of the "real world": "Hence they seemed to hold forth a real and accessible promise of power."[41] Confidence was indeed the most important ingredient in all these books of "experiments," horticultural or otherwise.

[39] Gervase Markham, *The English Husbandman* (London, 1613; rpt., New York: Garland, 1982), second book, p. 35.

[40] Ibid., second part of the first book, p. 58.

[41] Eamon, *Science and the Secrets of Nature*, p. 4.

But it was precisely for this confidence that the garden secrets writers later became figures of ridicule—both for exploiting the market and for meddling with nature. Even the men who proposed such tricks felt some stirrings of doubts: right after he wrote of the wonders of grafting and changing the colors and tastes of fruit, Markham cautioned that such "conceits and experiments" "more concerne the curious, than the wise," and he referred those who want to know more to those books that "have only strangenesse for their subject, resolved that this I have written is fully sufficient for the plaine English husbandman."[42] Although full of his own ideas for grafting and changing the qualities of plants, by the beginning of the seventeenth century Hugh Platt saw that although "all those fantasticall conceits, of changing the colour, taste, or sent of any fruite, or flower, by infusing, mixing, or letting in to the bark, or at the rootes of any tree, hearbe, or flower, of any coloured or aromatical substance, Maister Hill hath by often experience sufficiently controlled," it was clear that "though some fruits and flowers seeme to carrie the sent, or tast, or some aromatical bodie, yet that doth rather arise from the own natural infused qualities, then from the hand of man."[43] By the mid-seventeenth century we find Andrew Marvell's Mower condemning a garden culture in which men "with strange perfumes . . . did the rose taint, / And flowers themselves were taught to paint. / The tulip, white, did for complexion seek, / And learned to interline its cheek."[44]

While seventeenth-century horticultural writers such as John Parkinson, and later Samuel Gilbert and John Rea, sought to rank flowers in their classes and tribes and to exclude the vulgar ones, they also reacted against the earlier gardeners' claims to be able to alter a flower's nature—even while efforts at making rarities continued apace. Parkinson deplored "the wonderfull desire that many have to see faire, double, and sweete flowers, [which] hath transported them beyond reason and nature, feigning and boasting often of what they would have, as if they had it." This kind of "wonderfull desire," it seems, was improper, unlike the suitable desire he sought to manage in his gentle readers. His fulmination against the writers' "feigning and boasting" impugned both these gardeners' veracity and their presumption in de-

[42] Markham, *English Husbandman,* second part of the first book, p. 58.
[43] Hugh Platt, *Floraes Paradise* (London, 1608), pp. 141–42.
[44] Andrew Marvell, "The Mower Against Gardens," in *Andrew Marvell,* ed. Frank Kermode and Keith Walker (Oxford: Oxford University Press, 1990).

fiance of nature, God, and the social order.[45] From this viewpoint, even though Parkinson was writing his book to teach gentlemen and women how to produce a garden that both satisfied their desires and reflected well on them, he implied that there was something inherently presumptuous and almost blasphemous about the other unnamed gardeners' aspirations to improve nature.

By the time of the Restoration and the founding of the Royal Society, gentleman engaged in both collecting botanical rarities and producing them were caught up in a conflicting set of values concerning nature. On the one hand, the new virtuosi were delighted to play with nature, to see what new phenomena—and what new marvels—could be either observed or provoked in plants. Yet, at the same time garden writers and botanists, following Parkinson, protested that human beings could not alter nature or supersede God's design in creating new varieties of plants: the natural order is as it was given to us, and while plants may improve or degenerate with culture, they cannot change their "kind."

Part of the motivation for this reaction against the experiments of "curious" men sustained age-old interdictions against interference in God's creation. William Eamon relates a similar response to the introduction of *secreta* or technical "magic" in Europe in the Middle Ages, when "the word curiosity (*curiositas*) had a far more pejorative meaning than it has today. To be 'curious' about something was neither innocent nor virtuous. Instead it implied being a meddlesome, intellectual busybody who pries into things that are none of his business." The Church fathers, too, were suspicious of curiosity, since they believed that "God *intended* nature to be a mystery and had so fashioned the world as to make many of its secrets occult and unintelligible."[46] The curious man was accused not only of meddling but also of being too proud, insofar as he presumed to use "his illicitly won knowledge to glorify himself and impress the world with his 'marvels.'"[47] In response to comparable contemporary accusations, the Royal Society's apologist, Thomas Sprat, was careful to argue that the experiments of the Society were "not dangerous to the Christian religion," for having seen God's work for himself the true experimenter will "best under-

<hr>

[45] Parkinson, *Paradisi in Sole*, p. 22.
[46] Eamon, *Science and the Secrets of Nature*, p. 59.
[47] Ibid., p. 61.

stand the infinite distance between himself and his Creator, when he finds all things were produc'd by him, where he by all this study, can scarce imitate the least effects, nor hasten, or retard the common course of Nature."[48]

Yet more was at stake than religion when "pride" could also be interpreted as social ambition. Barbara Benedict has argued that, after the Restoration, "curiosity openly denoted ambition . . . : ambition for new truths engineered by new methods and wielded by new men."[49] Thus, Benedict believes, as a practice associated with acquiring rarities, the culture of curiosity was less identified with gentlemanly inquiry into the "book of nature," and more with consumer culture and a rapidly changing society, where "curiosities are not considered manifestations of morality but items for pleasure and personal prestige; curiosity itself is the search for personal advancement, not for a wonderful God."[50] The defenders of the Royal Society were, of course, at pains to distance the members and their experiments from any low desire for profit or self-aggrandizement. Stephen Blake (about whom we know very little personally) protested in his book *The Compleat Gardeners Practice* (1664) that his own intent in writing was for the "preventing of publick dangers, not for the gaining of filthy lucre, or the purchasing of vain glory, but for the gaining of a free conscience, and purchasing of the society and love of just and wise men."[51] Thomas Sprat praised the majority of gentlemen in the Royal Society who were "free, and unconfined," because they were neither stultified by theories of philosophical schools nor driven by a desire for profit, which "busies [some men] about possessing some petty prize; while Nature itself, with all its mighty Treasures, slips from them."[52] There was anxiety expressed here, to be sure, about what it meant to accumulate and investigate the wonders of nature.

Indeed, for some men, becoming a virtuoso and a collector of rari-

[48] Thomas Sprat, *History of the Royal Society* (London, 1667), ed. Jackson I. Cope and Harold Whitmore Jones (St. Louis: Washington University Press, 1958), pp. 345 and 349.

[49] Benedict, *Curiosity*, p. 70: "Satirical literature indicts curious men for distorting public values, for naïvete, corruption, and arrogance, and for mistaking the real for the ideal, the seen for the unseen."

[50] Ibid., p. 8.

[51] Stephen Blake, *The Compleat Gardeners Practice, Directing the Exact Way of Gardening in Three Parts* (London, 1664), preface to the reader.

[52] Sprat, *History*, pp. 67–68.

ties was in fact a handy way of establishing a superior social status. As Marjorie Swann and others have contended, even if being a "curious" man was socially ambivalent, men still wanted to take this path to a higher social status.[53] In particular, Swann reads the collecting efforts of both the elder and younger Tradescants as their attempt to create a "gentle" identity for themselves, even while they worked for others, charged admission to their collection, and sold their plants.[54] To move from merely collecting rarities to trying to produce them would intensify both the advantages and the risks associated with participating in this culture. Bettering a plant or producing a rarity would thus not only be a metaphor for disruption of the social order; it could also mark a transgressive desire for self-advancement.

Grafting Gillyflowers

The ambivalence about meddling in nature expressed in early seventeenth-century garden manuals may explain why Perdita's debate with Polixenes over the grafting of gillyflowers emerges out of her ordering of flowers. In early modern England, grafting was a common metaphor for conjunctions of disparate things. Many examples suggest a positive usage of the term, implying the indissoluble marriage of what had been separate or alien: so religious writers could speak fervently of God's love being grafted in our hearts. When it came to matters of sex and reproduction, however, the connotations were almost always unpleasant, associated with bastards and cuckoldry. Plays circulated jokes about the cuckold with horns "grafted" to his head, and grafts were also metaphors for bastard children. In John Webster's *Duchess of Malfi*, a conversation between the Duchess and the spy Bosola about grafted apricots is really a coded exchange about her pregnancy, the product of her secret marriage with her steward. She calls grafting "a bettering of nature," but Bosola mutters darkly to the audience and himself that, as far as he is concerned, this kind of graft

---

[53] Swann, *Curiosities*, p. 77: "The virtuoso *was* what he collected: he was a curiosity, a rare individual who deserved admiration for his very anomalousness. Paradoxically, however, in displaying his ostensible uniqueness, the English virtuoso was also creating and exhibiting his membership in a specific social group: curiosity and curiosities were seventeenth-century class markers."

[54] Ibid., pp. 27–38.

improperly joins what is cultivated and wild: "To make a pippin grow upon a crab, / A damson on a black-thorn: how greedily she eats them!"[55] In Shakespeare's history plays, grafting is used as a negative metaphor for the mixing of classes and for social transformation, whether the bastard scion is being grafted on a royal stock or a better plant on a wild one. In *Henry V*, the French Dolphin contemptuously refers to the English as Norman bastards and grafts gone wrong,

> the emptying of our father's luxury,
> Our scions, put in wild and savage stock, [who]
> Spirt up so suddenly into the clouds
> And overlook their grafters
>
> (*Henry V*, 3.5.3–6)

Richard III reverses the metaphor, when Buckingham theatrically complains that England's "royal stock [is] graft with ignoble plants" (3.7.125–27). Protests against grafting thus encode a concern for purity of blood and race (see also 2 *Henry VI*, 3.3). Given these associations, we can see what Perdita, the true princess, means when she pronounces that she will never set slips of "our carnations and streak'd gillvors, / (Which some call Nature's bastards) . . . For I have heard it said / There is an art which in their piedness shares / With great creating Nature" (*The Winter's Tale*, 4.4.80–89). She protests that she will not plant even one of them, implicitly declaring herself in favor of purity and "nature."

In an attempt to draw Perdita out, the disguised king Polixenes professes to defend such grafting, offering the example that "we marry / A gentler scion to the wildest stock, / And make conceive a bark of baser kind / By bud of nobler race"; so "Nature is made better by no mean / But Nature makes that mean." Thus, he claims, grafting "is an art / Which does mend Nature—change it rather; but / The art itself is Nature" (4.4.89–97). Polixenes is being disingenuous here, since the point of his spying on the sheep-shearing festival is to break up the marriage of the noble scion and base stock, that is, the uniting of Perdita and Florizel as he understands it. But, apparently for the purposes of testing Perdita, like Della Porta Polixenes defends grafting on

[55] John Webster, *The Duchess of Malfi* (London, 1613), ed. Elizabeth M. Brennan (New York: Hill and Wang, 1966), 2.1.149–51.

the grounds that it is a kind of paradoxical natural art—not because it is art alone.[56]

All this fuss about the carnation or gillyflower is not incidental or unique. The gillyflower, or july-flower, an umbrella (and confusing) category of flowers that often embraced pinks, carnations, and stock, came to obsess many gardeners from the sixteenth through the end of the seventeenth century. Carnations were long considered to be among the aristocrats of the early English plant world: Charles Evelyn and Worlidge called them "the pride of the summer."[57] The gillyflower was also seen as an emblematic English flower (even though in fact the cultivated form, the carnation, came from the east and was imported into Western Europe only in the fifteenth century).[58] Parkinson paid especial attention to them because they were "the chiefest flowers of account in all our English Gardens,"[59] and he began his discussion of "carnations and gillyflowers" with a description of "the great Harwich or old English Carnation," "this goodly great old English Carnation . . . who for his neatness and stateliness is worthy of a prime place."[60]

However, not all gillyflowers were alike. Double stock gillyflowers were valued over the common single form, the variegated (or "pied") over the monochrome. As Samuel Gilbert declared, "the single colours are flowers little esteemed, in comparison of those striped, flaked or powdered upon white or blush."[61] And all the flower books assume that a gardener would prefer to grow a fuller "double" or multilayered flower rather than a single one. George London and Henry Wise commented in *The Retir'd Gardener* that it is up to gardeners to increase the number of double stock gillyflowers, since nature seems not to have intended every one to be so: "For this Flower being in no esteem unless it be Double, and since Nature has not imparted to all of them that advantage . . . we may then govern them according the Methods following."[62] Even though they did not understand what they were do-

---

[56] See Terry Eagleton, *William Shakespeare* (Oxford: Basil Blackwell, 1986), p. 92.

[57] Evelyn, *Lady's Recreation*, p. 25; Worlidge, *Systema*, p. 133.

[58] Ruth Duthie, *Florists' Flowers and Societies* (Haverfordwest, Dyfed: C. I. Thomas and Sons, 1988), p. 82.

[59] Parkinson, *Paradisi in Sole*, p. 17.

[60] Ibid., p. 306.

[61] Gilbert, *Florist's Vade-Mecum*, p. 185.

[62] George London and Henry Wise, *The Retir'd Gardener* (translation of *Le Jardinier Solitaire* by François Gentil and *Le Jardinier fleuriste and historiographe* by Louis Liger) (London, 1706; rpt., New York: Garland, 1982), p. 576.

ing, like the Dutch breeders of tulips responding to tulipmania, growers of gillyflowers tried every imaginable technique to make new varieties.[63] So Parkinson may have listed 48 types of gillyflowers and carnations in 1629, but by the second half of the seventeenth century Rea counted over 350.[64]

Sixteenth- and early seventeenth-century manual writers recommended several ways of altering the color of a gillyflower: introducing a substance either into the stem or at the flower's root, soaking the seed in colored liquids, or grafting together the stems of flowers of different hues. In *The English Husbandman* Gervase Markham directed that his reader change the color of gillyflowers either by steeping the seeds in liquid or, more adventurously, by grafting: "If you please to have them of mixt colours you may also, by grafting of contrary colours one into another: and you may with as great ease graft the Gylliflower as any fruit whatsoever, by the joyning of the knots one into another, and then wrapping them about with a little soft sleav'd silke, and covering the place close with soft red Ware well tempered. And you shall understand that the grafting of Gylliflowers maketh them exceeding great, double, and most orient of colour."[65]

Other writers focused on producing a double stock gillyflower from a single one. Just as plain white was seen as a symptom of insufficient culture, so the single flower was believed to be a product of neglect. So the earlier writers were convinced that, through careful cultivation, they could manipulate the already growing plant to produce a double flower. In his *Floraes Paradise*, Hugh Platt directed the gardener to make a stock gillyflower double in the following way:

> Remove a plant of stock gilliflowers when it is a little wooded, & not too greene, and water it presently; doe this three daies after the full [moon], and remoove it twice more before the change [of the moon]. Doe this in barraine ground, and likewise three daies after the next full moone, remove againe; and then remove once more before the change: Then at the third full moone, viz. 8. dayes after, remove againe, & set in very rich grounde, and this will make it to bring forth a double flower.[66]

---

[63] See Anna Pavord, *The Tulip* (London: Bloomsbury, 1999), and Michael Pollan, *The Botany of Desire: A Plant's Eye View of the World* (New York: Random House, 2001), chap. 2.

[64] Duthie, *Florists' Flowers*, p. 83.

[65] Markham, *English Husbandman*, second book, p. 36.

[66] Platt, *Floraes Paradise*, pp. 78–79.

Even as late as the second half of the seventeenth century, this idea of producing double flowers by planting according to the phases of the moon was still popular. As John Worlidge later decided, why *not* take advantage of the obvious influence of the moon to control propagation of the gillyflower, which would show little improvement without human intervention, for if the moon "hath any such influence, then surely it is in the doubling of Flowers, for we daily observe that many sorts of double Flowers will degenerate themselves into single, and that most of those double we have (which are the kinds usually single) are propagated by Art and industry, and why may not the Lunar influence contribute much thereto?"[67] The temptation to believe that one could take charge of these flowers was clearly very powerful, even when it seemed too good to be true.

In all such recipes for doubling or coloring gillyflowers, the writer's rhetoric is self-assured, celebrating the gardener's skill and conveying through precise details experience in the field (whether the writer had such experience or not). The prose suggests, in Platt's case, the intricacy and difficulty of the procedure, planting and replanting, first three days after the full moon and then after eight days. This secret is sufficiently complicated that any failure could be attributed to not following the directions carefully enough, just as any success would be a fortuitous accident. Markham's prose in contrast evokes the necessary tenderness and delicacy (using a "little soft sleav'd silke") by which the gardener can make the single, small, or plain gillyflower change its nature to be "exceeding great." That is, in both cases the text draws attention to the gardener's technical skill and mastery in the face of a resistant nature. As Parkinson later described such recipes, they are "set downe in bookes, so confidently, as if the matters were without all doubt and question."[68]

In 1629, however, in *Paradisi in Sole*, Parkinson himself did question these matters, when he asserted, "I will assure you that they are all but meere idle tales and fancies, without all reason or truth, or shadow of reason or truth."[69] Unlike the earlier gardeners such as Markham and Hill, who had sought an audience ranging from the "plain English hus-

---

[67] Worlidge, *Systema*, pp. 142–43. Worlidge also thought that "if you have any gilliflowers that are broken, small, or single, you may graff on them other Gillyflowers that are more choice" (p. 139).

[68] Parkinson, *Paradisi in Sole*, p. 24.

[69] Ibid.

bandman" to the landed gentry, Parkinson wrote self-consciously for the gentry alone, and his book was conspicuously addressed to the queen as the most eminent of gardeners. The shift here from the plain English husbandman to the gentle gardener prepares the reader for the text that follows, which asserts that plants are given to us, as they are, by God and nature, and whether rare or common, grand or low, their "nature" cannot be changed by the hand of man.

Parkinson proclaimed defiantly that you could not permanently alter gillyflowers by grafting, planting at phases of the moon, or infusing color or scent, denying that such reports were "of any more worth than an old Wives tale, both nature, reason, and experience, all contesting against such an idle fancy, let men make what ostentation they please." First, he said of the idea that there is "any art to make some flowers to grow double, that naturally were single," "there is no such art in any mans knowledge to bring it to passe." As for planting at the change of the moon, he ruefully told his reader that he had tried it, but "I could never see the effect desired, but rather in many of them the losse of my plants." The improvement seen in gillyflowers by planting and transplanting, he judged, may be only an illusion: "single flowers have only been made somewhat fairer or larger, by being planted in the richer and more fruitful ground of the Garden, than they were founde wilde by nature, but never made to grow double, as that which is naturally so found of it selfe." Similarly, regarding the changing of flowers' colors and scents, Parkinson scoffed that such experiments could not hold up to trial: "Concerning colours and sents, the many rules and directions extant in manie mens writings, to cause flowers to grow yellow, red, greene, or white, that never were so naturally, as also to be of the sent of Cinamon, Muske, &c. would almost perswade any, that the matters thus set down by such persons, and with some shew of probability, were constant and assured proofes thereof: but when they come to the triall, they all vanish away like smoake."

Parkinson's reaction against writers like Hill, Della Porta, and Markham must be set in the context of his view of a ranked society in the natural world, couched in the language of English social class. As we saw in chapter 2, Parkinson particularly valued his own book for distinguishing the common from the rare flowers, whereas earlier herbal and botanical works did not make such a distinction. His book itself is all about status: status in the world of plants, regarding which types and forms of plants are fine and desirable and which are not, but also the status of his reader, who is assumed to be a lady or gentleman concerned to create a garden that reflects his or her estate. Parkinson's explanation of what constitutes a plant's nature, drawing on a notion of an inalterable "spiritual" essence, has a distinct social inflection; one senses that he felt the same way about people, and that those who claim to interfere in the garden world would be just as threatening to the world of man. He refused to say how it is that how some gillyflowers have come to be double, "if they were not made so by art": "we onely have them as nature hath produced them, and so they remaine." He reasoned that something added to a plant cannot change it permanently, for such added substances are "corporeal . . . and whatsoever should give any colour unto a living and growing plant, must be spirituall: for no solide corporeall substance can joyne it selfe with the life and essence of an herbe or tree . . . For no heterogeneall things can bee mixed naturally together." That is, unnatural "copulation" was impossible and unfruitful, and nature abhors "heterogeneity" in reproduction. A plant may be temporarily improved by culture, especially by being raised in rich ground or in hothouse conditions, but one cannot alter its God-given essence. It would be dangerous, or even blasphemous, to think otherwise, "for sents and colours are both such qualities as follow the essence of plants, even as formes are also, and one may as well make any plant to grow of what forme you will, as to make it of what sent and colour you will, and if any man can forme plants at his will and pleasure, he can do as much as God himself that created them."[70] The gardener's agency is thus strictly curtailed, as a threat to the very idea of God's creation and the order he has bestowed on it.

Parkinson set the direction for later writers who did want to provide the rules of propagating and "improving" plants yet couched these directions in terms of respect for leaving nature as it is, in the name of "essence" and the status quo. Stephen Blake objected that "some men are of the opinion when they see this beautifull Flower [the gillyflower], as to think it of an art of their own or others, but they are mistaken, [for] all the art of man is to find out the art of nature itself, for if any thing be not used in its own nature and season it will come to no effect."[71] Blake denied that one could change the color of a carnation by adding something between the bark and the body. He did

---

[70] Ibid., pp. 21–24.
[71] Blake, *Compleat Gardeners Practice*, pp. 26–27.

confess that he did try applying "Camomil, Valeran, Flag-Roots, Solendine-leaves, these beaten together into a salve to the roots," and thus "hath made it as big again as any of the ordinary natural flower, but I could never find that I could alter the form of them; sometimes the colour of them will alter that are thus ordered, but the alteration or mixtures of colours is a law in nature more than experiment in art."[72] Grafting, he concluded, could do nothing to really change a gillyflower, despite what earlier writers advertised: "I could not give any credit to their words, as to believe them, for why, each of them keeps their own nature"; an apricot grafted to a plum tree "keepeth his own nature, and bringeth forth an Apricock"; so gillyflowers grafted "must need brings forth flowers according to their kinds." Culture can make something temporarily larger or fuller, but it cannot change its "kind." Flowers are thus credited with a kind of inherent identity and value, and men are indeed mistaken to think of any flower's beauty as an art of their own.

Earlier in the seventeenth century, in his own speculations about propagating gillyflowers, Francis Bacon had directed the reader's attention to the roles of seed and soil in causing effects of color and fullness as another way of thinking about what causes one flower to be common and another exceptional. He thought that differences in color and form had much to do with "nourishment in the earth; so that the gardeners find that they may have two or three roots amongst an hundred that are rare and of great price; as purple, carnation of several stripes"; if so the cause must lie "in earth, though it be contiguous and in one bed, there are very several juices; and as the seed doth casually meet with them, so it cometh forth." For Bacon, this would explain how one could conceivably transform the flower through replanting, and thus he offered the gardener some possibility of controlling the production of gillyflowers that are "rare and of great price."[73] (This is apparently the kind of thinking Marvell was referring to when he wrote, in "The Mower Against Gardens": "The pink then grew as double as his mind; / The nutriment did change the kind.")[74]

[72] Ibid., pp. 22–23.
[73] Bacon, *Works*, 2:504–5: "It is a curiosity also to make flowers double; which is effected by often removing them into new earth: as, on the contrary part, double flowers, by neglecting and not removing, prove single. And the way to do it speedily, is to sow or set seeds or slips of flowers; and as soon as they come up, to remove them into new ground that is good."
[74] Marvell, "Mower Against Gardens."

However, in *His Observations upon some part of Sr. Francis Bacon's Naturall History, as it concerns Fruit-Trees, Fruits, and Flowers*, published in 1658, Ralph Austen countered that the cause of color variation must be hidden in the seed, since how could it be that "two or three very small seeds that lye as close together as can be, in the earth, should draw severall juyces, from the very selfe same mould, so as to cause them to vary in the colour of the flowers?" While Austen admired such "variety and choice" in flowers as God's gift to us, he believed that "for men to find out, and shew a particular Cause in Nature, of this variety, will be as hard to do, as to shew a Cause why several kinds of Grafes, upon one tree, drawing to the one and the self same sap, do yet bring forth different fruits, other than to say, they keep their several Natures."[75] Bacon had thus ultimately avoided resolving the question of man's interference, while evaluating causality in soil or seed. While subjecting Bacon's experimental speculations to rational critique, Austen remystified nature, making it resistant to human interference.[76] To say that the "kind" thus originates in the seed, so that a flower may grow large or dwindle but may not change fundamentally with culture, suggests a vision of a world where all God's creation—including people—can never escape their "kind."

In 1659 Robert Sharrock, who was a member of the Oxford scientific circle that included Austen and Robert Boyle, published his *The History of the Propagation and Improvement of Vegetables by the Concurrence of Art and Nature*, which he described as a corrective to "romances" of natural magic in propagation. When he republished the work in 1672, his protests still faintly echoed Polixenes' ambivalence about art and nature, in stipulating that "in the wayes of Propagation that are most artificial, there is more of Nature than of Art. Industry and Art may

[75] Ralph Austen, *His Observations upon some part of Sr. Francis Bacon's Naturall History, as it concerns Fruit-Trees, Fruits, and Flowers* (Oxford, 1658), p. 30.

[76] In his manuscript treatise of flowers (circa 1720) Peter Aram noted that seedling gillyflowers "will now & then deviate or varie from that colour they first appeard in at their first blowing, but generally to the worse," but, when they are good, one should save them, for "the best in all probability will produce the best, whatever some others may imagin[e] to the contrary" (p. 56 [90]). There may indeed be change, but the change originates from this "mutative or changing Power [that] was given them at their first formation by the Omnipotent Author of their being." Change may be "much excited and promoted by the Change of Air & Soil" and judiciously "managed" by "Industrious and Skilful Florists," but people cannot make it happen (p. 64 [98]) (*A Practical Treatise of Flowers*, by Peter Aram, edited from Ingilby MS 3664, ed. Frank Felsenstein [Leeds: Leeds Philosophical and Literary Society, 1985]).

bring Materials, and place them fitly for it, but Nature works them. And therefore, as one sayeth, it is the great Art of Man to find out the Arts of Nature."[77] So Sharrock hardly wanted to reject all curious experiments: among the changes he made in that edition was to add Blake's experiment of applying "salves" to the roots of gillyflowers, and he was delighted that "sometimes the colour of them will alter that are thus ordered." He cites Virgil to the effect that "wild plants be meliorated by transplantation to better soil." But Sharrock, like many other contemporary authors, still emphasized that the virtue lies in "the Seed . . . , being taken from the best Flowers," which can be "much meliorated by alternation and change of Ground."[78] Samuel Gilbert observed that "the most variety of double flowers are raised from seed of double flowers, though many times the seed of a single one will produce double," and only then did he repeat the rule about moving them according to the phases of the moon.[79] Like other gardeners of their time, Blake, Gilbert, and Sharrock were all thus torn between their earnest desire to control the "melioration" of plants, and their hesitancy in venturing too far to suggest that, in William Harrison's words of 1587, they were nature's "superiors."

In 1674, the botanist John Ray read two papers to the Royal Society, one on the character of seeds and the other on "the specific differences of plants," which addressed the relationship between culture and nature in "melioration." In the latter paper, Ray made a critical move to distinguish between "accidents" and real differences of species in plants, "having observed, that most herbarists, mistaking many accidents for notes of specific distinction, which indeed are not, have unnecessarily multiplied beings" (and he found both Gerard and

---

[77] Robert Sharrock, *The History of the Propagation and Improvement of Vegetables by the Concurrence of Art and Nature* (Oxford, 1672), p. 4. On the issue of transmutation he notes (although he reserves the right to doubt and says he needs to have sufficient proof): "It is usually believed that divers single flowers may be changed to double by frequent transplantation, made into better grounds" (p. 60). On changes in color and producing striped effects, he says it is effective to weaken flowers, which he has done with a group of "ordinary flowers" and "commonly found the success to answer my expectation in many, and some of them to come so well marked, that they might be taken for better flowers than they are: some think to produce variety of colors by grafting, or joyning artificially the stems of Carnations or Cloves of Tulips of divers colours. But this cannot hold, for every bud and clove that groweth will send forth leaf and flower after its own kind, as it happens in the inoculation and grafting of Roses and other plants" (p. 94).

[78] Ibid., pp. 237–39.

[79] Gilbert, *Florist's Vade-Mecum*, p. 197.

Parkinson at fault in this regard). Among the "accidents" of flowers he named variety of color and multiplicity of leaves, and of fruit, difference of magnitude, taste, figure, and color, all of which were understood in the past as defining different "kinds" or species. According to Ray, "accidents" in plants are like skin or hair color in people, not markers of different species, but rather "occasioned either by diversity of climate, and temperature of the air, or of nourishment and manner of living." So he noted that a plant "standing in one place without culture, will by degrees degenerate, becoming of double, single-flowered, and changing from rare to common colours," but in so doing, it does not change its kind. Ray then took on the question of *creating* rarity: "But because these varieties of flowers, for their beauty and rarity, are highly prized and desired by the curious; and those of fruits do no less gratify by the pallate than these the eye, it were desirable to know certainly, how such varieties might be produced." Ray in fact noted, as some of the practical gardeners had done, that, no matter how much you hope, you cannot rely on a seed, for it will not always come true to the plant that produced it. Ray recommended a secret of frequent replanting or using special colors of water, but he concluded that "the most sure and facil way to get plants different, either in color or multiplicity of flower, is to sow the seeds of those plants, of which you desire such varieties, in rich soil"; of these, some shall randomly bear double flowers, which you can then propagate by slips. Thus, the only reliable method for creating variety is to provide the favorable conditions for "accidents," which you can then cultivate through reproducing an offshoot.

All this effort, however, according to Ray, was not inconsistent with respect for the order of nature or God, since thus "many new varieties of flowers and fruits be still produced in infinitum, which affords me another argument to prove them not specifically distinct, the number of species being in nature certain and determinate, as is generally acknowledged by philosophers, and might be proved also by divine authority, God having finished his works of creation, that is consummated the number of species, in six days."[80] In this argument, which detaches the manipulation of "accidents" and "varieties" from the manipulation of God's creation (unlike Parkinson's approach, which did not distinguish between "accidents" and real differences among

[80] Thomas Birch, *The History of the Royal Society of London*, 4 vols. (London, 1757), 3:169–73.

species), Ray created a space for experimentation with plants, while holding back at the notion that one can meddle with creation itself.[81] While it is not clear that the practical gardeners who continued to prescribe both old and new ways of altering the color and form of gillyflowers knew about Ray's conclusions, the uneasy compromise he reached between innovation and conservatism, science and religion—and science and desire—reflects the spirit of many of his hard-working contemporaries.

It is fitting that the first English plant hybrid deliberately created through cross-pollination should involve a gillyflower. In his *New Improvements of planting and gardening, both philosophical and practical*, first published in 1717, Richard Bradley reported how

a curious Person may [through pollination] produce such rare Kinds of Plants, as have not yet been heard of, by making Choice of two plants for his purpose, as near alike in their parts, but chiefly in their Flowers of Seed-Vessels; as for Example, the Carnation and Sweet William are in some respect alike, the Farina of the one will impregnate the other, and the Seed so enliven'd will produce a Plant differing from either, as may now be seen in the Garden of Mr. Thomas Fairchild of Hoxton, a Plant neither Sweet William or Carnation, but resembling both equally, which was raised from the seed of a carnation that had been impregnated by the Farina of the Sweet William.[82]

The creation of Fairchild's "mule" or cross between a sweet william and carnation was reported to the Royal Society in 1720, if not by Fairchild himself (though he was present) and not as an intentional act.[83] Following Marcello Malpighi's publication of his *Anatomia Plantarum* in 1671, Nehemiah Grew's work *The Anatomy of Plants* (1682), which describes the stamen and its male "sperm," and the research of Rudolf Camerarius in Germany on sexual reproduction in plants, Bradley himself had made many observations concerning plant sexuality, and recorded experiments to demonstrate how hybridization by

81 See Charles E. Raven, *John Ray, Naturalist: His Life and Works* (Cambridge: Cambridge University Press, 1942; rpt., 1986), pp. 188–91, on this speech and Ray's later reservations about the fixity of species.

82 Richard Bradley, *New Improvements of planting and gardening, both philosophical and practical* (London, 1724), p. 20.

83 On Fairchild's "mule," and the controversy that has surrounded the question of whether he did this accidentally or intentionally, see Michael Leapman, *The Ingenious Mr. Fairchild: The Forgotten Father of the Flower Garden* (London: Headline, 2000), and Zirkle, *Beginnings of Plant Hybridization*, pp. 107–14.

pollination works. So he saw that it was from this "accidental Coupling that proceed the Numberless Varieties of Fruits and Flowers which are raised every Day from Seed. The yellow and black Auriculas, which were the first we had in England coupling with one another, produced Seed which gave us other varieties, which again, mixing their Qualities in like manner have afforded us little by little, the Numberless Variations which we see at this day in every curious Flower garden."[84] With Fairchild's mule and Bradley's "improvements," we thus return with some irony full circle to Della Porta and his infinite "copulation" of plants to produce new kinds. What these and other men opened up was a whole new future for the practice of the gardener's art, only dreamed of by the gardeners who came before them.

The alliance of Bradley and Fairchild in producing hybrids was emblematic of both the past and future of producing marvels in nature. Bradley was a person of obscure background and no advanced academic training, who became the first Professor of Botany at Cambridge (where he failed to provide them with a promised botanical garden). He was a prolific writer and journalist and elected a member of the Royal Society when he was only twenty-six years old. Bradley himself straddled the worlds of scholars and gentlemen, botany and practice, the Royal Society and the popular press. In this balancing act, he was also exactly the kind of ambitious man who embodied the multiple threat of "curiosity" to an orderly world of plants and people, and even today he is remembered more as a schemer than as a scientist.[85] Outside of those interested in the history of plant nurseries or garden manuals, most people have never heard of Thomas Fairchild and his hybrid. He was a prosperous and a practical man who wrote an original book on city gardening and made a good living selling rarities to richer men. But it was Fairchild who succeeded where others had failed in controlling the creation of a wholly new flower. Despite Bradley's recognition of his work, Fairchild's contribution to this science of plant hybridization was lost in the telling of a story of botany that led to Linnaeus, Koelreuter, and Mendel. But we should not forget how the creation of new plants began in a culture of green desire, fueled equally by a love of beauty and rarity, commerce, and ambition.

[84] Bradley, *New Improvements*, p. 19.
[85] See Leapman, *Ingenious Mr. Fairchild*, chap. 3.

❦6❦

Telling the Truth

When John Parkinson, Robert Sharrock, and Stephen Blake fumed about what they saw as the "ostentation" of earlier garden writers, they meant both contemporary meanings of the word: a false show and "showing off." Not only were the old writers seen as meddling with nature, but they were also accused of spreading "false tales and reports" and "boasting often of what they would have, as if they had it."[1] These accusations fit squarely into the midst of a century-long debate over the facts and fictions of natural history. This is a topic that may seem indeed foreign to today's reader of garden books, accustomed to quarrels over the desirability of organic as opposed to chemical horticulture, or the relative appeal of informality or formal design. But English gardening manuals of the sixteenth and seventeenth centuries, however mundane, reflect a passionate interest in historiography and early experimental science, fields where men fought about how we come to know and say what is true in natural and civil affairs.

Natural and human history meet in gardening books where they connect people with the land and where they are concerned with telling the truth about human interaction with nature. Herbals are meant to describe and classify plants; gardening books, however, tell how people worked in the field and with fruits and flowers and how they changed them. When gardening books detailed the diversity of soils and practices in England's shires, households, and estates, at

---

[1] John Parkinson, *Paradisi in Sole: Paradisus Terristris* (London, 1629; rpt., New York: Dover, 1991), p. 22.

stake was how the English man or woman was tied to a particular place and way of life, and thus linked to the nation as a whole. The gardening books thus functioned as a companion literature to chorography, a kind of early modern writing focused on the history and landscape of England's counties. As Andrew McRae has commented, "from its beginnings, chorography yoked scholarly concerns of history and topography to an eminently practical interest in the land."[2] In this yoking, the books also defined a distinctly English form of gardening.

While authors of early gardening books thus all promised to write for the English gardener, as we have seen, they increasingly diverged in their accounts of what was possible in the garden. Gardening books differed from natural history books insofar as they instructed the reader what to make of his or her land rather than just describing it. Yet all the gardening rules found in these books are tied to the story of the English land. Gardening books show that people knew that English "nature" differed from that of classical or foreign treatises. But they themselves do not concur as to what that "nature" really is. Chapter 5 explored how competing gardening writers, all claiming to speak from experience, argued vehemently about the extent of human power to transform nature. Precisely because gardeners' "experimental" manipulations seemed artful to the point of being fantastic, critics insisted that they were merely imaginary. The question of art's domination over the garden here dovetailed with the debate over the role of the imagination in writing history and poetry.

When, at the beginning of the seventeenth century, Bacon linked history with experience in his *Advancement of Learning*, he cut to the heart of the contemporary debate over truth, imagination, and authority in the writing of both natural and human history.[3] Bacon himself rejected both Greek natural philosophy (because "at that period there was but

---

[2] Andrew McRae, *God Speed the Plough: The Representation of Agrarian England, 1500–1660* (Cambridge: Cambridge University Press, 1996), p. 246. See, in general, McRae's insightful analysis of chorography as "agrarian discourse" in the chapter titled "Chorography: The View from the Gentleman's Seat" (pp. 231–61).

[3] See D. R. Woolf, speaking of Bacon's four types of idols and Bacon's thought as "the culmination of a Renaissance tendency to reduce all empirical knowledge (cognitio) to various types of 'history'" (D. R. Woolf, *The Idea of History in Early Stuart England: Erudition, Ideology, and "The Light of Truth" from the Accession of James I to the Civil War* [Toronto: University of Toronto Press, 1990]), pp. 147–48.

a narrow and meagre knowledge either of time or place")[4] and folk wisdom, for he claimed to be

> a more cautious purveyor than those who have hitherto dealt with natural history. For I admit nothing but on the faith of eyes, or at least of careful and severe examination; so that nothing is exaggerated for wonder's sake, but what I state is sound and without mixture of fables or vanity. All received or current falsehoods also (which by strange negligence have been allowed for many ages to prevail and become established) I proscribe and brand by name; that the sciences may be no more troubled with them. For it has been well observed that the fables and superstitions and follies which nurses instill into children do serious injury to their minds.[5]

In this passage, the wisdom of the classics and the follies of nurses are linked together as imaginative fables (similarly, Sir Thomas Browne believed that classical writers were ultimately responsible for the errors of rural folks and old wives' tales).[6] The "faith of eyes" and the "experiments of the mechanical arts" (however "low and vulgar") were to replace the accounts of women, antiquity, and mere scholars.[7]

Early modern English garden books reveal the social and political stakes in saying who is an authority on nature. As I have suggested in previous chapters, over the course of a century and a half, gardening books tried to map out the appropriate roles of the gentleman farmer and the "plain English husbandman," the man of science and the rural folk, men and women, in an increasingly complex English economy and social system. This chapter focuses on the question of who was to be credited with telling the truth about gardening, when everyone offered to speak out of some kind of experience, for their people and for England.[8] While the writers of the earlier books did claim quite firmly

[4] Francis Bacon, in *The Works of Francis Bacon*, ed. James Spedding, Robert L. Ellis, and Douglas D. Heath, 14 vols. (London, 1859), 4:73.

[5] Ibid., 4:30.

[6] See Keith Thomas, *Man and the Natural World: A History of the Modern Sensibility* (New York: Pantheon, 1983), p. 77; from Thomas Browne, *Pseudodoxia Epidemica* (London, 1646), book 1, chaps. 6–9.

[7] Bacon, *Works*, 4:29.

[8] For a thorough discussion of the meaning of "experience" versus "experiment" in seventeenth-century Europe and, in particular, the definition of "experience" in

that they spoke from local knowledge, they seemed less concerned about veracity in their imaginative explorations of gardening. The later garden writers of the seventeenth and early eighteenth centuries, however, professed that they alone could convey the truth of what worked in the garden, against the assertions of their predecessors.

In *A Social History of Truth*, Steven Shapin has argued that, by the late seventeenth century, credibility was closely linked to gentility. According to Shapin, while "gentle" empirical scientists admitted depending on the common folk's knowledge and manual labor, they distrusted them as informants. This distrust arose, as Shapin puts it, because gentlemen thought that "greed, ignorance, and bias" could interfere with the search for truth, "transforming direct experience into deceit or delusion."[9] In his *History of the Royal Society* Thomas Sprat praised the Society for including among its members "very many men of particular professions," but he admitted that "the far greater number are Gentlemen, free, and unconfin'd," a condition that he thought protected them from the "corruptions of learning" because they had no masters and they were not concerned with profit.[10] In the 1717 preface to his *New Improvements in Planting*, Richard Bradley welcomed the entrance of John Evelyn and John Laurence into garden book writing, because these were men who were "studious and capable of obliging the world, free from the narrow views of self-interest," and who had given us "something equally new and just, built upon Experiment."[11] Scholars do not agree about Shapin's description of the Royal Society's beliefs as solely tied to class and character. In particular Barbara Shapiro has protested that "social status was one but not the sole criterion of reliability," for the Society relied on travelers' and merchants'

---

scholastic philosophy as opposed to Baconian science, see Peter Dear, *Discipline and Experience: The Mathematical Way in the Scientific Revolution* (Chicago: University of Chicago Press, 1995).

[9] Steven Shapin, *A Social History of Truth: Civility and Science in Seventeenth-Century England* (Chicago: University of Chicago Press, 1994), pp. 264–65. I have also been enlightened by Julie Solomon's work on the rhetoric of "disinterest" in Baconian empirical science, where she follows the links between the new science and a "commercial class discourse" that "preserves a central place for self-interest but renders it fluid, unformulaic, and powerfully invisible." See Julie R. Solomon, "'To Know, to Fly, to Conjure': Situating Baconian Science at the Juncture of Early Modern Modes of Reading," *Renaissance Quarterly* 44 (1991): 513–58.

[10] Thomas Sprat, *History of the Royal Society* (London, 1667), ed. Jackson I. Cope and Harold Whitmore Jones (St. Louis: Washington University Press, 1958), p. 67.

[11] Richard Bradley, *New Improvements of Planting and Gardening both Philosophical and Practical* (London, 1717), preface.

reports and drew on the standards of law rather than civility.[12] Without deciding this question, this chapter will explore how, in the case of gardening manuals, who you were—by nation, rank, or occupation—might ground your authority to write such a book.

In looking at the arguments over grafting and other fantastic arts of the garden, chapter 5 focused on the social values of that quarrel, when confidence in human agency was seen to violate "natural" decorum. This chapter builds on that analysis by looking at the gardening books' rhetoric of fact. Just as altering plants teetered between nature and art, the process of writing about it oscillated between truth and fiction. If being English was supposed to make one better at writing about English gardening, experience and occupation also shaped that authority. If changing nature through grafting or culture started social reverberations, the act of recording or reporting such acts was also bound up with social concerns.

The story is indeed a complicated one, since by the late sixteenth century, almost every author wanted to argue that he was writing a practical book, useful for men of all degrees. As we have seen, the early writers were not shy about admitting that they wrote for profit as well as pleasure. Francis Bacon sought profit as well as knowledge in the inventions of a new experimental science, a compromise that would significantly influence later writers. Yet in the latter part of the seventeenth century, gentlemen writers increasingly cast aspersions on any "vulgar" men who wrote or gardened for profit. It is curious, however, that their explicit targets (rarely naming any names) were not the practical men of the earlier century, whom they largely ignored. Instead these new writers attacked what they called "scholars" or "schoolmen" who composed "romances" about gardening in their studies, since they wanted to claim the authority of experience for themselves. The late seventeenth-century garden books thus carved out a place for what they fashioned anew as the plain-speaking and practical—but gentlemanly—English gardener, who was content to work in the garden for enlightenment and recreation but not for gain.

---

[12] Barbara J. Shapiro, *A Culture of Fact: England, 1550–1720* (Ithaca: Cornell University Press, 2000), pp. 139–42. On the connections between a culture of curiosity, class, and matters of truth, see Marjorie Swann, *Curiosities and Texts: The Culture of Collecting in Early Modern England* (Philadelphia: University of Pennsylvania Press, 2001); also Barbara M. Benedict, *Curiosity: A Cultural History of Early Modern Inquiry* (Chicago: University of Chicago Press, 2001), p. 45.

The English Experience

When Gervase Markham wrote in his *English Husbandman* "that contrary to all other Authors, I am neither beholden to Pliny, Vergil, Columella, Varo, Rutillius, Libault, nor any other Forrainers, but onely to our owne best experienst Countreymen, whose daily knowledge hath made them most perfect in their professions," he reflected a new trend in linking vernacular horticulture with experience. This kind of experience was less the scholastic notion of a universal statement of "how things are or how they behave"[13] and more the idea of directly observing and participating in a given activity. Markham insisted that these "countreymen" were better qualified to teach the practice of gardening, "being men of our owne neighbourhood, acquainted with our Climate and Soile": why, for example, should we resort to "strangers helpe," who recommend we use asses' dung for manure, when England has few such animals?[14] Just as his idea of being a gardener was tied to his life in the field, he claimed to tell the truth because he was an Englishman, who garnered his knowledge from other hard-working Englishmen.[15]

Markham's letter of dedication to Lord Clifton, Baron of Leighton, in *The English Husbandman* suggests some hesitation in pushing the claims of experience, especially when writing for a double audience of noble patron and English husbandman: what served as authority for one audience might not impress another. Markham himself came from a decayed gentry family and had turned to gardening to support his large family, while also producing a prodigious number of instruc-

---

[13] Dear, *Discipline and Experience*, p. 22.

[14] Gervase Markham, *The English Husbandman* (London, 1613; rpt., New York: Garland, 1982), second book, p. 13. For Markham's additional comments on these matters, see "second part of the first book," p. 89, where he insists that in the matter of hop-growing, "I thus farre consent with Maister Scot, that I doe not so much respect the writings, opinions, and demonstrations, of the Greeke, Latine, or French authors, who never were acquainted with our soyles, as I doe the dayly practice and experience which I collect, both from my owne knowledge, and the labours of others my Countrymen, best seene and approved in this Art."

[15] See Wendy Wall, "Renaissance National Husbandry: Gervase Markham and the Publication of England," *Sixteenth Century Journal* 27 (1996): 767–85, for an excellent discussion of "Markham's role as an author in a print marketplace in which he competed with foreign writers of agrarian guides, his use of print to model a new class readership united by nationality, and his insistence that 'English thrift' informed his own process of compiling and organizing information" (p. 767).

tional manuals as well as some poetry and plays.[16] In his letter, he presented his book as "an account of the expence of my idle time," while protesting that "if your Lordship shall doubt of the true tast of the liquor because it proceedeth from such a vessell as my selfe, whom you may imagine utterly unseasoned with any of these knowledges, beleeve it (my most best Lord) that for divers yeers, wherein I lived most happily, I lived a Husbandman, amongst Husbandmen of most excellent knowledge; during all which time I let no observation over-slip me."[17] Markham cared to describe himself as having "idle time," allying himself as a gentleman by birth with the aristocrat whom he addressed, while also grounding his authority to speak on this matter in his work as a husbandman.

Markham's appeals to experience reach back to the empiricist turns taken in the meditations of Juan Luis Vives and Michel de Montaigne (Vives, for example, recommended that scientists consult "gardeners, husbandmen, shepherds and hunters"), but they were also connected with the "science" of the technological writers on exploration, astronomy, and navigation to whom Bacon had turned.[18] As Markham's frequent invocation of the "plain English husbandman" indicates, he was trying, in his own way, to define a new category of natural knowledge. The appeal, however, was also specifically national, separating English custom and present practice from the classical rule, as well as from other "outlandish" or foreign models. Like the poets Samuel Daniel and Gabriel Harvey, who had argued for English poetry that "all our understandings are not to be built by the square of Greece and Italie," men such as Markham wanted to write English gardening advice for Englishmen, whether husbandmen or gentlemen.[19]

For gardening writers, the "English experience" was local and na-

---

[16] See the biography of Markham by F. N. L. Poynter, in *A Bibliography of Gervase Markham, 1568?–1637* (Oxford: Oxford Bibliographical Society, 1962), pp. 1–32.

[17] Markham, *English Husbandman,* epistle dedicatory.

[18] *Vives: On Education: A Translation of the De Tradendis Disciplinis of Juan Luis Vives,* trans. Foster Watson (Cambridge: Cambridge University Press, 1913), pp. 169–70.

[19] Samuel Daniel, "A Defence of Ryme," in *Poems and A Defence of Ryme,* ed. Arthur Colby Sprague (Chicago: University of Chicago Press, 1965), p. 139. For the argument in English poetics about the vernacular versus classical models, and how that debate might be correlated with attention to locality, see Richard Helgerson, *Forms of Nationhood: The Elizabethan Writing of England* (Chicago: University of Chicago Press, 1992), chaps. 1 and 3. While I would argue that the parallels are not as strict as Helgerson constructs them, I am much indebted to his discussion of the politics of "localism" in early modern England.

tional. After its beginnings in the late medieval period, when herbalists inserted descriptions of local plants in classical manuscripts and renamed well-known herbs, the horticultural vernacular movement gained momentum in the sixteenth century.[20] William Turner wrote his herbals in English about native plants so that they would be useful for English physicians.[21] In his preface to *The Names of Herbes* (1548), he neatly delineated the connection between writing in the vernacular, describing English flora, and experiencing an English place. In his preface he told the reader that having

> axed the advise of Phisicianes in thys matter [of whether to write in Latin or in English], their advise was that I shoulde cease from settynge out of this boke in latin tyll I had sene those places of Englande, wherein is moste plentie of herbes, that I might in my herbal declare to the greate honoure of our countre what numbre of sovereine and strang herbes were in Englande that were not in other nations, whose counsell I have folowed deferryng to set out my herbal in latin, tyl I have sene the west contrey, which I never sawe yet in al my lyfe, which countrey of al places of England, as I heare say is moste richly replenished wyth al kindes of straunge and wonderfull workes and giftes of nature, as are stones, herbes, fishes and metalles.[22]

This passage celebrates the uniqueness of the "sovereine and strang" botanical riches of England, and most of all those of the West country.

The natural history practiced in horticultural books and herbals thus depicted England in its particulars. In his *English Husbandman*, Markham took care to detail England's types of soil by county and to specify how they should be treated differently. If your soil is generally

[20] See A. G. Morton, *History of Botanical Science: An Account of the Development of Botany from Ancient Times to the Present Day* (London: Academic Press, 1981), pp. 96–98, 118; for example, see Otto Brunfels's *Herbarum vivae eicones* (Strasburg, 1530–36), which was notable for its illustrations drawn from life.

[21] On Turner, see Frank J. Anderson, *An Illustrated History of the Herbals* (New York: Columbia University Press, 1977), p. 152: "Over 200 species native to England are described in Turner's pages, and some of them were first named by him. . . . Turner was well aware that the local northern floras did not agree with those written about by Dioscorides, Galen, and Pliny, and that the British flora was often distinct from the Continental floras."

[22] William Turner, *The Names of Herbes in Greke, Latin, Englishe, Duche & Frenche wyth the commune names that Herbaries and Apotecaries use* (London, 1548; rpt., London: The English Dialect Society no. 34, 1888), sig. a2r.

of good condition, he wrote, "in this case it is best to lay your lands flat and levell, without ridges or furrowes, as is done in many parts of Cambridge-shire, some parts of Essex, and some parts of Hartford-shire"; if it is somewhat wet, "then you shall lay your lands large and high, with high ridges and deep furrows, as generally you see in Lincolne-shire, Nottingham-shire, Huntington-shire, and most of the middle shires in England"; but if it is very wet and heavy, then "you shall lay your land in little stiches, that is to say, not above three or foure furrowes at the most together, as is generally seene in Middle-sexe, Hartford-shire, Kent and Surrey."[23] Similarly, amidst his rules for ordering the orchard in his *New Orchard and Garden,* William Lawson described the planting of fruit trees in hedges in Worcestershire[24] and told the tale of a giant toppled oak in Brooham Park.[25] In his *Surveior's Dialogue* John Norden always took local considerations into account: "For the first, namely your low and spungie grounds, trenched, is good for hoppes, as Essex, and Surrey, and other places do find to their profit. The hot and sandy, (omitting graine), is good for Carret roots, a beneficial fruit, as at Oxford, Ispwich, and many sea townes in Suf-folke."[26]

This habit of gardening books had its closest analogues in chorog-raphy and topography, genres of writing that focused, in Richard Helgerson's words, on "places" and their differences.[27] Gardening books and chorographies relied a great deal on direct study, and choro-graphic descriptions of husbandry in different shires sound much like the contemporary garden books. In Richard Carew's *Survey of Corn-wall,* we not only hear about the nature of the Cornish soil, but we also are told how the Cornishmen till it.[28] William Lambarde likewise opened his *Perambulation of Kent* with praise of its air, soil, and typical

---

[23] Markham, *English Husbandman,* "a former part," sig. e2v.

[24] William Lawson, *New Orchard and Garden* (London, 1618; rpt., New York, Gar-land, 1982), p. 10.

[25] Ibid., p. 42.

[26] John Norden, *The Surveiors Dialogue* (London, 1610), p. 168.

[27] See Helgerson, *Forms of Nationhood,* chap. 3. See Barbara Shapiro, *Probability and Certainty in Seventeenth-Century England* (Ithaca: Cornell University Press, 1983), pp. 128–30, on chorographic and topographical literature that "slid back and forth be-tween natural history, chorography, history, and simple description without any sense that these subject matters should not be mixed together" (p. 130). On chorography, see also Swann, *Curiosities and Texts,* chap. 3.

[28] Richard Carew, *The Survey of Cornwall,* in *Richard Carew of Anthony: The Survey of Cornwall, &c.,* ed. F. E. Halliday (London: Andrew Melrose, 1953), pp. 86 and 102.

produce. Michael Drayton's *Poly-Olbion*, too, mentions the "sundry varying soyles" as the very first of Britain's wonders.[29] Drayton's poet then imagines his Muse taking flight over the English countryside, surveying its riches: she

> Now, in the finnie Heaths, then in the Champains roves;
> Now, measures out this Plaine; and then survayes those groves;
> The batfull pastures fenc't, and most with quickset mound,
> The sundry sorts of soyle, diversitie of ground;
> Where Plow-men cleanse the Earth of rubbish, weed, and filth,
> And give the fallow land their seasons and their tylth:
> Where, best for breeding horse; where cattell fitst to keepe;
> Which good for bearing Corne; which pasturing for sheepe:
> The leane and hungry earth, the fat and marly mold,
> Where sands be alwaies hot, and where the clayes be cold;
> With plentie where they waste, some others toucht with want:
> Heere set, and there they sowe; here proine, and there they plant.[30]

Drayton's Muse sounds as if she is preparing to write a gardening book, as much as a poem of Britain, in her careful consideration of the land's fitness and its agricultural traditions.

At other parts Drayton's *Poly-Olbion* converges even more narrowly on local herbs and flowers. In the section on Warwickshire, Drayton depicted the forests inhabited by a hermit who collects local herbs, including fumitory, eye-bright, vervain, hore-hound, mugwort, and dill. The speaker comments on his own list that "of these most helpfull hearbs yet tell we but a few, / To those unnumbered sorts of Simples here that grew. / Which justly to set downe, even Dodon short doth fall; / Nor skillfull Gerard yet, shall ever find them all."[31] The marriage of the rivers Thames and Isis serves as a catalogue of local cultivated and wild flowers: the bridegroom Isis is decked in flowers "only such as sprong / From the replenisht Meads, and fruitfull Pastures

---

[29] Michael Drayton, *Poly-Olbion*, in *The Works of Michael Drayton: Tercentenary Edition*, vol. 4, ed. J. William Hebel (Oxford: Basil Blackwell, 1961), p. 1 (song 1, ll. 1–2: "Of Albions glorious Ile the Wonders whilst I write, / The sundry varying soyles, the pleasures infinite").

[30] Ibid., p. 57. For other relevant texts from *Poly-Olbion*, see the discussion of the production of pear trees and perry in Worcestershire (p. 296); the description of the meal in Peryvale, in Middlesex (p. 319); and an account of English produce (p. 410).

[31] Ibid., pp. 280–81.

neere," that is, with the lily, daffodil, cowslip, oxslip, columbine, eglantine rose, lady-smock, crow and clover flowers, daisy, darnell flower, and blue bottle; in contrast, the bride, the Thames, is decked in "flowers of gardens," among which are found the red and white rose, the crown imperial, the carnation and pink, the purple violet, pansy, marigold, bachelor's button, sweet william, campion, lavender, rosemary, bay, and marjoram.[32] This passage records not only a sense of place in its flowers, but also a distinction between the flowers of the English garden and the wild flowers similar to that which appears in many seventeenth-century gardening books.

This kind of focus on the local and vernacular implied a very different source of knowledge than classical literature. Not only would these writers want to see for themselves, but they would also rely on local informants to supplement or even supplant the information to be gained from books. As Keith Thomas tells the story, "It is not surprising . . . that natural history at first depended for its progress on absorbing much popular lore. . . . Sir Joseph Banks, the future President of the Royal Society, as a schoolboy paid herb-women to teach him the names of flowers. Physicians and apothecaries had long depended for their supplies upon such persons, what William Turner called 'the old wives that gather herbs.'"[33] However, writers were also anxious about the reliability of such sources.[34] Praise of rural experience might impress the yeoman farmer, but it might mean something else when the better sort came to garden. Further, what might in other contexts be considered another sign of England's great diversity—the variety of English regional names for plants and their culture—also came to be considered a liability in the pursuit of science.[35] At the end of the seventeenth century, by all accounts, rural knowledge of natural history was tarnished. When Bacon cheerfully admitted his dependence on the "low and vulgar" mechanical arts, while he dismissed antiquities, "citations or testimonies of authors" together with "all superstitious stories" and "old wives' fables," he marked a middle point in the process of change. By the end of the century, it had become necessary

---

[32] Ibid., p. 307.

[33] Thomas, *Man and the Natural World*, pp. 73–74.

[34] As Thomas puts it, "popular knowledge was soon eclipsed by the more thoroughgoing inquiries of the scientists, whose viewpoint was not narrowly utilitarian and who rapidly became disillusioned to discover that there were limits to rural curiosity" (ibid., p. 74).

[35] Ibid., pp. 83–84.

to appear to reject local "stories" and "fables" in favor of the "chastity and brevity" of scientific truth.[36]

Fancies in Nature

For Francis Bacon, who influenced so many of the seventeenth century's men of practical science, the work of the imagination could not be entirely separated from the technologies of knowledge. Bacon's interest lay in the instances where art and nature intersect, or in "nature under constraint and vexed; that is to say, when by art and the hand of man she is forced out of her natural state, and squeezed and molded."[37] He deplored the error of "considering art as merely an assistant to nature, having the power indeed to finish what nature has begun, to correct her when lapsing into error, or to set her free when in bondage, but by no means to change, transmute or fundamentally alter nature"; he had hopes, indeed, that art could do what Puttenham's imaginative gardener might accomplish in transforming nature. Bacon insisted that "the artificial does not differ from the natural in form or essence, but only in the efficient; in that man has no power over nature except that of motion; he can put natural bodies together, and he can separate them; and therefore that wherever the case admits of the uniting or disuniting of natural bodies . . . man can do everything."[38] In this praise of art, which echoes Della Porta's celebration of "copulative" natural magic, these words suggest Bacon's uneasiness about the power balance between art and nature; in effect he blurs the distinctions between them, where art can do all and nothing with nature.[39]

[36] Bacon, *Works*, 4:254–55. On "weeding" natural history of "fables, antiquities, quotations, idle controversies, philology and ornaments," see p. 299.

[37] Ibid., p. 29. On the value of the vexations of art, see also p. 257; here he sets out more directly the three branches of natural history, as of nature "free," "perverse" (e.g., monsters), and "constrained and moulded by art and human ministry" (p. 253). On Bacon on art and nature, see Horst Bredekamp, *The Lure of Antiquity and the Cult of the Machine: The Kunstkammer and the Evolution of Nature, Art, and Technology*, trans. Allison Brown (Princeton: Markus Wiener, 1995), chap. 4.

[38] Bacon, *Works*, 4:294–95.

[39] See Michèle Le Doeuff, "Man and Nature in the Gardens of Science," in *Francis Bacon's Legacy of Texts: "The Art of Discovery Grows with Discovery,"* ed. William A. Sessions (New York: AMS, 1990). Le Doeuff argues that we misread Bacon if we see him as "the philosopher of a triumphant domination of man over nature": rather, her view is that "Bacon challenges both the minimalist idea that the power of art is restricted to

But a similar slippage occurs in Bacon's differentiating history—including natural history—from "poesy." History, *The Advancement of Learning* states, is related to memory, and "is properly concerned with individuals"; poesy "is also concerned with individuals . . . with this difference, that it commonly exceeds the measure of nature, joining at pleasure things which in nature would never have come together, and introducing things which in nature would never have come to pass. . . . This is the work of Imagination."[40] The terms of this passage effectively link the experimental practices—"uniting and disuniting bodies"—that Bacon outlined in the *Great Instauration* and advocated in *Sylva Sylvarum* with the effect of the imagination or "poesy." The *Sylva Sylvarum*, Bacon's own book of secrets, repeatedly advises its reader how "to bring things together," and it does not deny the possibility of "the transmutation of plants one into another . . . certainly it is a thing of difficulty, and requireth deep search into nature; but seeing there appear some manifest instances of it, the opinion of impossibility is to be rejected, and the means thereof to be found out."[41] Like the work of so many men before him and Puttenham's poetic gardener, Bacon's experiments in horticulture explored ways of making things that would never have come to pass in nature, including the "curiosities" of having several fruits upon one tree, "fruits of divers shapes and figures," "inscriptions or engravings in fruits or trees," or changing the hue and form of flowers.[42]

Robert Ellis acknowledges with some embarrassment in his preface to the *Sylva Sylvarum* that, even while Bacon may have boasted of the rigor of his new science, he was really depending on Della Porta: "If we did not know the channel through which his information is derived, we might give him credit for much curious research."[43] In his preface to the edition of *Sylva* published a year after Bacon's death in 1627, William Rawley cautiously explained how Bacon's practice

---

the perfecting of that which nature has already almost completed on her own, *and* the maximalist idea of art's discretionary power of transfiguration" (pp. 122–23). In this context, gardening is "that supreme craft which consists in denaturing things with nature's assistance" (p. 126).

[40] Bacon, *Works*, 4:292.

[41] Ibid., 2:507.

[42] Ibid., 2:501–3. See Le Doueff, "Man and Nature," pp. 132–34, on *Sylva Sylvarum*.

[43] Bacon, *Works*, 2:328. See William Eamon, *Science and the Secrets of Nature: Books of Secrets in Medieval and Early Modern Culture* (Princeton: Princeton University Press, 1994), pp. 285–91 on Bacon's attitude toward the "books of secrets" and natural magic.

might differ from Della Porta's. He first rather anxiously defended the "baseness" and "vulgarness" of the experiments laid out in *Sylva:*

> And as for the baseness of many of the experiments; as long as they be God's works, they are honorable enough. And for the vulgarness of them, true axioms must be drawn from plain experience and not from doubtful; and his lordship's course is to make wonders plain, and not plain things wonders; and that experience likewise must be broken and grinded, and not whole, or as it groweth. And for use; his lordship hath often in his mouth the two kinds of experiments, *experimenta fructifera* and *experimenta lucifera:* experiments of Use and experiments of Light: and he reporteth himself, whether he were not a strange man, that should think that light hath no use, because it hath no matter.

The passage expresses concern about "use" or profit and its relationship to "light" (knowledge or truth), and with this doubts about the vulgarity of *Sylva*'s experiments, which should not contaminate their "honor." But, Rawley argued, Bacon's works surely differed from those of the books of secrets and base gardening manuals, because "his lordship thought good also to add unto many of the experiments themselves some gloss of the causes" meant to produce axioms.[44] In Bacon's *Sylva* a rhetoric of "experiment" designed to produce light through the extraction of natural axioms is thus superimposed on the stratum of Della Porta's ambitious *Natural Magic* and its own rhetoric of "experience."

While Bacon stole from Della Porta, he was concerned to mark some distance from him. He began the section "touching curiosities about fruits and plants" by indicating his distaste for "impostures and curiosities," yet intimating that they can produce something—if not profit, then knowledge.[45] His accounts of these curiosities demonstrate his simultaneous attraction to such "wonders" and his suspicion of them as fantasies. He does seem to have been loath to abandon the possibilities and the profit that might be gained. When he introduced the section on "making herbs and fruits medicinable," at first he demurred once again that these recipes were really mere "curiosities," but then he added, "lest our incredulity may prejudice any profitable

---

[44] Bacon, *Works*, 2:336.
[45] Ibid., 2:501.

operations in this kind (especially since many of the ancients have set them down) we think good briefly to propound the four means which they have devised of making plants medicinable" (he then went on to cite liberally from book 3, chapter 20, of *Natural Magic*).[46]

Yet, when it came to drawing out the "causes" and the axioms, Bacon had to then label parts of the older literature "imaginative." For example, where he borrowed from Della Porta on grafting, he drew a line at the idea that you can manipulate the time of fruiting by grafting:

> Men have entertained a conceit that sheweth prettily; namely, that if you graft a late-coming fruit upon a stock of a fruit-tree that cometh early, the graft will bear fruit early; as a peach upon a cherry; and contrariwise, if an early-coming fruit upon a stock of a fruit-tree that cometh late, the graft will bear fruit late; as a cherry upon a peach. But these are but imaginations, and untrue. The cause is, for that the scion over-ruleth the stock quite, and the stock is but passive only, and giveth aliment, but no motion, to the graft.[47]

Implicitly, Bacon's experimental "curiosity" was meant to differ somehow from other men's "fancies" of manipulating nature. The rhetoric implies that while their fancies were mere effects of the mind, reporting what might only be possible in nature, his "curiosity" was grounded in an analysis of natural processes and causality. Like the Baconian type of the civil historian, who distilled the order of men's lives by interpreting the data of human experience,[48] the Baconian natural historian and experimentalist was to seek the axiom of the generation of plants, which would ground invention.[49]

Bacon's curious scientist thus oddly resembles not only Puttenham's gardener but also Philip Sidney's poet, who "disdaining to be tied to

---

[46] Ibid., 2:499.

[47] Ibid., 2:480, referring to Della Porta, *Natural Magic*, book 3, chaps. 9–10.

[48] For Bacon, invention also served for the writing of civil history. As Stuart Clark puts it, "in reducing all sciences to natural science, Bacon in effect transformed all history into natural history" (Stuart Clark, "Bacon's *Henrie VII*: A Case-Study in the Science of Man," *History and Theory* 13 [1974]: 97–118; p. 104).

[49] See Eamon on the efforts of the member of the Royal Society to turn experiments from "wonders" to disciplined demonstrations so that "as one of the fellows put it, 'an Artist or Experimenter, is not to be taken for a maker of gimbals, nor an observer of Nature for a wonder-monger'" (*Science and the Secrets of Nature*, p. 338).

any such subjection [to nature], lifted up with the vigour of his own invention, doth grow in effect another nature, in making things either better than nature bringeth forth, or, quite anew, forms such as never were in nature, as the Heroes, Demigods, Cyclops, Chimeras, Furies, and such like: so as he goeth hand in hand with nature, not enclosed within the narrow warrant of her gifts, but freely ranging only within the zodiac of his own wit."[50] It may seem a long way from Sidney's demiurge poet to Bacon—or natural magic—but both were made possible by and contributed to a culture that dreamed that the pleasures of the imagination could exceed the mundane attractions of the given world.

Sidney and Bacon may have wanted to oppose imagination and art to nature and history, but their analogies between poetry and horticulture inevitably betrayed them. In Renaissance poetics, the notion that expresses the coalescence of nature and art they sought is "invention," which uses reason to construct images never thought before but preexisting in nature. Inventions are found, discovered rather than created, and at the same time they are new.[51] While invention was a rhetorical term, understood as "a fabrication" or "fiction," it also had a mechanical application, signifying "something devised or produced by original contrivance . . . an instrument, an art, etc., originated by the ingenuity of some person, and previously unknown" (Oxford English Dictionary). The equivalent in Bacon's natural history was experimentation that produces a new nature through "vexation," or the altering of its conditions. Invention was thus as important to natural history as it was to poetry: both were to make something new of what was always there.

Who Tells the Truth?

In the later seventeenth century, Bacon's successors more severely restricted the imagination, when invention was linked with neither the

[50] Philip Sidney, A Defense of Poetry, ed. Jan Van Dorsten (Oxford: Oxford University Press, 1966), pp. 23–24. See Edward William Tayler, Nature and Art in Renaissance Literature (New York: Columbia University Press, 1964), on the parallels between poetics and gardening literature.

[51] See Grahame Castor, Pléiade Poetics: A Study in Sixteenth-Century Thought and Terminology (Cambridge: Cambridge University Press, 1964), on the subject of invention.

poet's golden world nor the experimentalist's vexed nature, but rather with lies, superstition, and vanity. Depending on the context, the object of attack might be the follies of old books or pedants, the boasts of "vulgar" writers, or the much-despised "old wives' tales." Paralleling neoclassical poetic treatises, which opposed the purified vernacular of the neoclassical but native poet to the crude language of the folk,[52] the new horticulturalists rejected both scholars and the "mechanicals" who wrote of transforming nature, and allied themselves instead with those who "wore virtuosity as a badge of honor that distinguished [them] from the scholastic 'pedant' and from the 'vulgar sort.'"[53] The rhetoric of experience so important to men like Gervase Markham gave way to the "experimental" methods of a purportedly disinterested science.[54]

But these later writers were certainly not the first to claim to have submitted horticultural advice to trial. Many of the sixteenth- and early seventeenth-century secrets books mark their advice as "proven." Even when the secrets were marvelous, readers had to believe, at least a little, that these marvels could be performed. So secrets often bore a stamp of empirical proof with the tag line of "a thing proved." A particularly distasteful recipe in Thomas Lupton's *A Thousand Notable Things of Sundry Sorts* directs that "if one use to rubbe chapped or rough lippes, with the sweat behind their eares, it will make them fine, smothe, and well culloured: a thing proved."[55] In Hugh Platt's *Floraes Paradise* the tag line is often "Probatum," followed by the name of the secret's source, where *probatum* carries the connotation of both experience and proof: a secret on sowing radishes is followed by *"Probatum per Tomkins the gardiner,"* and one on dusting corn with lime is said to come "per my coosen Matthew of Wales."[56] Even though they were usually just stealing from other books, the writers and compilers of these secrets felt compelled to insist that their knowledge came from practice rather than ancient philosophy or hermetic books. It was all

[52] See, for example, Joachim Du Bellay, *La deffence et illustration de la langue francoyse* (1549), ed. Henri Chamard (Paris: Marcel Didier, 1948), pp. 108–9.

[53] Eamon, *Science and the Secrets of Nature*, p. 301.

[54] For a discussion of distinctions in notions of empiricism, and in the links between empiricism and theory, see Frederick O. Waage, "Touching the Compass: Empiricism in Popular Scientific Writing of Bacon's Time," *Huntington Library Quarterly* 41 (1978): 201–16.

[55] Thomas Lupton, *A Thousand Notable Things of Sundry Sortes* (London, 1590), p. 2.

[56] Hugh Platt, *Floraes Paradise* (London, 1608), p. 86.

the more important since most of these writers had no academic background, and they were thus seeking a rhetoric and a reason to authorize their own rules.[57]

As early as the late sixteenth century, some garden writers did begin to doubt the reliability of the more fantastic recipes. Chapter 2 described the ways in which the secrets books indeed often advertised the entertainment value of their "inventions" and "conceits," even when they appealed to the reader's practical side. A secret writer's boast of his invention as a "thing proved" was inevitably compromised by the implication of fiction that the term invention itself carried. The 1595 edition of *The Booke of Secretes of Albertus Magnus* puts it pretty frankly: "Use this book for thy recreation (as thou are wont to use the book of Fortune) for assuredly there is nothing herein promised but to further thy delight."[58] By the 1590s, we find Hugh Platt himself protesting that *his* recipes are based on "true" experiments, unlike those found in other secrets books. In *The Jewell House of Art and Nature* he criticized what he calls the "magical crew" of Albertus Magnus, Della Porta, and others for not always telling the truth, and for composing "whole Volumes by imagination only, in their private studies."[59] In *Floraes Paradise* he promised his reader that in this book he or she would find only his "laborious collections, not written at adventure, or by an imaginary conceit in a Schollers private Studie, but wrung out of the earth, by the painfull hand of experience."[60]

When John Parkinson reacted vehemently in his *Paradisi in Sole* against earlier, unnamed gardeners' assertions about transforming plants, he much more strongly accused them of arrogance and lying. In describing the earlier confident reports of success in making single flowers double, he denied that such reports were "of any more worth than an old Wives' tale, both nature, reason, and experience, all contesting against such an idle fancy, let men make what ostentation they please." He mocked any claims that gardeners made to achieve such results, deploring "the wonderfull desire that many have to see faire, double, and sweete flowers, [which] hath transported them beyond both reason and nature, feigning and boasting often of what they

---

[57] Eamon, *Science and the Secrets of Nature*, p. 259.

[58] *The Booke of Secrets of Albertus Magnus* (London, 1585), "to the reader."

[59] Hugh Platt, *The Jewell House of Art and Nature* (London, 1594), preface.

[60] Platt, *Floraes Paradise*, preface to the reader. See also Eamon, *Science and the Secrets of Nature*, pp. 311–14.

would have, as if they had it." He accused them of spreading "false tales and reports": some of these errors may be "ancient, and continued long by tradition, and others are of later invention: and therefore the more to be condemned, that men of wit and judgement in these dayes should expose themselves in their writings, to be rather laughed at, then believed for such idle tales." Parkinson considered himself brave in countering these tales and expected to "undergo many calumnies," but he still hoped to "by reason perswade many in the truth."[61] Most important, Parkinson insisted that he knew these stories to be false from "mine own experience in the matter." When he asked if anyone could prove their claims, "I never could finde any one, that could assuredly resolve me, that he knew certainly any such thing to be done: all that they could say was but report." When planting at the change of moon or infusing colors or scents come "to the triall, they all vanish away like smoake." All these "are mere idle tales & fancies, without all reason or truth, or shadow of reason or truth."[62]

When Parkinson condemned what he saw as the false tales of the earlier horticulturalists, and when he offered to tell the "truth" of his own experience, his contention expressed his own conservative view of the natural world, which constructed a nature fixed in its ranks, and where no "hetereogeneal" things could be mixed together (see chapter 5). Parkinson's anger against the writers' "feigning and boasting" combined a slight against their social presumption with the attack against their veracity. The representation of his predecessors' reports as "idle" fancies undercut both their claims of practice and their masculine rhetoric of instruction, when their reports became no better than the old wives' tales that Bacon had rejected in favor of technical experience.

In criticizing the earlier writers' art in telling their story of nature, Bacon and Parkinson foreshadowed the direction taken by garden writers of the later seventeenth century, such as Stephen Blake, Robert Sharrock, and Samuel Gilbert, who all turned against their forebears. They professed (in Gilbert's words) that they were now "able to Judge what was Legendary, and impos'd falsities on the belief of the ignorant, and what was truth from my own experience."[63] Either directly

---

[61] Parkinson, *Paradisi in Sole*, pp. 21–22.
[62] Ibid., pp. 23–24.
[63] Samuel Gilbert, *The Florist's Vade-Mecum* (London, 1682), epistle to the reader.

or indirectly, all three were influenced by the style and practice of the "new science," as advocated both by the Hartlib circle and later by the Royal Society in their professed campaigns to "separate the knowledge of Nature, from the colours of Rhetorick, the devices of Fancy, and the delightful deceit of Fables."[64] Thomas Sprat described the members of the Royal Society as occupied with the "plainest" things as well as marvels. Too much focus on "curiosities," he judged, infects "the mind, and mak[es] it averse from the true Natural Philosophy: It is like Romances, in respect of True History; which, by multiplying varieties of extraordinary Events and surprizing circumstances, make that seem dull, and tasteless."[65] As Michael McKeon has reminded us, one should, of course, be suspicious of the "easy simplicity" of such oppositions between old romances and true histories of nature. In the eyes of their contemporaries, the curious works of the Royal Society might too have seemed like marvels, and Henry Stubbe ridiculed the new scientists as "novellists."[66] Sprat himself worried that what he related of the Society's work might sound more like "Romances, instead of solid Histories of Nature."[67] It was then all the more important for these writers to insist upon their distance from the "fantasies" of their predecessors.

In 1664, in his *Compleat Gardeners Practice, Directing the Exact Way of Gardening,* like Parkinson, Stephen Blake reported that he had consulted the works of earlier writers and found them deficient:

> The reason why I undertook this Work is this; I have made diligent enquiry after such Books of such Authors as might help me in my Practice, and I could find very few, and for those that are they did not answer my desires, because they only treated of the use and vertue of Herbs, the beauty, variety and preheminence of Flowers, and the goodness and profit of Fruit-Trees; but they have written little or nothing as to the practical part of the advancement of nature and growth of Flowers, and Trees; and for that which is written, seems to me, and other Men which have experience, as fancies, dreams, and conceits which might come into their heads as they were sitting in their Studies.[68]

[64] Sprat, *History*, pp. 61–62.
[65] Ibid., pp. 90–91.
[66] Michael McKeon, *The Origins of the English Novel, 1600–1740* (Baltimore: Johns Hopkins University Press, 1988), pp. 69–71.
[67] Sprat, *History*, p. 214.
[68] Stephen Blake, *The Compleat Gardeners Practice, Directing the Exact Way of Gardening* (London, 1664), epistle dedicatory.

In this judgment, he seems to reject both herbals and the old secrets books of Albertus Magnus or Della Porta as "uncreditable as the stories of Robin Hood."[69] He considered in turn each of the recipes that earlier writers gave to create new colors, scents, and forms, and rejected them.[70] Anticipating readers' complaints that he himself gave no recipes for such exotic practices, Blake retorted "that these intercisions and supplies, are but conceits took up upon trust, and never made good by practice, and therefore I shall not dispense with the time to answer them in particular, and swell up my Book about such uncertain, vain, and needlesse curiosities which are unpractical, and that is more, they were never affected, and so I wave the Discourse."[71]

Remarkable in Blake's criticism is his silence about men like Hill, Markham, Platt, and Lawson, who also had claimed to write out of "experience," even when they merely passed on some of the sort of secrets that you might find in Magnus, Della Porta, or even Pliny. Blake boasted that "mine is the Gardeners practicall part, which hath never been written by any."[72] His blindness cannot be explained by the books' having disappeared after the Restoration: William Lawson's *New Orchard and Garden* was reprinted throughout the Interregnum and again in 1660 and 1665; Hugh Platt's *Garden of Eden* (a retitled and repackaged *Floraes Paradise*) reappeared in 1660; and Markham's *Way to Get Wealth* (a compendium of several works, including Lawson's *New Orchard*) was also published in 1660.[73] Either Blake *chose* to ignore them or he did not recognize them as practical works because of what he saw as their irrational errors.[74]

69 Ibid., p. 71.
70 See for example, ibid., p. 23, on the altering of scent.
71 Ibid., p. 65.
72 Ibid., epistle to the reader.
73 As Michael Leslie notes, one finds that after the Restoration, with the disgrace of Hartlib, "with him fell a whole range of husbandry and horticultural authors, whose works suddenly ceased to be reprinted," including Hartlib's own works and those of Blith and Weston, while "Gervase Markham, whose star had waned in the 1640s and 1650s, returned to the bookseller shelves as though nothing had happened" (Michael Leslie, "'Bringing Ingenuity into Fashion': The 'Elysium Britannicum' and the Reformation of Husbandry," in *John Evelyn's "Elysium Britannicum" and European Gardening*, ed. Therese O'Malley and Joachim Wolschke-Bulmahn [Washington, D.C.: Dumbarton Oaks, 1998], pp. 139–40).
74 He described these errors as failures of reason whereby "Noblemen are deprived of their pleasure, their minds are discontented and the place is disgraced, if in propagating of Plants they will follow old errors, by reason of the dullness of their brains and stubbornness of their wills, which will not let reason work, to know the times and

While we cannot identify Blake's reading or his intellectual circles, his complaints closely resemble those of Robert Sharrock, who five years earlier wrote the first version of his *History of the Propagation and Improvement of Vegetables*, containing a similar blanket condemnation of all previous work on plants (he redid the work in 1672, adding many new experiments). Sharrock himself was a member of Wilkins and Boyle's Oxford experimental science group and had been influenced by the agricultural reforms advocated by the Hartlib circle in the 1650s. As Webster comments, it was the Hartlib group who first found fault with earlier agricultural writing and thought it "was necessary to replace the traditional compilations of rules of doubtful authenticity and ambiguous phraseology, by systematic guides to the specialist areas of husbandry, couched in 'plaine sound Experimental terms.'"[75] Sharrock wrote in his dedication to Boyle that, when looking at all extant books on the subject, all he found was "a multitude of monstrous untruths, and prodigies of lies, in both Latine and English old and new writers, worse in their kind then the stories in Sir John Mandevel's Travels or in the History of Fryer Bacon and his man Miles; or else what may be more, ridiculously removed not only from truth, but from any semblance therof," thus echoing his colleagues' criticism of both the follies of an earlier age and the dreams of a new one.

In his preface to the reader Sharrock drew on Bacon's critique of the "deficients of Natural History" to lambaste their "neglects and rejection of experiments," and he proceeded to condemn every sort of previous garden writer, educated or unlearned, elevated or common:

> some prove altogether useless; as being so full of their natural Magick and Romantic stories, that we know no more what to credit in those relations, in the Natural, then what in civil history we may believe of King Arthur, Guy of Warwick in ours; or of Hector and Priam in the Trojan story: Others elevated in their fancies, write in a Language of their own, addressing their Discourse to the Sons of Art, speaking rather to amuse, than instruct, and prove like blazing Stars, that distract many, and direct few. Many of those who would write for Universal Instruction, either

---

the seasons, the difference in Climates, the moisture, the operations of the Earth, and the vast difference in the vertue of Plants" (Blake, *Compleat Gardeners Practice*, epistle dedicatory).

[75] Charles Webster, *The Great Instauration: Science, Medicine, and Reform, 1626–1660* (New York: Holmes and Meier, 1976), p. 140.

know the things that might make up the matter of their History, but want the skill to draw up such an Inventory, as my Lord Verulam requires, to common Tradesmen and Artisans, or else indeed are learned enough to draw up the writing, but want the knowledge of most of the particulars therein to be ingrost; which is commonly the cause of such of us as have pretensions to Scholarship.[76]

Sharrock targeted here a manifold set of antagonists: ancient and medieval scholars (writing in both Latin and English); books of "natural magick" (with a dig at Della Porta); purveyors of secrets (who wrote to amuse or distract); insufficiently educated men of experience; and insufficiently experienced scholastic philosophers. He did not even believe, he confessed, what he had read in recent books on the subject that appeared to be based on experience, for he complained that he "found in the Shops Authors newly set forth (I hope against their own wills) who seriously professed to have made a select choice of experiments of this nature, and to report nothing, but what from observation and experience they have certainly found true; yet deserving not to have the credit of Wecker and Porta." (In the copy of the 1672 edition I consulted, which was owned by a John Harwood, a handwritten marginal note comments here "Digby," probably referring to Sir Kenelm Digby's "philosophical" *Discourse concerning the Vegetation of Plants,* which had been published in 1661.)[77] While Sharrock represented his own project as based on experience, it was meant to differ from both the former generations' "undigested" reports and the new generation's "curious" speculations: his own are supposed to be "common and devoid of curiosity." In the same copy, the marginal annotator apparently understood the lesson, for he or she wrote next to Sharrock's observation that lilies and roses no longer rise without seed, the correction "Not so," for, on the contrary, "Lilies and Roses still do in the hotter climates."[78] The book itself thus stands as a record of "observation," when the values of practice and experience were thus reappropriated for a new generation of gardeners.

At the same time that they claimed the authority of experience, the post-Restoration garden writers also saw themselves as introducing

[76] Robert Sharrock, *The History of the Propagation and Improvement of Vegetables by the Concurrence of Art and Nature* (2d edition, Oxford, 1672), epistle dedicatory, and p. 2.
[77] Ibid., epistle dedicatory.
[78] Ibid., p. 5.

into garden writing the plain style that was meant to be the distinct voice of the new science. Long forgotten, it appears, were the early English gardening and husbandry books, which in their effort to reach readers ranging from husbandman to queen had also promised to offer their advice in simple terms. In his book on growing hops, Reynolde Scot had said that he wanted "to write plainly to playne men of the Countrie,"[79] and Leonard Mascall's book on cattle was to be "plainely and perfectly set forth, as well to bee understood of the unlearned husbandman, as of the gentle learned man."[80] In the epistle of *The English Husbandman* Gervase Markham proclaimed that, in these days, "nothing is happy or prosperous, but meere fashion and ostentation, a tedious fustian-tale at a great mans table, stuft with bigge words, with out sense, . . . yet not withstanding in this apostate age I have adventured to thrust into the world this booke, which nothing at all belongeth to the silken corner, but to the plaine russet honest Husbandman."[81]

Most notably Hugh Platt had mocked the European writers of secrets for writing figuratively and wrapping their recipes up in "clowdes of skill." And so he asked, in *The New and Admirable Arte of Setting of Corne*, of Della Porta's relation of a secret for soaking corn in wine: "And what if all this mysticall marriage between the God Bacchus and the Goddess Ceres . . . what I saie if all this great mysterie or Magistrie of nature, as Baptista Porta would have it to appeare, bee nothing else but a soaking of Corne in Wine . . . ? Might this not without the prophaning of Nature, or her sacred Maxime, beene safelie and without offence in playne termes delivered to the publike view of the world?"[82] In response, Platt proudly offered his own vernacular plain style, which he asserts gives immediate gratification, without the need for puzzling it out. He would cast his secrets, as he said in *The Jewell House of Art and Nature*, in "plain termes" into the open laps of the ladies.[83] We often think of the plain style as the voice of honesty and sincerity, conveyed in simple words, or in terms of the elegant brevity

[79] Reynolde Scot, *A Perfite Platforme of a Hoppe Garden* (London, 1574), preface to the reader.

[80] Leonard Mascall, *The First Book of Cattell* (London, 1587), preface to the reader. See McRae, *God Speed*, p. 145.

[81] Markham, *English Husbandman*, epistle to the reader.

[82] Hugh Platt, *The Newe and Admirable Arte of Setting of Corne* (London, 1601), preface.

[83] Platt, *Jewell House of Art and Nature*, p. 3.

of the "Attic style." But Platt's books construct a plain style for science in terms of accessibility and thus quick profit.

After the Restoration when Thomas Sprat wrote his *History of the Royal Society*, he celebrated what he saw as the members' success in separating natural knowledge from rhetoric, fancy, and fables. They are to be commended, he wrote, for their reform of extravagant language and their intention

> to reject all the amplifications, digressions, and swelling of style: to return back to the primitive purity, and shortness, when men deliver'd so many things, almost in an equal number of words. They have extracted from all their members a close, naked, natural way of speaking; positive expressions; clear senses; a native easiness: bringing all things as near the Mathematical plainness as they can, and preferring the language of Artizens, Countreymen and merchants, before that, of Wits and Scholars.[84]

Many scholars have commented upon this passage, noting its connections to the history of language reform and new economic values. For example, Mary Poovey sets it in the context of the enlisting of merchants in the cause of the new science,[85] while for Michael McKeon, this passage is to be read as defining a new style of natural history: "in Sprat's view the plain style of the new philosophy's 'records' is paralleled by the simplicity and humility of its recorders, a new breed of philosophers not 'skilled in all Divine and human things, but plain, diligent, and laborious observers: such, who, though they bring not much knowledge, yet bring hands and their eyes uncorrupted.'"[86] As William Eamon has pointed out, this pose of transparency was a bit insincere, since the members of the Society were hardly as eager to open up their own organization or reveal secrets as they might protest.[87] But it was important to the new rhetoric of fact that it was "plain" and the product of the "uncorrupted" hand and eye, qualities now attributed to the new gentleman scientist, who was neither "vulgar" nor a pedant.

So, just as he ignored the earlier books' rhetoric of experience in or-

---

[84] Ibid., p. 113.
[85] Mary Poovey, *A History of the Modern Fact: Problems of Knowledge in the Sciences of Wealth and Society* (Chicago: University of Chicago Press, 1998), pp. 118–19.
[86] McKeon, *Origins of the English Novel*, pp. 104–5.
[87] Eamon, *Science and the Secrets of Nature*, chap. 10.

der to promote his own experiments, Stephen Blake was happy to confess that he was "wanting in scholarship," to make the point that he was ready to replace such earlier horticultural "treatises as are so full of Oratory of words and so filled and varnished (as it were) with Quirks, Quiblets and Paradoxes, speaking little absolutely, but imaginations very obscure and promiscuously written and composed together, running far wide of the practice, and for the major part suspitious and incredulous." He would write instead for "the unlearned sort of men . . . this plain and extempory Work . . . , which was meerly drawn from the very practicall part, that it might redound to an extraordinary and publick profit."[88] Samuel Gilbert, too, professed that he had written in "plain English," avoiding "Bumbastick" words,[89] and Robert Sharrock argued that his plainness opened up to daylight the truth that had hitherto been obscured by the darkness of "alchemical" rhetoric:

> I intend my directions so plain, as if appointed for the instruction of
> some Artists rude and untaught Apprentice: and yet in the second, if not
> so homely, yet as easie and evident; being a little disgusted with any
> thing intended for the use of Philosophy, when overgarnished with
> Rhetorical Tropes, which like Flowers stuck in a Window for whatsoever
> intended (either cheat or ornament) certainly create a darkness in the
> place. Bebemenical, Paracelsian, and such Phrases as many Alchymists
> use, I must for the same reason avoid.[90]

Both Blake and Sharrock, thus, did not want to be seen as mere "scholars" (though Sharrock was a fellow of New College): as Blake puts it in his epistle dedicatory, he demurred that "to give you a description [of the work] in metaphorical expression I have not Scholarship enough, but I have confidence enough to speak and publish the truth of these experiments, which I have gathered, with a diligent Eye and a painfull Hand from all such Plants as are cultivated in Gardens now in England."[91] In the context of the intellectual reform movement of their time, of course, the rejection of "scholarship" suggested their distaste for scholastic philosophy. When these men said that they wrote

88 Blake, *Compleat Gardeners Practice*, preface to the reader.
89 Gilbert, *Florist's Vade-Mecum*, epistle to the reader.
90 Sharrock, *History of the Propagation*, p. 3.
91 Blake, *Compleat Gardeners Practice*, epistle dedicatory.

out of experience rather than book learning, and that they were pleased to write in a "homely" or "evident" style, they were not saying that they themselves were humble men. Rather, they wanted to send a signal that they were gentlemen;[92] writing as men of "free conscience" and free of desire for gain, they believed that they served others like them. Like the new gentleman who did not need to garden but worked there for pleasure and knowledge, these authors too implied that they did not need to write but published instead for the benefit of their countrymen.

By the beginning of the eighteenth century, Richard Bradley was far more willing to condemn directly the English garden writers who came before him, rather than aiming for the general target of "scholars" in their studies. Like everyone else, he attributed the need for his new work to the deficiencies of the old:

> Some of these Writers have bestowed their Pains in collecting from Antiquity and foreign Soils, as though they had perform'd great Matters by heaping together a load of Observations from Varro and Pliny, without carefully considering wherein their Experiments differ from the Genius of our Soils and Climates. Others have employ'd their Time in copying from our old English Systems, and these have generally transcrib'd one another without the least Acknowledgment of their thefts, or adding one single improvement to the Knowledge of their Fore-fathers: And indeed, how should it happen otherwise, when the undertakers of this subject have been covetous or illiterate Gardeners and Planters; some, that if they knew anything New or Curious, had not the Spirit to communicate their Notions; and some that jogged on in the old beaten Track, without any Ambition to excel their predecessors. We have now and then, it is true, a Gentleman studious and capable of obliging the World, free from the narrow Views of Self Interest, and employing his Hours for a more diffusive Benefit than the Culture of his own private Estate or Garden: an Evelyn, a Nourse, and a Laurence, have given us something equally New and Just, built on Experiment, upon the beneficial Subject of Planta-

[92] See also Stephen Switzer's dismissive comments on Platt's and Bacon's writing as "full of the old Philosophical Tenets, now exploded" (p. 49); in contrast, "The laborious works of Gerard and his Commentator Johnson, of Mr. Parkinson and Ray, deserve our utmost Tribute of Thanks; as likewise to Mr. Rea, the Author of *Flora, Ceres and Pomona*, the practical and plain Method in which he has deliver'd his Precepts, are admirable" (Stephen Switzer, *Ichnographia Rustica, or, The Nobleman, Gentleman, and Gardener's Recreation* [London, 1718; rpt., New York: Garland, 1982], p. 56).

tion. But what are these when compared with that useless number of unimproving authors?[93]

Bradley traced his own genealogy—whatever the obscurities of his background and training—to these latter gentlemen: public-spirited, disinterested, and free to cultivate their own gardens. Despite his own constant struggles for money and position and his collaborations with men like Thomas Fairchild, the story of gardening books that he chose to tell was one that started with Evelyn and Laurence. Like Stephen Switzer's history of gardening, Bradley's obscures the history of the old "practical" writers, who are called "covetous or illiterate Gardeners and Planters." For Bradley they were to be condemned, because they were "covetous": what they lacked, he thought, was intellectual ambition, or the proper type of curiosity. It is a shame that he could not in fact see that it was these men who had made his own work possible.

[93] Bradley, *New Improvements of Planting and Gardening,* preface.

Conclusion

The condemnations of the earlier gardening manuals found in eighteenth-century books left their mark on the history of English gardening. In his anthology *The English Garden*, Michael Charlesworth divides his English texts into the categories of descriptions, prescriptions, and reflections: he briskly dismisses most books of "prescription," calling them "tedious" and repetitive of "existing lore."[1] From another point of view, Michael Leslie has also questioned the connection of books like Gervase Markham's *English Husbandman* to the "grand tradition" of English garden writing. Commenting on the inclusion of books by Hill, Markham, and Lawson in the Garland series of English gardening books, Leslie observes that "one of the most interesting features of the list of texts it contains is the paucity of material worthy of inclusion from barely 100 years before the great period of the English landscape garden. Even among those deemed worthy, it is difficult to identify more than one or two that are principally focused on the aesthetic, rather than the practical."[2]

Garden history in search of "theory" and "art" has always looked elsewhere. John Dixon Hunt begins his account of seventeenth-cen-

---

[1] Michael Charlesworth, ed., *The English Garden: Literary Sources and Documents*, vol. 1: *Chronological Overview, 1550–1730* (Mountfield, East Sussex: Helm Information, 1993), pp. 6–7.

[2] Michael Leslie, "'Bringing Ingenuity into Fashion': The 'Elysium Britannicum' and the Reformation of Husbandry," in *John Evelyn's "Elysium Britannicum" and European Gardening*, ed. Therese O'Malley and Joachim Wolschke-Bulmahn (Washington, D.C.: Dumbarton Oaks, 1998), p. 134.

tury English garden theory with Samuel Hartlib, John Beale, John Evelyn, and Stephen Switzer, crediting them with the first ambitious and sophisticated theorizing of English garden art, meant "to educate humans in the appreciation of the ideal perfection of God's handiwork in the larger world of nature."[3] All this is true, but can we deny that the country housewife and the English husbandman, the writers of "secrets," and the nurseryman practiced art in their own ways? All the garden manuals discussed in this book have shown sensitivity to the fundamental questions underlying later garden theory: the balance between art and nature, our need for art in ordinary life, the role of pleasure, profit, and contemplation in the garden, and the relationship between God and our gardens. I have argued here that the books of practical gardening were in fact deeply engaged with art in their pursuit of profit and delight. It may not always appear in the form and the language in which we are accustomed to recognize it, but we cannot ignore these books when telling the history of the human struggle to wrest art out of nature.

Perhaps we do not think about these men as artists because they were not primarily garden designers, and the art of gardening is most often thought of in terms of arraying plants and objects in a plot or landscape: that is, we see the garden as an art object, not gardening practice as an "art." Certainly some early garden manual writers did speculate about the art of garden design, while they may not have imagined themselves building on a vast scale. William Lawson and Gervase Markham provided a design in nature when they included woodcuts for knot gardens in their books, what Lawson called those "few, choice, new forms." Several wrote about the arrangement of walks, walls, and fences or the building of garden mounds, and they speculated about what were the most pleasing and effective arrangements of plants. But for the most part, these writers were concerned with cultivating and propagating their most precious plants and not with their disposition in a landscape.

But this book has argued that there was art, too, in this kind of plantsmanship, whether in the shaping of nature into delightful or regular form or the production of new fruits and flowers. I am not merely speaking here of the fine line between art and craft, insofar as in the early mod-

[3] John Dixon Hunt, *Greater Perfection: The Practice of Garden Theory* (Philadelphia: University of Pennsylvania Press, 2000), p. 183.

ern period, art could indeed be as defined in the *Oxford English Dictionary* as "skill in doing anything as the result of knowledge and practice" or "anything wherein skill may be attained or displayed." The *OED* appears at first quite firm in stating that the notion of art as "the application of skill to the arts of imitation and design, painting, engraving, sculpture, architecture; the cultivation of these in its principles, practice, and results; the skilful production of the beautiful in visible forms . . . does not occur in any English Dictionary before 1880, and seems to have been chiefly used by painters and writers on painting, until the present century." But later in its long entry on "art," the *OED* softens its stand, allowing that people thought of art in the seventeenth century as "a pursuit or occupation in which skill is directed towards the gratification of taste or production of what is beautiful." While the early garden manual writers never neglected what was profitable or practical, they also pursued the "gratification of taste" and beauty—especially where they saw that such a pursuit was entirely compatible with profit. In this they were not that different from all the other artists of the time—poets, painters, architects, workers of metal and gems—who celebrated the Horatian pursuit of profit and delight (while there was considerable vagueness about just what was meant by "profit").

We should give credit to these earlier garden writers as artists, too, because their books arose as much from a written tradition and the powers of the imagination as they did from experience and practice. People often ask me whether some of the more fantastic recipes and instructions included in these books could work, and then whether the writers really believed that they could work. While the answer to the first question is most often no, the answer to the second must be that we cannot know for sure—but that this is not the point. Some writers clearly reproduced these instructions with some reservations, while others promulgated them confidently, but we can tell that the writers knew that their readers would derive pleasure from reading as much as doing them. My point is that we should care less about the truth value of any prescription about buried toads warding off hail or the grafting of gillyflowers than we should think about why we would want these recipes to work. The art of gardening will always be inseparable from the art of the imagination; we would never be able to face that plot of bare dirt in early spring and plant a seedling without being able to dream of what might be. More often than not, the seed of that dream has come from a book.

While I wouldn't necessarily follow their advice in my own garden, I have argued that these early gardeners were in fact garden artists and that we should take seriously their contribution to the imagining of early modern English gardens. Further, their works reveal how early gardening, whether practiced in great or common places, was influenced by social and political changes in its time. For these garden dreams were not merely fancies of garden plots. For writers and readers alike, they were dreams about their selves and their world: dreams of power and self-improvement, visions of God and Eden, reveries of beauty without work or of beautiful work, and fantasies of order in an unpredictable world. These are not so different, indeed, from the dreams of so many gardeners today, however they take their pleasure in gardening. It may be that we can find the seeds of our own fantasies in these reveries of long ago, if we can see through the sometimes banal surfaces of the garden manuals to the hopes that shaped them.

Index

Note: Italic page numbers indicate illustrations.

Garden book writers: and art, 190–92; and book design, 51, 61; and cultivation, 146; and desire, 15–16; and experience, 12–13, 152–53, 162; and histories of garden work, 16, 42–48; and imagination, 14, 179, 191; nurserymen as, 23; and pleasure-work balance, 10; and readership, 9, 16, 32, 35–42, 49, 165, 191; scholars as, 165, 183, 186, 187; self-image of, 10, 42. *See also* Truth; *specific writers*

Garden dreams: and aristocrats, 33–34; and art, 192; and control over nature, 83; and English gardening manuals, 9, 14, 16, 48, 58; and imagination, 191; and natural order, 63, 87; and reading, 13, 87

Garden theory, 7, 17, 190

Gardeners: and book design, 51–52, 59, 61; and class, 10, 17–22, 26, 34, 85; and garden labor, 83, 84–85, 101; identity and status of, 16, 17–19, 34, 89–90, 130; salaries of, 20, 90; types of, 9, 16–34, 49. *See also* Pleasure-work balance; *specific types*

Gender: and flowers, 124–26, 128, 131, 139–40; and garden desire, 108; and hierarchy of natural difference, 137; and histories of garden work, 45; and images of gardeners, 110, 121, 123, 130–31; and pleasure-work balance, 95–97, 117; and readership, 63, 126. *See also* Women

Gentlemen: and cultivating curiosities, 140; and flowers, 125, 129; as garden book writers, 165, 187; as gardeners, 8, 10, 25, 31–32, 34; and histories of garden work, 45–47; and pleasure-work balance, 10, 32–33, 86–91, 93–94, 94n. 24, 98–99, 101–2, 104–5, 107, 187; and pocket companions, 83; and profit, 32–33, 136, 165; and readership, 40–41, 167, 184; and truth, 164–65

Gentry: as gardeners, 9, 18, 30, 34, 95; and georgic moralization of labor, 86; and histories of garden work, 45; and Parkinson, 153; and pocket companions, 82; and Rea, 128; and readership, 37; and seasonal gardening manuals, 77–78

Georgic, the, 8, 86, 94, 106n. 60, 110

Gerard, John: as gentleman gardener, 25–26, 27, 29; and herbals, 39n. 75, 61; and Johnson, 113; Parkinson on, 62; and pleasure-work balance, 99–100, 101; and Ray, 157; and Tuggy, 23

Gilbert, Samuel: and cultivating curiosities, 141; and earlier garden book writers, 179; and flowers, 94, 134–35, 150; and gender, 125, 127; as gentleman gardener, 32–33; and human being–nature relationship, 157; and monthly format, 77–78; and nature as book of God, 101, 102; and plant ranking, 134–35, 145; and pocket companion, 80–81; style of, 186

God: and gardening as spiritual recreation, 32, 101–4, 107; and grafting metaphor, 148; and interference in creation, 146–47, 153–54, 156, 158–59; and scientific knowledge, 100

Grew, Nehemiah, 29, 31, 159

Hanmer, Thomas, 23, 129

Harrison, William, 140, 157

Hartlib, Samuel: and agricultural reforms, 30, 32, 81, 96n. 29, 182; and Austen, 82; disgrace of, 181n. 73; and Hunt, 190; science advocated by, 7, 180

Henrey, Blanche, 35, 82

Henrietta Maria (queen of England), 52, 59, 124, 126, 128, 128n. 51

Henry VIII (king of England), 22, 33

Herbalists, 25

Herbals: and book design, 59, 61; and botanists, 18; cost of, 38–39, 39n. 75; and English experience, 168; and Hill, 41, 55; and illustrations, 64, 68; and language of flowers, 138; and Parkinson, 59, 62; and plant rankings, 134; and public service, 39, 81; purpose of, 9, 161; and Rea, 74; and readership, 37–38, 41, 82; and truth, 181; and women gardeners, 113

Heresbach, Conrad, 43, 44–45, 47, 112

Hill, Thomas: appeal of, 6, 41; and cultivation, 143; and experience, 181; and histories of garden work, 43–47, 112; and illustrations, 68, 69, 70; and pleasure-work balance, 93, 98, 105; and readership, 41, 51n. 4, 55, 152–53; and secrets book, 56; and women as gardeners, 112

Hoby, Margaret, 113–14